The
Executioner's Men

The Executioner's Men

Los Zetas, Rogue Soldiers, Criminal Entrepreneurs,
and the Shadow State They Created

George W. Grayson and Samuel Logan

With a new introduction by George W. Grayson

Transaction Publishers
New Brunswick (U.S.A.) and London (U.K.)

Library of Congress Catalog Number: 2011034932
ISBN: 978-1-4128-4617-2 (cloth); 978-1-4128-5484-9 (paper)
Printed in the United States of America

Library of Congress Cataloging-in-Publication Data

Grayson, George W., 1938–
    The executioner's men: Los Zetas, rogue soldiers, criminal entrepreneurs, and the shadow state they created / George W. Grayson and Samuel Logan.
        p. cm.
    Includes bibliographical references and index.
    ISBN 978-1-4128-4617-2
    1. Zetas Cartel.   2. Drug traffic—Mexico.   3. Organized crime—Mexico.   4. Narco-terrorism—Mexico.   I. Logan, Samuel.   II. Title.

HV5840.M4G727 2012
364.1060972—dc23
                                                          2011034932

Dedication

We dedicate this book to the US law-enforcement community, and their Mexican allies, who are seeking to combat Los Zetas, the deadliest criminal organization based in the Americas. In addition, we will be forever in debt to our long-suffering loved ones without whose sacrifices and encouragement this volume would never have seen the light of day: Bryan Holt Grayson and Sam's wife and children, Barbara, Iris, and Enzo.

Contents

List of Illustrations

List of Maps

List of Figures

List of Tables

Acknowledgments

The journey to bring this book to press involved the assistance of experts in security issues, drug Mafias, and the political, cultural, economic, and social contexts in which criminal organizations operate. Their help greatly benefited the authors' attempt to unravel the layers of mystery that suffuse Los Zetas.

It is difficult to persuade anyone in Mexico, the United States, or Central America to talk openly and frankly about Los Zetas, much less speak at length about a group of men and women who incite unvarnished fear. As such, we are indebted to our friends and sources across the Americas who offered what information they could and enabled us to fill in the blanks left between various media stories, think tank reports, white papers, books, and other items in print that mentioned Los Zetas with some level of veracity.

Among those to whom we owe a debt of gratitude are Don Pollo Suárez and his wife Margarita, Rubén Olmos, Alexander Renderos Vásquez, Steven Dudley of *InSightCrime*, Ildefonso Oritz of *The Monitor* (McAllen, Texas), "Manuela," and a plethora of Mexican journalists, politicians, diplomats, and scholars, who, in the interest of their safety, will not be mentioned by name.

Law-enforcement officials on both sides of the border aided us enormously with "off the record" interviews. Many of these men and women risk their lives every day to combat Los Zetas and other venal criminal organizations.

We also thank Lorraine Jablonsky Floyd for research assistance.

Lindsey C. Nicolai, a College of William & Mary graduate, who is bound for law school, conducted research, prepared tables, tracked down maps, edited chapters, and provided ideas on shaping the text. For this reason, her name appears on the title page.

Lucinda H. Baker, associate director of Creative Services at the College of William & Mary, did a magnificent job of preparing a diagram of the "Structure of Los Zetas."

Above all, gratitude is owed to Transaction Press and its distinguished publisher, Professor Louis Irving Horowitz. He and his superb colleagues consistently, enthusiastically, patiently, and astutely encouraged and supported our venture every step of the way.

With so many helping hands, we must attribute any errors of omission or commission to Hurricane Irene, who struck with a vengeance as we were completing the manuscript. No doubt, this vicious lady injected questionable entries that neither we nor the publisher discovered.

Map 1 Map of Mexico

Source: Congressional Research Service, "Mexico: Issues for Congress," by Clare Ribando Seelke, June 9, 2011. http://www.fas.org/sgp/crs/row/RL32724.pdf.

Introduction to the Paperback Edition

The United States maintains diplomatic relations with 194 independent nations. Of these, none is more important than Mexico in terms of trade, investment, tourism, natural resources, migration, energy, and security. In recent years, narco-violence has ravaged this cornucopia-shaped country with more than 65,000 drug-related murders since 2007 and some 26,000 men, women, and children missing. Los Zetas are the deadliest of the drug trafficking organizations (DTOs) on Mexico's criminal stage. The founders of this group, trained to combat the Gulf Cartel, deserted from Mexico's elite Airborne Special Forces Group in the late-1990s. Higher pay, better food, and the chance to profit from selling small amounts of cocaine enticed the thirty-one khaki-clad Benedict Arnolds to become a praetorian guard for Osiel Cárdenas Guillén. He was the overlord of the Gulf Cartel based in Matamoros, Tamaulipas, across the Rio Grande from McAllen, Texas. The paranoid Cárdenas acquired the nickname "The Friend Killer" because he ordered goons to pursue and execute real and imagined foes believed to be plotting his demise. Although the tough-as-nails Zetas formed protective circles around their boss, an informer revealed his whereabouts. This betrayal enabled the military to capture the kingpin on March 14, 2003.

After Cárdenas' imprisonment, a disoriented troika endeavored to control the reins of the Gulf Cartel. The ineffectiveness of the threesome prompted an attack from the Sinaloa Cartel, headed by the notorious Joaquín "El Chapo" Guzmán, who lusted for dominance over Nuevo Laredo, Matamoros, Reynosa, and other border cities that provided access to the United States.

In helping fend off the Sinaloan invaders, the diabolical Heriberto "The Executioner" Lazcano Lazcano emerged as the head honcho of Los Zetas. Yet, these villains, like a cadre of Frankensteins, gradually turned with a vengeance on their Gulf Cartel masters—with the final rupture occurring in the first half of 2010. Earlier they had entered situational pacts with the rival Beltrán Leyva Organization (BLO), former allies of the Sinaloa Cartel. Cárdenas had never taught the paramilitaries the intricacies of the drug racket, and they had modest success importing cocaine from Colombia. Thus, they set out to brand themselves as the meanest, leanest, most ghastly underworld outfit in the Americas.

Thanks to instruction from ex-Kaibiles, the Guatemalan army's ruthless commandos, Los Zetas learned to savage victims—with an emphasis on chopping off heads, performing castrations, and skinning bodies. An especially apt student of these macabre techniques was Miguel Ángel "El 40" Treviño Morales who, like The Executioner, thrived on aggression, manipulation, and the infliction of unspeakable pain on others.

Random incidents of such atrocities often made only local news. To attract widespread print and electronic media coverage, these emissaries of Satan began decapitating multiple enemies, arraying their corpses in patterns convenient for TV cameras and newspaper photographers. In December 2008, Los Zetas captured and executed eight army officers and enlisted men in Guerrero, a violence-torn, impoverished southern state that is home to Acapulco. Pictures of the headless cadavers lying side-by-side flashed around the world on television and YouTube. In addition, Los Zetas adeptly employed Google, Facebook, Twitter, and other social media outlets both to alert authorities and the populace to their viciousness and to stalk victims.

In July 2009, Los Zetas assaulted the home of a police chief in Veracruz, a state that lies below Tamaulipas. Within five minutes, they blasted their way into the house and murdered the law-enforcement officer, his wife, their son, and a policeman. They then torched the residence, incinerating the remaining three children, all girls.

The following year, Los Zetas slaughtered seventy-two Central and South American migrants—fifty-eight men and fourteen women— leaving their remains in a farm outside of San Fernando, Tamaulipas. In the spring of 2011, authorities discovered 193 bodies near the same crossroads municipality in what came to be known as San Fernando II. These high-profile abominations, including the September 2010 killing of US citizen David Hartley on Falcon Lake and the February 2011 attack on two US Immigration and Customs Enforcement personnel that left one of the agents dead, helped "bring Los Zetas to the attention of the American government and public." [1]

In December 2009 they stormed Monterrey, the cosmopolitan capital of Nuevo León known for giant corporations, bilingualism, museums, and art galleries. For years the residents lived on an island of tranquility amid an ocean of turmoil. Then Los Zetas began blocking streets, undertaking kidnappings, practicing extortions, and engaging in atrocities. For instance, on April 27, 2011, they torched the Casino Royale, burning at least fifty-two occupants beyond recognition. The following February, imprisoned cadres of this hyperviolent cartel stabbed and bludgeoned to death forty-four members of the rival Gulf Cartel as they staged a mass escape. On May 13, 2012, authorities reported that the evildoers had decapitated and mutilated forty-nine people near Cadereyta, a Monterrey suburb. These horrors sparked such an outcry from the business community that the unpopular governor, Rodrigo Medina de la Cruz, established the Fuerza Civil (Civil Force) to take over security functions from the military. The Fuerza Civil is composed of young people without previous police experience, who were recruited outside the state. In return for attractive salaries and educational opportunities, the cadets submit themselves to rigorous training and agree to be housed in special barracks. Most observers view the initiative as an achievement.[2]

Despite the success of projects like the Fuerza Civil, Los Zetas continued to hone their intimidating slaughter tactics. They mastered the preparation of a "guiso," the Spanish word for a stew. The simple recipe entailed plunging a tortured child or adult into a pig cooker or 55-gallon oil drum, dousing the body with gasoline, and setting their quarry on fire. Los Zetas employ gruesome artifices to gain "cartel cred"—that is credibility that they will carry out whatever deed is necessary to achieve their goals. For instance, they may inform a physician who runs a profitable clinic that he needs their protection for, say, $25,000 a month. The doctor will either comply or relocate his practice, knowing that failure to pay could mean that, say, his six-year-old son will be seized, sliced, and diced—with body parts dropped onto his parents' doorstep.

Furthermore, their heinous behavior discourages deserters, and, ironically, assists the recruitment of youngsters who gravitate to the toughest band of brigands in the country. No wonder the White House labeled them a "global menace" comparable to the Camorra secret society in southern Italy, the Yakuza mob in Japan, and the Brothers' Circle of Eastern Europe.

Like the dominant Sinaloa Cartel, traditional Mexican narco-traffickers emphasize the economic aspects of their trade. The Gulf Cartel also stressed profitability over gratuitous carnage. The increasing tendency of Los Zetas to brutalize their adversaries was bad for business, and further strained Gulf-Zeta relations.

The takedown of top leaders, discussed below, has decimated Los Zetas' vertical organization, and the fiendish paramilitaries have assumed a lower profile. Still, younger men and women, often unknown to law-enforcement agents, continue to use the cartel's diabolical reputation to achieve their ends. "The cartels have been able to recruit tens of thousands of killers in part because poor neighborhoods have been systematically abandoned over decades and lack sufficient schools, community centers and security—in short they lack opportunity," the International Crisis Group said in a report on cartel violence.[3] Los Zetas' bloodlust has facilitated their access to Central America and other regions where they work with established gangs and crime families. Guatemala has become a haven for the miscreants, who have incurred the wrath of local security forces, the military, the United States, and the Sinaloa and Gulf cartels.

In March 2012, Guatemalan officials reported the capture of the Zeta chieftain in the country, Gustavo Adolfo Colindres; however, this arrest did not stanch the bloodletting. A study released by the National Economic Research Center found that firearm-related homicides in Guatemala over the previous ten years had soared 82 percent. This figure is nearly double the global average of 42 percent, and above even Central America's relatively high average of 70 percent. Los Zetas, the Sinaloa Cartel, and a dozen other deadly groups have turned Guatemala into a Tennessee-sized killing field. The US Drug Enforcement Administration (DEA) described Los Zetas as possibly "the most violent, sophisticated, and technologically advanced of these paramilitary groups."

Enrique Peña Nieto, who swore Mexico's presidential oath on December 1, 2012, has tried to divert national attention from the mayhem by stressing reforms in energy, education, telecommunications, health care, tourism, labor, and other areas rather than hunting down heads of DTOs.

Blows continued to rain down on these villains on his watch. On October 7, 2012, Mexican Marines killed Zeta kingpin "The Executioner" Lazcano in a withering gunbattle on October 7, 2012. With the aid of intelligence supplied by the DEA and other US agencies, Lazcano was discovered while nonchalantly watching a baseball game in Progreso, Coahuila, a state infested with Zetas.

What ensued is worthy of a best-selling "Whodunit." Believing they had gunned down a common criminal, the Marines deposited his remains at a private funeral home in Sabinas, Coahuila, 80 miles from the US border. A day after the slaying, a band of masked, heavily armed thugs burst into the funeral parlor, overpowered the staff, shoved Lazcano's decaying body into a hearse, and forced the owner to drive to a yet-to-be discovered venue. Such melodramatics aside, there is no evidence that the demonic Mafioso lives on.

On July 15, 2013, Marines captured "El 40" Treviño Morales on a dirt road near Nuevo Laredo, his hometown and a Zeta bastion. The most sadistic hombre in Mexico, he delighted in dealing out excruciating pain before delivering the coup de grâce. As one analyst said: "He deserves to rot for eternity in the lowest rung of hell."

These takedowns thrust Omar "El 42" Treviño Morales into the leadership of the Zetas. Lacking the skills and legitimacy of his older brother, Miguel Ángel, Omar has watched the dismantling of the venal syndicate's command and control apparatus. The publication *Borderland Beat* has speculated on El 42's possible allies: Sergio Ricardo "El Grande" Basurto Peña (Nuevo Laredo) and Maxiley "El Max" Nadales Barhona (Veracruz, Chiapas, and Tabasco). Although the current government makes reporting extremely difficult in the blood-drenched North, Los Zetas continue to incur casualties. The successes against the desperados included:

• On July 26, 2012, Marines arrested Mauricio Guizar Cárdenas, suspected of serving as the organization's chief in the southeastern states of Veracruz, Tabasco, Chiapas, Campeche, and Quintana Roo.

• On March 27, 2014, police and military killed ten Zetas, who accomplished kidnappings in Veracruz.

• On May 14, 2014, authorities apprehended Fernando "Z-16" Martínez Magaña, an original Zeta who specialized in smuggling migrants to the United States.

• On May 17, 2014, soldiers and federal police captured Juan Fernando "El Ferrari" Álvarez Cortez, a confidant of Omar Treviño Morales and plaza boss in central Tamaulipas, where he had fueled a surge of violence. He had been taken into custody exactly four years earlier, but managed to escape from prison.

Another aperçu into the villains' change of fortunes took place in early April 2014 when Iván "El Talibán" Velázquez Caballero, a notorious assassin and once-mighty Zeta regional chieftain, confessed to narcotics commerce and money-laundering conspiracies in a courthouse in McAllen, Texas. According to stellar journalist Ildefonso Ortiz, the former grandee who is also known as "Z-50," dressed in disheveled khaki pants, a wrinkled T-shirt, and light brown boots, softly responded: "Sí, Señora," when US District Court Judge Micaela Alvarez asked whether he was pleading guilty to the charges. A plea agreement to cooperate with law-enforcement officials may reduce a sentence that could range from ten years to life in prison.

In August 2012, Velázquez Caballero allegedly formed the "Sangre Zeta" or "Blood Zeta" cell that rebelled against El 40 in San Luis Potosí and later began working in Coahuila and Nuevo León. This splinter group, calling themselves Los Legionarios, even dared to hang anti-Morales Treviño banners in Nuevo León.[4]

El Talibán's minions may have perpetrated a barbarous act against a valiant woman in a north-central state. After her marriage evaporated, Isabela left the impoverished Huasteca region of San Luis Potosí for Texas, where she became a superb cook in a Houston restaurant. Ten years later, she returned home to open a restaurant—Las Isabelas— where she masterfully whipped up Tex-Mex creations that she had learned to prepare in the United States, combining these recipes with scrumptious local dishes. The combination of finger-licking entrees, affordable prices, and a clean establishment earned her a devoted following. Moreover, family, friends, and customers took pride in the achievement of a local person who not only made good in "El Norte," but returned to her community to share her culinary creations.

The poignant story ended in the fall of 2013, when a group of Los Zetas barged into her eatery. Isabela was away, so the intruders approached her daughter who was the on-duty manager and demanded a payoff for safeguarding the premises. The young woman said, in effect, "I know nothing of such affairs." At that point, the desperados raped and murdered her. Then they burned the building to the ground and set off in pursuit of Isabela.

Even though suffering reverses since the 2012, these brigands continue to pose a viral menace to individuals, businesses, and institutions in a dozen or more Mexican states, as well as in Central America.

At approximately the same time as El Talibán's trial, Guatemalan police apprehended Wilmer Arnulfo Cabrera Franco, a suspected Zeta boss in Alta Verapaz, Baja Verapaz, and Ixcan in the northwestern province of Quiché. "We have struck a really hard blow with this capture," boasted government minister Mauricio López Bonilla, who emphasized that security forces had devoted months tracking their prey.

Weakness has reduced Los Zetas' drug-trafficking capability, which was never as great as that of other major cartels. As a result, they have zeroed in on migrant smuggling, contraband, murder-for-hire, loan-sharking, selling protection, child prostitution, extortion, investments in "legal" businesses, and, above all, abductions—often in collaboration with local police and insidious gangs that are mushrooming apace with the fracturing of Mexico's major DTOs. Although the government placed the figure at 1,317, Mexico's quasi-independent National Institute of Statistics and Geography concluded that 105,000 people were kidnapped in 2012, but only a small fraction of cases were reported.[5] Surveys indicate that citizens perceive that the number is soaring into uncharted territory. Narco-related murders are alarming, but they mainly involve the cartel members, hoodlums, the military, police, judges, prosecutors, and so forth. But anyone now faces the nightmare of being snatched from his or her automobile, workplace, home, school, or neighborhood streets.

Increasingly vulnerable are average Mexicans, who lack expert drivers, state-of-the-art security devices, platoons of bodyguards, the wherewithal to send their youngsters abroad to study, and relocate their businesses to the United States. Foreigners also find themselves at risk—with nationals of Spain, Colombia, and the United States having been stalked in recent years. "Virtual" kidnappers, who may conduct their trade from behind bars, fake the ability to pull off the crime. As part of their bluff, these mercenaries have offered to accept smaller ransoms payable to an accomplice outside the prison walls. In exchange for this discount, the wily inmates demand that targets provide the names of ten or so friends and relatives, who will then become the next wave of abductees—a pyramid scheme of shakedowns, so to speak. If the victim fails to play this game, the desperadoes threaten to dismember him or a family member.

From their redoubts in Nuevo León and Tamaulipas, Los Zetas have targeted Petróleos Mexicanos (Pemex), the state oil monopoly. The scoundrels have tapped into oil and gas pipelines, undoubtedly with the aid of company personnel; hijacked gasoline tanker trucks; stolen TNT and other explosives acquired for well blasting; and purloined such solvents as toluene and xylene. These chemicals are acquired for hydraulic fracking, but they can also be used to process cocaine and methamphetamines. While not involved in methamphetamine commerce, Los Zetas can sell their booty to producers of synthetic drugs, as well as to legal, but complicit, pharmaceutical firms, dye-makers, and soap manufacturers eager to reduce input costs.

Penetration of Pemex pipelines spiraled from 213 in 2006 to 1,449 in 2012, giving rise to losses of hundreds of millions of dollars annually. "The illegal trafficking in large quantities of natural gas, gasoline, aviation fuel and diesel has surged as one of the principal sources of financing for Los Zetas, the Gulf Cartel, and other criminal cells," Carlos Mendoza Mora, president of a Mexico City security firm, told the Coahuila newspaper *Vanguardia*.

An ambitious reform of the energy sector will spur imports of vital materials from outside the country, thus magnifying prospects for theft, extortion, and other criminality. Will foreign firms be willing to hire companies to protect their managers, workers, and resources? Pemex Director General Emilio Lozano Austin has expanded the role of the company's security chief, Eduardo León Trauwitz; however, the retired brigadier general has failed to stem losses since his 2012 appointment. It's important to remember that Los Zetas' presence in the Petén territory has severely constricted Guatemala's ability to entice investment in its hydrocarbon reservoirs.

Although pursued by the Federal Police, the armed forces, US law-enforcement agencies, and others, Los Zetas have benefited from the reverses of their rivals. On February 22, 2014, Marines took into custody Joaquín "El Chapo" Guzmán Loera, the infamous jefe of the Sinaloa Cartel, which—in concert with the Tamaulipas-based Gulf Cartel—had waged all-out war on the rogues, who once served as the latter's paramilitary arm. Moreover, the Gulf Cartel has suffered a blood-drenched schism between its Matamoros (Cyclones) and Reynosa (Metros) factions. This internecine conflict has emboldened Los Zetas to seek to recover lost territory in Monterrey, Nuevo León, and the Tamaulipas municipalities of Matamoros, Reynosa, and Río Bravo.

Pressure from law-enforcement agencies in Mexico has led Los Zetas to expand further their presence in Central America. The UN Office against Drugs and Crime has called Los Zetas the "dominant" narco-traffickers in the region. While the arrest of Cabrera Franco was a thorn in the side, it was not dagger in the heart of the marauders, who continue to deepen and widen their inroads into the isthmus. In late April 2014, El Salvador's Public Security and Justice Minister Ricardo Perdomo denounced Los Zetas for selling high-powered rifles to the Mara Salvatruchas (MS-13) and other gangs in Honduras and Guatemala. They are also accused of training these heinous outfits. The Salvadoran official said that in exchange for weapons, Los Zetas turned over small amounts of cocaine to the gangs for street-level sales known as *menudeo.*

Moreover, branding has helped keep the debilitated Zetas on the map. El 40 and The Executioner inculcated their followers with a vile approach to victims, competitors, and law-enforcement personnel. The very mention of "Los Zetas" in many urban and rural zones in Mexico and Central America strikes fear in the hearts of men, women, and children. What accounts for the bloodlust? One theory, which requires in-depth research, is that The Executioner and El 40 were afflicted with Sadistic Personality Disorder (SPD), which, according to mental-health professionals, involves abusiveness, violence, a lack of concern for people, and the derivation of pleasure from the suffering of others, including babies and young children.[6]

For better or worse, the arrest of chieftains has dramatically altered Los Zetas's structure. As analysts Dwight Dyer and Daniel Sachs pointed out: "Instead of developing a strong vertical hierarchy, they have built a horizontal, decentralized one. The Zetas do not have identifiable leaders, but its individual cells have always been empowered to exploit opportunities available to their respective locales."[7] This means that parochial jefes, who may be young, inexperienced, and ill trained in the use of AR-15s and AK-47s, can act without waiting for orders from a commander. At times advantageous, this flexibility may trigger imprudent moves, which can result in the capture or killing of the aggressors, even as "zetanization"—mimicking Los Zetas' heinous antics—gains greater acceptance in Mexico's ever-expanding underworld. Washington policymakers, who overwhelmingly concentrate on Asia and the Mideast, would be well advised also to focus on the acute dangers that lie below the Rio Grande, but whose deadly avatars are spilling into the United States.

The takedown of "El Chapo" Guzmán sparked a chain reaction in northern Mexico—to the point of precipitating an attempted comeback by the sadistic Zetas. This bloodlust attracted a plethora of enemies: the armed forces, the Federal Police, US security agencies, and rival cartels. For instance, the Sinaloa and Gulf cartels—once akin to two scorpions in a bottle—joined forces against the villains. El Chapo's Sinaloans sought access to Nuevo Laredo, the busiest portal with the United States; the Gulf Cartel endeavored to maintain control of Matamoros, Reynosa, and other frontier crossings in Tamaulipas.

Just when it seemed that Los Zetas were doomed, El Chapo's arrest sidelined the one strongman who could forcefully impose cooperation on the Gulf Cartel factions that increasingly resembled gangs lunging at one another's throats, according to Ildefonso Ortiz. Subsequently, however, warfare has erupted within Los Metros, allowing Los Cyclones a chance to lick their wounds. One of the fatalities in the intra-Metro brawl was Galindo "Z-9," an original Zeta who remained with the Gulf Cartel and held a prominent post in the Reynosa area.

During the first half of 2014, officials reported dozens of deaths in firefights in Reynosa, Matamoros, and other cities of Tamaulipas. The fatalities included average citizens, federal policemen, soldiers, and gunmen. The figure may have been higher, according to an anti-crime specialist who lamented the image-conscious regime's under-reporting of casualties.

The tsunami of killings and a barrage of social media complaints about insecurity led Interior Minister Miguel Ángel Osorio Chong to jet to Reynosa on May 13 to unveil a security program for Tamaulipas. Among other items, he said the state would be configured into various areas (border, coast, center, and south)—with federal prosecutors and special military personnel assigned to each zone. In addition, urban areas will be patrolled twenty-four hours a day, seven days a week, and vigilance will be further strengthened in ports, airports, and customs. Local police forces will also be reviewed in order to eliminate corruption. Osorio Chong said these moves by the government marked the coming of a "new phase" in the battle against the drug cartels.[8] A Tamaulipas state government spokesman also promised the establishment of a new police academy. Several thousand troops have been deployed to reassert control over what has the makings of a failed state.

The civilian and military personnel will have to be on their guard. For instance, on May 5, 2014, hoodlums ambushed and killed the state police intelligence chief, Col. Salvador Haro Muñoz.[9] A week later, it was announced that Tamaulipas Governor Egidio Torre Cantú had sacked his top bodyguard for allegedly masterminding the assassination that Zetas allegedly carried out. Confidence in federal and state authorities is almost nil. So concerned was southern Texas congress-man Filemon Vela that he wrote Secretary of State John Kerry, who visited Mexico in May, stating that "the Tamaulipas security crisis lies at our very doorstep and it has had a profound impact on citizens on both sides of the US-Mexican border. He urged the nation's top dip-lomat to inform his Mexican counterparts that our country "strongly supports their efforts to bring security to Tamaulipas."

In all fairness, Mexican authorities confirmed on May 25, 2014, the apprehension in Nuevo León state of Juan Manuel Rodríguez García, also known as "Juan Perros," one the twelve most wanted criminals in Mexico and a Gulf cartel boss in Tamaulipas. "There is proof that this individual ordered the mass kidnappings of undocumented im-migrants, who he forced to work for his group, or murder them if they refused," said Mexico's commissioner of public safety, Monte Alejandro Rubido, according to Reuters.[10]

With the Marines, the DEA, and other law-enforcement agencies on his tail, the prospects for Omar Treviño Morales, who is reportedly ill, are not promising. Still, dispersed bosses such as the leader of the "Sangre Zetas" or "Blood Zetas" will continue to spew their venom on rival cartels, politicians, public officials, the police, and average citizens.

George W. Grayson
Class of 1938 Professor of Government Emeritus
College of William & Mary
Williamsburg, Virginia
gwgray@wm.edu
June 1, 2014

Notes

1. Scott Stewart and Tristan Reed, "Mexico's Zetas Are Not Finished Yet," *Security Weekly*, October 24, 2013.
2. Alma Vigil, "Nuevo León: en las entrañas de Fuerza Civil," *El Universal*, April 3, 2014.
3. "A Grisly Crime Surges into Spotlight as Mexico Shifts Drug War Strategy," CNN, March 27, 2013.
4. "Sangre Zeta and Other New Groups Complicate Drug War," *Borderland Beat*, March 1, 2013.
5. Instituto Nacional de Estadística y Georgrafía, "Nota Técnica: Encuesta Nacional de Victimización y Percepción Sobre Seguridad Pública" (ENVIPE 2013), October 28, 2013.
6. PsychNet-UK, Sadistic Personality Order Criteria" http://www.psych-net-uk.com/x_new_site/personality_psychology/a_diagnostic_criteria/criteria_personality_sadistic.html.
7. "Los Zetas Spawn: The Long Afterlife of Mexico's Most Ruthless Drug Gang," *Foreign Affairs*, August 5, 2013.
8. "New Security Plan for Mexican State," BBC, May 13, 2014.
9. Joshua Partlow, "A Frightened Mexico City Tries to Survive Drug War," *Washington Post*, June 1, 2014; and "Tamaulipas: SSP Chief of Intelligence Killed by Zetas," *Borderland Beat*, May 6, 2014.
10. Jorge Cavillo, "Mexican Drug War News: Capture of Gulf Cartel Leader 'Juan Perros' in Nuevo León Confirmed," *Latinos Post*, May 26, 2014.

Introduction

In 2009, Miguel Ángel Morales Treviño convened a meeting of corrupt police in Nuevo Laredo, a drug-smuggling Mecca across from Laredo, Texas. No sooner had these law-enforcement officers, who constituted 70 to 80 percent of the municipality's force, slouched into their seats than "El 40," as Morales Treviño is called, admonished them against betraying Los Zetas, one of Mexico's most powerful drug trafficking organizations (DTOs) that he cocommands.

After this harangue, a brace of thick-necked toughs dragged into the dimly lit room a distraught female officer whom El 40 condemned as a "government informant." Rather than allowing her to defend herself with a single word, the thugs tied her hands and prevented her from moving. Morales Treviño stepped forward, grabbed a two-by-four and, after a couple of practice swings as if he were batting clean-up, methodically began to beat her, beginning with her tear-stained face. Once released, the alleged traitor's body collapsed into a broken mass, so mangled, bruised, and bloodied that it was impossible to recognize that she had ever been a living human being. The stunned and frightened onlookers got the message.

Such savagery has not always been part of life in Nuevo Laredo and other criminal enclaves such as Reynosa, Matamoros, Tampico, and Ciudad Victoria in the South Carolina-sized state of Tamaulipas. Decades of neglect, economic malaise, the unintended consequences of government policies, and the effect of enormous criminal wealth on an impoverished populace have weakened the government's presence and power in this northeastern region, one of the most criminally active in Latin America.

Its proximity to the United States has long made Tamaulipas an enticing venue for criminal organizations. Its geographical location has subjected the state to shocks of violence as wave after wave of Mexican lawbreakers have pushed and pulled against one another in an underworld dance of power and influence. The first modern era capo to rise out of this dusty border region was Don Juan Nepomuceno Guerra, who became a legend for cold-blooded executions. One tale claims that he gunned down Pancho Villa's son. It is also rumored that he killed a man for talking too loudly in his presence.[1]

Juan bootlegged whisky during Prohibition along the Gulf Coast before founding the Gulf Cartel in the 1970s with the complicity of Rafael Chao López and Rafael Aguilar Guajardo, commanders in the notoriously corrupt Federal Security Directorate (DFS). Through political connections that he had nurtured, Don Juan, who reportedly never spent more than "a few hours in jail," smuggled contraband into South Texas via established routes through the border cities of Nuevo Laredo and Matamoros. He also amassed a fortune in the arms trade, prostitution, protection, and gambling. The kingpin, who conducted business under a gilded cage of chirping canaries in his "Piedras Negras" restaurant in Matamoros, tutored his American-born nephew Juan García Abrego in the art of stealing automobiles. An apt student, the young man drew upon his uncle's latticework of trusted contacts to expand the family's illicit business into trafficking a more lucrative product—cocaine.[2] García Abrego entered into a new relationship with Colombian producers whom US authorities were successfully targeting in Florida and Mid-Atlantic states. Operations "Impunity" (1997–99) and "Millennium" (1998–99) resulted in the arrest of ninety-three individuals linked to the Amado Carrillo Fuentes drug-trafficking organization headquartered in Juárez and the arrest of thirty-one individuals, including Fabio Ochoa-Vasquez and Alejandro Bernal-Madrigal, former members of the original Medellin Cartel. At the time of their capture, they were considered two of the most powerful cocaine traffickers in the world.

García Abrego guaranteed the suppliers delivery anywhere in America in return for 50 percent of the load. After his arrest in early 2006, Osiel Cárdenas Guillén clawed his way to the summit of the affluent Gulf Cartel.[3]

Decades before Cárdenas' rise to power, economic booms and busts had shredded the social fabric of Tamaulipas. These cycles helped impel the rise of a man who would eventually become one of the most remarkable trafficking bosses in Latin America, as organized crime increasingly became an important source of wealth, employment, and social welfare.

Tamaulipas lies along the Gulf of Mexico and once depended heavily on agriculture, construction, and light manufacturing in the North;

government activities, universities, and silviculture dominated Ciudad Victoria, the state capital nestled in the Sierra Madres. Highway 101, which runs through scrub forests of mesquite, prickly pear, and creosote, connects this picturesque city to Matamoros. Shipping, fishing, and petroleum production and refining power actuated the economy of the southern ports of Tampico, Altamira, and Ciudad Madero. Yet periods of feast and famine have swept across the state, especially the northern cities, since the Mexican–American War and the Mexican Revolution. During World War II, dollars poured into the area, thanks to the Bracero Program that allowed Mexicans to work lawfully in agriculture on a seasonal basis inside the United States. It replaced Americans siphoned into the war effort. Opposed by the AFL-CIO, the initiative also impeded the unionization of farm hands.[4] As a stream of unlawful workers paralleled their legal countrymen, the end of this guest worker initiative brought a major economic downturn to the area in the mid-1960s.

Map 2   Map of Tamaulipas

Source: Explorando México at www.explorandomexico.com.mx.

To address soaring unemployment, the Mexican and US governments launched the Border Industrialization Program or "Maquiladora" initiative. This scheme involved the construction of twin factories—one north of the frontier that accomplished the capital-intensive aspects of producing television sets, toys, clothing, furniture, plastics, auto parts, and footwear; south of the border, plants imported raw materials duty-free, performed labor-intensive tasks, and exported assembled products, lowering the cost of products in the United States and creating jobs that paid more than the Mexican average wage.

Arrival of these maquiladoras reshaped the state's socioeconomic landscape.[5] Cheap labor, peso devaluations, and the favorable legal framework made "in bond" industries appealing to domestic and foreign companies doing business in the United States. The program attracted tens of thousands of females because of their dexterity, malleability, and reliable work habits. Many of these women were young, unmarried, single mothers, and migrants from rural areas. Although earning substantially more than in the countryside, they were vulnerable to exploitation, unemployment, and violence.

Still, the number of attacks on females in Tamaulipas paled in comparison with Ciudad Juárez where approximately five hundred *feminicidos*, systematic murder of women, took place between 1993 and 2008. Tamaulipas did begin to catch up the following year, and jumped to fourth among Mexico's states for murders of and violence against females—with the greatest number of incidents taking place in Reynosa, Matamoros, and Tampico. Of course, most nonlethal attacks went unreported and with little recourse available, some of the victims turned to prostitution.[6]

A series of economic crises that coincided with presidential administrations in Mexico (1976, 1982, 1988, and 1994) strongly affected profits of the dual-plants. At the same time, access to even cheaper labor found companies—including those owned by Mexicans—pulling up stakes and relocating to Central America, China, and other Asian countries. Job-seekers who had made the trek from southern Mexico to the border region found themselves without employment, without families, and without local ties. Many of them tried to enter the United States illegally; others remained behind, resigned to their fates and determined to make the best of an onerous situation; and some embarked upon lives of crime.

The North American Free Trade Agreement (NAFTA), which took effect on January 1, 2004, was a godsend for Mexico's macroeconomy.

The trilateral pact ballooned the nation's trade with its continental partners and pulled in an unprecedented influx of foreign investment. Nevertheless, small businesses and subsistence farms could not compete with the influx of less expensive American and Canadian goods produced by vastly more efficient enterprises, such as many giant agribusinesses that enjoyed generous tax benefits and subsidies. The accord also gave smugglers such as Osiel Cárdenas Guillén unprecedented access to the global system for his Colombian cocaine. Even as NAFTA began to liberalize Mexico's once-cocooned market, many bottlenecks remained intact: virtual monopolies and oligopolies in telecommunications, the mass media, cement, processed foods, oil, electricity, education, and petroleum.

The disastrous "Christmas Crisis" plunged Mexico into another recession in late 1994. This traumatic event prevented the then president, Ernesto Zedillo (1994–2000), from implementing his promised modernization of agriculture through regional development that included research into new and improved crops, the establishment of small, rural industries, targeted subsidies, farm-to-market roads, and cooperatives.

Consequently, legitimate Mexican farmers shifted from traditional fruits, vegetables, and grains to the cultivation of drugs.[7] For decades, kaleidoscopic changes afflicted Tamaulipas, which languished amid stagnation and a sharp rise in unemployment in the debacle of the mid-1990s.

By the time this economic disaster had arrived, traditional social safety nets undergirded by the long-dominant Institutional Revolutionary Party (PRI) and the Roman Catholic Church had decayed. The flow abroad of workers, who had been migrating to the United States for decades, accelerated in the 1990s. Men, usually alone or with male counterparts, legally and illegally entered the United States to earn money required to support their families. As a result, many rural municipalities in the North were divested of men between the ages of eighteen and forty-five. Males who remained in the state gravitated to the narco-economy, which constituted far more than illegal agriculture—that is, "it [had] a huge multiplier effect in the vast array of other jobs it generates both directly (e.g., transportation, security, banking, and communication) and indirectly (e.g., construction, the service sector, and spin-off businesses)."[8]

The northern cities became portals for three-way commerce among Mexico, the United States, and Canada. Every day, more than ten thousand cargo trucks and freight cars rumble across the International Bridge, the Juárez-Lincoln Bridge, and the Libre Comercio Bridge. In addition, the Texas Mexican Railway and Kansas City Southern de México own the Laredo International Railway Bridge. The Laredo-ColombiaSolidarity Bridge, located twenty miles northwest of Nuevo Laredo, provides yet another bilateral link. All told, fifteen bridges—from Matamoros to Nuevo Laredo—connect Tamaulipas to Texas. These road and rail links constitute "the spinal cord of Pan-American trade."[9] Traffic from San Luis Potosí, Saltillo, and Monterrey converge at Nuevo Laredo before crossing to its sister city, Laredo, Texas, en route to Interstate 35 and states and provinces to the north. Another ten thousand trucks transit the border at other points, totaling over twenty thousand vehicle-crossings a day. At such high volumes, it was impossible for US customs to stop, inspect, and process more than 5 percent of every automobile, tractor-trailer rig, or boxcar. Increased pedestrian traffic contributed to drug smuggling. With the enactment of NAFTA, ever-larger quantities of narcotics, migrants, guns, and other contraband moved across the Rio Grande. At the same time, it was economically and politically destructive to close down the crossing even for a few hours. "The Nuevo Laredo–Laredo border [is] a smuggler's paradise."[10]

The paradise became even more appealing when, in October 2011, the United States began allowing Mexican trucks to travel throughout its northern neighbor without changing cabs at the border. The first such long-haul tractor-trailer left Apodaca, Nuevo León, crossed the World Trade Bridge in Laredo, and headed 450 miles north to Garland, Texas, carrying a large steel drilling structure.

Sometimes a container aboard a truck will be configured to include hidden compartments. "Other times," said a [driver] over breakfast, "they just roll up with guns and say: 'Open the door!'" Lorries are forced to resume their journeys with drugs on board. The drivers complain that haulage companies' efforts to outwit criminals are inevitably met with countermeasures. "They give us GPS systems to make sure we don't go anywhere off the route, but some people are told to switch them off. They have special seals now, but the bad guys know how to break them and make them look as before."[11]

As NAFTA opened the world to Osiel Cárdenas and his cohorts in crime, shoot-outs and killings by competing syndicates became a regular occurrence during the latter years of the Vicente Fox Quesada presidency (2000–06). Infamous capo El Chapo Guzmán Loera headed the Sinaloa Cartel, also called the Sinaloa Federation. He and his allies in the Arturo Beltrán Organization (ABO) sought to break the grip of the Gulf Cartel (CDG) on the Tamaulipas transit points.

Meanwhile, groups such as Carrillo Fuentes' Juárez Cartel, mentioned earlier, and the Tijuana Cartel specialized in extreme violence and accepted zero tolerance for slights of honor. They had staked their criminal empire on controlling access to the United States, creating a "have" and "have not" environment within Mexico's underworld. They would not give up this prized position easily when newcomers invaded their terrain. Conflict escalated dramatically under Fox's successor, Felipe Calderón Hinojosa, who took office on December 1, 2006. Soon after his inauguration, the new chief executive dispatched large contingents of the army and Federal Police to the violence-plagued northern states. These incursions coincided with an upsurge in narco-related killings along the border from 651 (2007) to 2,648 (2008) to 2,853 (2009), to 5,283 (2010), and 5,283 (2011).[12]

In the past, Mexicans seeking to flee untenable situations made haste to the United States. The porosity of the border ensured eventual success; if a migrant did not make it on his first or second attempt, he would usually accomplish the feat the third time.

Yet, a medley of factors—reaction to the September 11, 2001, attack on the Pentagon and the twin trade towers, the dispatch of US troops to Iraq and Afghanistan, and intractably high American joblessness—prompted Washington to devote more personnel and resources to securing its two-thousand-mile long frontier with Mexico. States such as Alabama, Arizona, Georgia, Indiana, South Carolina, and Utah enacted stringent legislation to stanch the inflow of illegal workers. Those who managed to sneak across the border found it extremely difficult to obtain work. Texas governor and presidential aspirant, Rick Perry, even threatened to send troops into Mexico to end cartel-related violence should he win the White House.[13]

The severe economic downturn that began in 2008 also beset migrants' family members and friends in the United States. As a result, the roughly one hundred thousand *tamaulipecos* residing abroad sent far fewer dollars back to Mexico—with Tamaulipas suffering one of the nation's sharpest declines in "remittances." These receipts plummeted from $490 million (January–June 2007) to $260.4 million (January–June 2008) to $95 million (January–March 2011).[14] Many immigrants who came to their native state for the 2009–10 Christmas holidays decided not to return to "El Norte" because bleak economic prospects in America exacerbated unemployment at home. For example, when some fifteen thousand people flooded into their small hometown of Tula, in southern Tamaulipas, the mayor complained that the returnees precipitated social problems and overburdened the municipality's budget, which depended heavily on funds from abroad. "As mayor I have a flow of people asking for money to buy food, medicine, gasoline, clothing, and even their electricity bills . . . here is where you find [economic problems] affecting families," he said.[15] An entrepreneur's attempt to organize "narco-tours" of sites of executions, gun battles, and other historical sites came a cropper in light of escalating bloodshed.[16]

The absence of opportunities accentuated the appeal of criminal groups. Perhaps, some reasoned, it was easier to break the law in Mexico, especially because of the ubiquitous corruption of police, prosecutors, and judges. In addition, the so-called Ni-Nis—teenagers who neither work nor study—abounded. Even wrongdoers who suffered arrest and incarceration frequently managed to escape from the state's sieve-like, overcrowded prisons, thanks to incompetent administrators, venal guards, and cartel-engineered breakouts. Imprisoned or not, dreadful conditions in the state could not meet the needs of the half million individuals of its 3,268,554 inhabitants who had been found to suffer mental illness.[17]

Drug abuse continued to climb. A Ministry of Education's National Survey placed Tamaulipas number one in the consumption of narcotics out of thirty-one states and the Federal District (DF). In an earlier study, the state ranked third in the use of crack cocaine and heroin.[18] So desperate was the addiction level that Antonio González Sánchez, bishop of Ciudad Victoria, called for legalizing the use of all drugs in Mexico. "Some say that this will lead to more addiction—I sincerely don't believe it; current addicts will continue being addicts and those who are going to be addicts will try drugs whether or not they are legalized. I don't believe that this [reform] will increase the problem." He emphasized that changing the law would reduce the high level of violence, the narco-trafficking, and the insecurity that devastated his country. He added that alcohol was legal and "does far more damage than any other type of drug."[19]

Bishop González Sánchez's views, which he stressed were personal, drew criticism from the Tamaulipas health secretary, who underscored the imperative to reinforce established programs. Yet the Mitofsky consulting firm found that 75 percent of respondents believed insecurity was increasing in the North.[20] And a November 2011 poll taken by *Reforma* newspaper found that 51 percent of those surveyed said the cartels were winning "the war against narco-trafficking."[21] Such results were music to the ears of Mexico's criminal elite, who rely on impunity as they conduct their multifarious criminal activities (Table 1 sets forth the number and types of crimes committed during the first quarters of 2009, 2010, and 2011).

The bloodletting tormenting Nuevo Laredo prompted the Laredo, Texas, Chamber of Commerce to delete its twin city from local road markers lest travelers encounter harm when crossing the border. In the face of an uproar from its Mexican neighbor, the city's mayor apologized and restored signs pointing the way to the Tamaulipas municipality.[22]

The recent economic, social, and political history of Tamaulipas reflected how decades of malfeasance, corruption, impunity, and a host of other embedded factors played out across Mexico in favor of criminals and a limited number of citizens and state officials. The eroded civil contract between state and populace engendered an environment where even the least ambitious criminals might thrive; the more predatory lawbreakers eventually formed their own social system, tilted toward violence and black market economics that

Table 1   Serious Crimes Committed in Tamaulipas (first quarters of 2009, 2010, and 2011)

Crime	2009	2010	2011
Robberies of homes[a]	81	100	103
Robberies of stores[a]	110	171	153
Robberies of vehicles[a]	390	257	823
Robberies of pedestrians[a]	104	142	226
Robberies in intersections	0	0	28
Murders	230	154	303
Premeditated murders (Homicidios dolosos)	71	126	188
Kidnappings	7	6	30
Rapes	125	95	132

[a]Involved violence.
Source: Henia Prado, "Crecen delitos en Tamaulipas," *Reforma.com*, April 24, 2011.

spurned all normal government services except one: employment. The opportunities offered by Osiel Cárdenas Guillén and his counterparts fomented a reality where criminals acquired more lethal force than law-enforcement agencies, which often devolved into snake pits of venality.

Men like Osiel become modern-day caudillos, and as many analysts have observed, over the past ten years, one criminal group has revealed itself as the most barbaric in Mexico, and indeed in several other countries. This book discusses the Gulf Cartel's recruitment of Latin America's most deadly and diverse transnational criminal organization, Los Zetas; analyzes the paramilitaries' structure and training as it has evolved from a Praetorian Guard into an independent entity; evaluates the resources at its disposal; discusses its "branding" as it has diversified into multiple criminal rubrics; describes its psychological operations (PSYOPS); compares Los Zetas with La Familia Michoacana/Knights Templars,[23] another relatively new syndicate; explores the "dual sovereignty" that Los Zetas have developed with elected state and municipal governments; examines the nation's "Zetanization"; traces the syndicate's expansion into other Latin American nations; probes the mercenaries' penetration of the United States; and, finally, focuses on its future in light of the warfare raging between Los Zetas and their foes in the Gulf and Sinaloa cartels, the Knights Templars, and the Mexican and US governments

Notes

1. Sam Dillon, "Matamoros Journal; Canaries Sing in Mexico, but Uncle Juan Will Not," *New York Times*, February 9, 1996.
2. Ibid.
3. Peter Lupsha, "Transnational Narco-Corruption and Narco-Investment: A Focus on Mexico," *Transnational Organized Crime* (spring 1995).
4. Cindy Hahamovitch, "The Politics of Labor Scarcity: Expediency and the Birth of the Agricultural 'Guestworkers' Program," *Backgrounder*, Center for Immigration Studies, December 1999.
5. Maquila owners, who have enhanced security, pay $8 to $16 per day; see Randal C. Archibold, "Despite Violence, Mexico Plants Hum at Border, *New York Times*, July 11, 2011.
6. "Superan a Ciudad Juárez en violencia contra mujeres," *El Siglo de Torreón*, November 24, 2009; and "Ocupa Tamaulipas cuarto lugar en agresiones hacia la mujer," *El Mañana*, August 5, 2009.
7. Bowden, *Down by the River: Drugs, Money, Murder, and Family* (New York, NY: Simon & Schuster, 2003).
8. Quoted in James H. McDonald, "The Narcoeconomy and Small-Town Rural Mexico," *Human Organization* 64, No. 2 (summer 2005): 117; although

McDonald wrote about Michoacán, the same situation applies to Tamaulipas.

9.   Quoted in Ed Vulliamy, "Mexico's Zetas: Lords of a Brutal Narco-State," *The Observer* (London), November 17, 2009.

10. Quoted in Sam Logan, "Mexico's Uppermost Threat is Organized Crime," *Mexidata.Info*, May 1, 2006.

11. Quoted in Ed Vulliamy, "The Zetas: Kings of their Own Brutal Narco State," *Mail&Guardian.online*, November 15, 2009.

12. "Ejecuciones 2010," *Reforma*, March 24, 2010.

13. Amy Gardner, "Perry: Send U.S. Troops to Mexico to Fight Drug Wars," *Washington Post*, October 1, 2011.

14. Banco Central de México.

15. Saúl Muñoz Vallejo, quoted in María Guadalupe Jaramillo Alanís, "Regreso de migrantes generará conflictos sociales, Alcalde de Tula," *Asi es Tamaulipas*, October 15, 2008.

16. Marc Lacey, "For Some Taxi Drivers, a Different Kind of Traffic," *New York Times*, March 1, 2009.

17. "Por la Inseguridad, más 500 mil con trastornos mentales en Tamaulipas," *Excélsior*, June 5, 2011.

18. Claudia Zapata Santiso, "Refuta SET resultados sobre adicciones," *MetroNoticias*, October 26, 2009; and Julio L. Guzmán, "Tamaulipas, tercer estados en consume de heroina," *El Universal*, August 27, 2008.

19. "Aprueba Obispo legalizar drogas," *PrimeraHora.com.mx*, April 14, 2009.

20. Consulta Mitofsky, "Percepción Ciudadano sobre la seguridad en México," August 18, 2009.

21. Alejandro Moreno and María Antonia Mancillas "Encuesta/Respaldan labor de Fuerzas Armadas, *Reforma*, December 1, 2011; in March 2011, the same analysts found that 54 percent of respondents believed that organized crime was winning the war; see "Ven fines distintos en Guerra al narco," *Reforma*, April 1, 2011.

22. Juan Manuel Reyes Cruz, "Se disculpa Texas; quita letreros de Laredo para evitar a 'extraños,'" *Excélsior*, May 20, 2011.

23. Since 2010, the majority faction of La Familia Michoacana refers to themselves as the Knights Templars.

1

Origins and Establishment of Los Zetas

In mid-1999, Osiel Cárdenas Guillén gave a hearty abrazo to the coleader of their Gulf Cartel, Salvador "El Chava" Gómez Herrera, whom he cordially welcomed into the passenger side of his shiny Dodge Durango. They bantered for a few minutes, exchanging laughs and quips. Gómez Herrera was in an expansive mood, having just organized and served as godfather at the baptism of Osiel's daughter, a service the capo had not attended.[1] Arturo Guzmán Decena, who was riding in the backseat, suddenly and coldly fired a bullet point blank into El Chava's head, splattering brains, blood, and tissue across the leather dashboard. Investigators later found the victim's decaying body, partially eaten by scavengers, in the brush near Matamoros.[2]

Osiel earned the nickname "El Mata Amigos" or "The Friend Killer" for ordering this and other executions. The treacherous act vaulted him into the leadership of the Gulf Cartel, which would become one of Mexico's most powerful and vicious organizations, inferior only to the Sinaloa Federation headed by the infamous Joaquín "El Chapo" Guzmán Loera, Carrillo Fuentes' Juárez Cartel, and the Tijuana Cartel, also known as the Arellano Félix Organization (AFO) because it was once dominated by the Arellano Félix brothers.

Since childhood, Osiel had harbored profound insecurities to the point of paranoia. Fathered by an uncle, he was born on May 18, 1967, on the impoverished "Caracol" ranch forty-five miles from the sweltering city of Matamoros. He suffered bouts of depression, obsessed over his lack of a real father, rebelled against his family, and left home at age twelve to live in Matamoros with his sister Lilia. He worked as a dishwasher, waiter, and messenger before beginning to climb the criminal ladder. Young Osiel loathed school, but demonstrated "street smarts" and a determination to become someone important.

Serving a brief stint in Great Plains prison in Arizona for drug running in 1992 only hardened Osiel as a criminal. One of the by-products of NAFTA was the transfer of Mexican inmates to Mexican prisons. On January 2, 1994, Osiel entered the Santa Adelaida penitentiary in Matamoros. The warden knew his brother, Mario "El Gordo" Cárdenas Guillén,[3] and the penal facility became an ideal venue for The Friend Killer to hone his skills in exporting narcotics. On April 13, 1995, he left prison as a businessman, vicious as ever.[4]

While behind bars, he had become enamored of the wife of Rolando Gómez Garza, the prison warden. When Gómez Garza learned of the affair, he beat his wife, which prompted Osiel to have the man executed.

His brother Mario helped Osiel set up a repair shop, from which the ex-convict peddled small amounts of drugs and functioned as an informant for the Federal Judicial Police (PJF), who, with crooked local cops, protected him. He stole luxury cars, counterfeited auto registrations, inflicted grotesque torture on his rivals, and concentrated on selling drugs in Miguel Alemán, a municipality of twenty-five thousand inhabitants in northeast Tamaulipas across the Rio Grande from Roma, Texas, a two-hour drive from Matamoros. Osiel eventually supplanted Gilberto "El June" García Mena, a devotee of Santa Muerte or Saint of Death, who is discussed later, as the top dog in the Miguel Alemán area.

Still, Osiel was a minor player compared with Juan García Abrego, who headed the Gulf Cartel until early 1996. Friends with Raúl, the so-called inconvenient brother of President Carlos Salinas (1988–94), the puffy-faced García Abrego became the first Mexican to appear on the FBI's Ten Most Wanted List, largely owing to his pathbreaking accord with Colombian cartels in the early 1990s. In lieu of receiving cash, the Colombians gave half of their shipments to the Gulf Cartel, which incurred the risk of marketing the cocaine in return for pocketing the profits derived from sales. The formula soon became the model for all major Mexican syndicates. "This deal was a major turning point in the fortunes of the Mexican cartels. With this new business arrangement, the power and wealth of the Mexican drug cartels exploded."[5] By renegotiating this pact with Colombia's Cali Cartel, García Abrego was able to derive 50 percent of a shipment from Colombia as payment for delivery, instead of the $1,500 per kilogram previously received. The new business model came with a price: the Mexicans would have to guarantee that Colombian exports reached their destinations. This deal, while risky, was a driving force behind exponential growth as kilos became tons, and thousands of dollars became millions in profits.

In the wake of this arrangement, García Abrego accumulated large quantities of cocaine along Mexico's northern frontier. At the same time, the agreement enabled him to design his own distribution network and with newfound profits, expand his political influence. By the end of the 1980s and into the early 1990s, it was estimated that García Abrego smuggled more than three hundred metric tons per year across the US–Mexico border. The Mexican Attorney General's Office (PGR) claimed that his organization was generating $500 to $800 million in gross profits by the early 1990s.[6]

Collaboration with Guillermo González Calderoni, a commander in the PJF who had won fame for killing drug honcho Pablo Acosta,[7] vouchsafed the organization's success and shielded its leaders from arrest. The devious cop never needed to prove his loyalty to the organization; he had grown up in Reynosa and was a boyhood friend of García Abrego's elder brother Mario. In a world where trust is worth more than life, he drew upon their shared history, transcended only by blood relations.

The Mexicans established distribution centers in Chicago, Dallas, Denver, Houston, New York, and Los Angeles. The Colombians agreed to the arrangement as long as the Mexicans left them alone in Miami and selected East Coast markets. The windfall allowed García Abrego to make additional investments to insulate his organization from law enforcement. In the early and mid-1990s, he loosed a cataract of millions of dollars on police officials, the army, and politicians.

He even stretched his corruptive influence across the Gulf of Mexico to Quintana Roo, where he and Governor Mario Villanueva Madrid facilitated the flow of drugs from the Yucatán Peninsula through Campeche, Tabasco, Veracruz, Tamaulipas, and ultimately to Nuevo León, paving the initial route where his organization would exercise significant territorial control and political pressure.[8] However, President Salinas' successor, Ernesto Zedillo, brought a swift end to the trafficking enterprise of García Abrego, who was taken into custody in early 1996. Mexican authorities immediately delivered him to the FBI in Texas.

At his October trial in a Houston Federal Court, the prosecution revealed that the Gulf Cartel had smuggled more than fifteen tons of cocaine and forty-six thousand pounds of marijuana into the United States and laundered approximately $10.5 million. His cousin testified that García Abrego routinely spent up to $80,000 on pricey watches and expensive suits for Mexican police and prosecutors during frequent shopping trips in Texas. A government witness alleged that the defendant paid $1.5 million a month to Javier Coello Trejo, the assistant attorney general in charge of combating narcotics—an accusation that Coello Trejo denied. García Abrego fought back tears as the jury, eager to make him the poster boy in the drug war, sentenced him to eleven life sentences and decreed the seizure of up to $350 million of his assets—$75 million more than the prosecution requested. Meanwhile, the PJF commander who made the arrest is believed to have received a bulletproof Mercury Grand Marquis and $500,000 from a competing cartel for accomplishing the takedown.[9]

Once García Abrego landed behind bars, Salvador Gómez Herrera, a squat, trigger-happy underling of the formidable drug lord, sought to seize Gulf Cartel operations. The proliferation of dangerous competitors for the top spot prompted El Chava to invite Osiel to assume joint dominance of Tamaulipas, which had become a key Gulf Cartel *plaza* or area for the importation, production, storing, and shipping of narcotics.

The men functioned well together, at first. They muzzled the press, bought off police, liquidated rivals, and forged alliances with law-enforcement officers, politicians, and army personnel. In addition, they acquired drugs from Guatemala through the southern state of Chiapas. At other times, they smuggled shipments through the port of Coatzacoalcos, Veracruz, from where the cocaine was trucked to Nuevo Laredo and Matamoros before entering the United States.

They boosted earnings in the lucrative zone by strong-arming small-time hoodlums into paying a *derecho de piso* or transit fee to transport drugs across their turf. El Chava's goons hustled those who failed to fork over the danegeld into the shabby Hotel Nieto in Matamoros. Passersby heard bloodcurdling screams and fervent cries for God and mercy, as captives were tortured, often choked by a gun barrel jammed down their throats, until they anted up the money.[10]

Although supposedly an equal to Osiel, El Chava acted as if he wielded the whip. Especially vexing to The Friend Killer was his continual request for loans from his "partner," who treated him as a subordinate or bootlicker. Such behavior offended the pride of a neurotic Osiel, who had assembled his own entourage. His confidants included Eduardo "El Coss" Costilla Sánchez, Víctor Manuel "El Memeloco"

Vázquez Mireles, and Arturo "Z-1" Guzmán Decena, who would play a pivotal role in Osiel's ascent to power.

Hooked on cocaine, the thirty-one-year-old Friend Killer's internal demons convinced him that assassins plotted his demise. Osiel yearned to rise from a criminal honcho to a feared capo. His rise to the top of the Gulf Cartel brought with it enemies—gangs and individuals who had suffered apace with his success—and accentuated his fear of violent death. Often on a whim, he ordered triggermen to hunt down real and imagined foes. His obsession with death at the hands of a traitor often "paralyzed" him, according to an astute biographer.[11] Burdened by the weight of his delusions, Osiel had earlier approached local military personnel seeking their protection. One of his first contacts was with Lt. Antonio Javier Quevedo Guerrero, a former member of the Twenty-First Cavalry Regiment in Nuevo León. After Quevedo's capture on March 29, 2001, Osiel increasingly relied on Guzmán Decena, who had acquired skills in explosives, counterinsurgency, and tracking down and apprehending enemies during his military career.

Growing distrust of the crude, impetuous, and imperious Gómez Herrera drove Osiel to mastermind the murder of his supposed confrere in crime. Guzmán Decena, an Osiel confidant who had delivered the coup de grâce to El Chava, devised a safety plan for his jittery, disturbed employer. Born in Puebla in 1976, Guzmán Decena had distinguished himself in the army and ascended through the ranks to become a lieutenant in the Airborne Special Forces Group (GAFES), an elite combat unit modeled on the US Special Forces.[12] After deserting the military, he became Cárdenas Guillén's protector. "In contrast to the timid, sometimes cowardly Osiel, [Guzmán Decena] exuded daring, a detail that was not lost on the almost absolute chief of the cartel, who saw in him a well-prepared man and began to encourage the creation of a security group that over the years became the most formidable of any Latin American cartel, including the Colombians."[13]

Osiel emphasized that he "wanted the best men possible" to protect him. The deserter replied, "They are only in the army." As a result, Guzmán Decena helped lure disaffected GAFES and other malcontents into the "Army of Narcos" to protect Osiel and his entourage.[14] Military personnel were vulnerable to this siren song. Soldiers endured measly pay, long hours, deplorable food and housing, harsh and arbitrary discipline, and low morale. Meanwhile, rank-and-file fighting men watched as many senior officers used their positions to steal from the government and ingratiate themselves with crime chiefs.

Ironically, a top military anticartel fighter would later become defenders of a different sort of organization, the Gulf Cartel. In late 1996, President Zedillo named Major General Jesús Gutiérrez Rebollo director of the National Institute to Combat Drugs (INCD). The bulldog-faced forty-two-year veteran had previously served as a member of the prestigious Presidential Guard and commanded the Fifth Military Region, which embraced several west-central states, including the drug trafficking emporium of Guadalajara in Jalisco state. The enigmatic officer—initially reputed to be a rugged leader brimming with personal integrity—had extensive experience in running army operations against drug traffickers. Among trophy capos whom he had captured were Guadalajara Cartel big shot Héctor Luis "El Güero" Palma Salazar and miscreants in the Tijuana-based AFO. Mexico's top-ranking drug interdiction chief won an encomium from Washington's own drug czar, General Barry McCaffrey, who lauded him for "a public reputation of absolute integrity. He is a strong leader. This is clearly a focused, high-energy man."[15]

The head of America's war on narcotics had to eat crow when investigators discovered, eleven weeks after his appointment, that Gutiérrez Rebollo was on the payroll of the Juárez Cartel. This syndicate, led by the obscenely successful drug trafficker "Lord of the Skies" Carrillo Fuentes, ferried drugs from Colombia to Chihuahua in Boeing 727s. The two-star Judas had assigned other double-dealing officers as "antidrug delegates" in the North where several answered the Gulf Cartel's call for recruits, including Guzmán Decena. He was serving in Miguel Alemán, Tamaulipas, as an appointee to the Special Prosecutor for Crimes against Health (FEADS). Gutiérrez Rebollo's nose for talent was surpassed only by his limited insight into what his men would ultimately become, and the deaths they would deal in the future.

In a house in Reynosa in February 1999, Osiel instructed Guzmán Decena to round up twenty thugs to assassinate his rival Rolando "El Rolys" López Salinas. When spearheading the mission, Guzmán and his men encountered gunfire. One man in the crew, Heriberto "The Executioner" Lazcano Lazcano, blew up a gas tank, killing those in their prey's hideout. The municipal police never reported the incident. Guzmán proceeded to attract more than thirty other deserters enticed by princely salaries—referred to a *cañonazos de dólares* or "cannon balls of dollars"—compared with the pittance they earned in uniform.[16] Osiel gave each new recruit $3,000, called *la polla* (a pullet or young chicken), with which to buy cocaine, enter the United States, and round up distributors. This artifice acquainted the newcomers with the drug trade and broadened the cartel's market. The turncoats could reinvest their profits in more cocaine and multiply their earnings, according to "Rafael," a protected witness. It was said that The Executioner, who was destined to lead the mercenaries, purchased eighteen kilograms of the white powder.[17] Guzmán Decena also offered opportunities for advancement, which—after his death—became even more rapid. By 2011, new Zetas could reach the position of hit man in a month, a process that used to take several years, at best.[18]

Many of the original deserters had been assigned to the Fifteenth Motorized Cavalry (Reynosa) and the Seventieth Infantry Battalion (Puebla).[19] In contrast, Óscar "El Winnie Pooh" Guerrero Silva held a bureaucratic post in the General Services Group of the Defense Ministry's General Staff (Appendix 1 lists the names, specialties, and status of the original GAFE traitors). Guzmán Decena's original platoon had grown to more than three hundred cadres by 2003.[20] The thirty-one men who composed the Gulf Cartel's security detail in mid-2003 included lieutenants or second lieutenants (five), sergeants (three), corporals (three)—with the rest being privates.[21]

Guzmán Decena's code name "Z-1" gave rise to "Los Zetas," the eventual name of Osiel's first-class bodyguards.[22] Initially, they provided three to five protective circles around Osiel, who, for the first time in his life, began to feel a modicum of security. The paramilitaries later added to their ranks defectors from the Guatemalan Army. Edin José "El Ponchado" Aragón Stwolinsky alone rounded up a dozen fellow deserters, each of whom the Gulf Cartel paid Mex$13,000 per month ($1,083) plus benefits—more than six times the amount they received from the military (Mex$2,000). The newcomers were handed voting cards and other bogus credentials with which they could open bank accounts in Mexico.[23]

While Osiel was content to place his life in the hands of Los Zetas, other Gulf Cartel notables spawned a hodgepodge of personal defenders: the "Sierras" and the "Tangos" protected Jorge Eduardo "El Coss" Costilla Sánchez and Víctor Manuel "El Meme" Vázquez Mireles; Gabriel Montes, the Gulf's top man in Tampico, relied on the Sierras; and Osiel's brother, Ezequiel "Tony Tormenta" Cárdenas Guillén, depended on the "Escorpiones" or "Scorpions," two of whose members—Marcos Antonio "Escorpión 37" Cortes Rodríguez and Josue "Escopión 43" González Rodríguez—were taken into custody when the navy killed Osiel's brother and four bodyguards on November 5, 2010.[24] Members of these units also had access to "la polla," depending on the plaza and their importance to the cartel, which rose as their deeds deemed the men trustworthy and battle tested.[25]

Systematically infused brutality pushed Los Zetas well beyond the tasks learned during army training. Among the renegades' first assignments was eradication of Los Chachos, a group led by Dionicio "El Chacho" Román García Sánchez. El Chacho had double-crossed García Abrego by switching allegiance to the powerful Sinaloa Cartel headed by El Chapo Guzmán.

Originally composed of fifty or sixty cross-border auto thieves, Los Chachos competed for control of Nuevo Laredo with the Flores Soto gang, headed by Mario Flores Soto. The Gulf Cartel sought unfettered access to this border portal, as well as the absolute right to charge other groups that traversed its turf. For instance, they levied as much as a $200,000 fee to allow one airplane to fly over their bailiwick.[26]

When Los Chachos kidnapped and killed Mario Flores Soto's youngest brother and ten of his associates, Los Zetas responded by systematically decimating the gangsters. They began with four policemen believed to be linked with El Chacho. Z-1, The Executioner, and other Zetas seized the officers, tortured them until they confessed their association with Los Chachos, and then burned them to a crisp in a two-hundred-liter metal drum. A heavily armed contingent eventually tracked down El Chacho, who was found dead reportedly clothed in women's underwear, in Tamaulipas on May 13, 2002. Los Zetas also killed his right-hand man, El Juve.[27] Nuevo León authorities attributed to the paramilitaries twenty-one of the forty-two homicides committed in the state between January 2002 and June 2003.

Rescuing prison inmates constituted another type of operation. The first occurred on December 27, 2002, to free Daniel Pérez Rojas (Santa Adelaida, Matamoros); the second on November 15, 2003, to rescue Antonio Román Vega (Mexicali prison hospital), and the third on January 5, 2004, to liberate twenty-five prisoners (Apatizingán). These successful assaults functioned as trial runs, looking to the day when the paramilitaries might have to engineer the escape of capos.[28] Their early major offensives quickly demonstrated that a new criminal element had emerged. In view of the relative ease with which Osiel's bodyguards expelled the car thieves from the Nuevo Laredo plaza, potential rivals quickly grasped that they were well trained, keenly motivated, and prepared to shoot first and ask questions later.

Osiel gradually expanded the responsibilities of Los Zetas to encompass collecting debts, securing cocaine supplies, protecting trafficking routes, keeping his subordinates in line, and executing opponents—often with unspeakable savagery. Although a Gypsy fortune-teller supposedly claimed to see neither death nor prison bars in his future, Osiel became even more despondent—to the point of seeking to kill as a "traitor" his ally who had suggested the session with the soothsayer. The capo even stated that he was going to retire, turning over the reins to "El Coss" Costilla, currently a *jefe* of the Gulf Cartel. However, Osiel failed to conquer his destructive addiction to power.[29] Rather than step aside, he consolidated his strength in 1999 and began to create what he referred to as "my business," as his brothers looked on.[30]

Osiel's younger brother Mario was even less adept than was Osiel's sibling, Tony Tormenta. Mario's forte was testing the quality of drugs and moving them to the United States, a mission that he continued to perform even after his 1995 capture. He carried on other criminal activities while in Matamoros' Cereso II penitentiary. These included as many as ten cockfights a day with bets up to $3,000 a contest, the sale of drugs, and the distribution of benefits such as television sets and conjugal visits. Mario's own cell measured sixty square meters and accommodated automobiles, trailers, and stocks of cocaine and marijuana. Every Sunday, forty distributors doled out Mex$1,000 to the prison administrators for the opportunity to pick up drugs from Mario and his allies. Osiel assisted these activities, as did Rogelio "El Kelín" González Pizaña and others. El Coss and El Meme Vázquez Mireles ensured that customs officials would not interfere with their northbound exports. The naming of some twenty different wardens between 1995 and 2002 illustrated the corruption that engulfed the penal institution. "Prison as a party"—the caption of a newspaper article—ended on May 28, 2000, when Mario was suddenly transferred to the La Palma maximum-security penitentiary, outside of Mexico State's capital, Toluca.[31] He obtained his freedom in 2007 but was too late to support his brother or the Gulf Cartel. By then, Los Zetas had already begun to act independently.

In 1999, Osiel had reached the top of his game. He had garnered support from an ever-changing array of gangs, including Los Flores Soto, Los Ortiz Medina, and the Mexican Mafia, known as "La Eme." At the same time, he had severed ties with the execrably corrupt PJF Commander Guillermo González Calderoni and other erstwhile confidants of García Abrego. In addition, Osiel supplemented Los Zetas with Los Sierras and Los Tangos. While the paramilitaries concentrated on protection, the other bands controlled clandestine air flights, robbed automobiles, tapped telephone lines, and involved themselves in smuggling illegal immigrants.[32] Osiel's small-time criminal organization acquired more turf, and its leader more importance. The Friend Killer's bravado, swagger, and self-delusion, though, bred notions of invincibility, even in the face of US law enforcement.

In May 1999, Osiel threatened to kill a Cameron County sheriff's deputy who, working in an undercover capacity for a US agency, refused to deliver a load of approximately 988 kilograms of marijuana. Six months later, Osiel again stepped further out of bounds by confronting Federal Bureau of Investigation (FBI) Agent Daniel Fuentes and Drug Enforcement Administration (DEA) Agent Joseph DuBois. The explosive standoff occurred as a local informant was giving the law-enforcement officers a tour of cartel members' homes, stash houses, and hangouts in Matamoros. After cruising through the Aurora neighborhood where Osiel resided in a gaudy pink house adorned with towering walls and state-of-the-art security cameras, a black Lincoln Continental pulled in behind them along with a pickup truck with Texas plates.

At least three vehicles blocked the path of the Americans' Ford Bronco, which was fortified solely with diplomatic license tags. More than a dozen men, some wearing bulletproof vests and hoisting assault rifles, surrounded the vehicle as the snitch-turned-guide cowered in the backseat.

"The only way we were getting out was to talk our way out," DuBois later recalled. Osiel jumped from a white Jeep Cherokee and sauntered toward the Americans. He gripped a gold-plated AK-47 and had a Colt pistol with a gold grip bulging from his waistband. At first he pounded on the Bronco and ordered the agents to get out and hand over their passenger. Fuentes flashed his FBI shield, and in a fusillade of profanity, Osiel demanded that the agents surrender. He again told them to hand over their Mexican companion, who was cowering in the backseat. Again, the Americans denied his demand. "He kept saying, 'I don't give a damn who you are!'" recalled Dubois. The agent replied, "You don't care now, but tomorrow and the next day and the rest of your life, you'll regret anything stupid that you might do right now. You are fixing to make 300,000,000 enemies." Meanwhile, Fuentes, an accomplished marksman, fondled his handgun. If he and his partner were going to die, Osiel was "coming with us."[33] Osiel finally released them, saying, "Don't return to my territory, you sons of whores, because you will die."[34]

News of this toxic encounter ricocheted through the FBI and DEA headquarters like a photon in a laser cavity. It revived memories of the kidnapping, torture, and execution of DEA agent Enrique "Kiki" Camarena in early 1985.[35] The agency, which had previously regarded Osiel as a marginal player, quickly lofted him to number one on its priority list of Mexican narco-traffickers. Within a few days, the DEA purchased eight armored, bulletproof Chevrolet Suburbans, and sixteen agents drove them from Cincinnati to each of the organization's offices in Mexico. They simultaneously began to pressure Mexico City to apprehend Osiel, who continued to make furtive glances over his shoulder, even as the Gulf Cartel dispatched fifty tons of cocaine to the United States each month.

US authorities offered a $2 million reward for the criminal's capture. Acting as if nothing had happened, Osiel wasted no time in organizing a twenty-two-man team, some dressed as policemen, to free four of his associates from jail. The bounty on his head may have exacerbated Osiel's chronic paranoia. Realizing that he was in the spotlight, in September 2001, Osiel ordered Los Zetas, who then numbered fifty elements, to take enhanced military preparation in Nuevo León.[36] A year later, Attorney General Rafael Macedo de la Concha estimated that Osiel commanded at least three hundred hit men and traffickers in Tamaulipas alone.[37] On January 14, 2002, the army managed to nab Rubén "El Cacahuate"/"The Peanut" Sauceda Rivera, the Gulf Cartel's financial guru and most sophisticated money launderer, who was later extradited to the United States. The Mexican government registered its first significant success against Los Zetas when soldiers killed Guzmán Decena in November 2002. Unsubstantiated reports from within the organization claimed that his own men murdered the ex-lieutenant on orders from The Friend Killer, who had grown wary of Decena's might.

After these actions, the PGR and the military made yet another attempt to track down Osiel, who was believed to be hiding in Reynosa. Somehow, either he had disappeared from sight, or the pursuers had looked the other way. Authorities dragged the Rio Grande, split open cement blocks, and dug holes in empty terrain in an exhaustive attempt to find his body.[38] Osiel had hundreds of lookouts and infiltrators in Tamaulipas. The six-month investigation, which culminated in Osiel's arrest, was kept secret from everyone but President Fox—who ordered the raid—and the attorney general. The state's governor, Tomás Yarrington Ruvalcaba, whose fortunes rose and fell with Osiel's, knew nothing of the initiative.[39]

The prophetic Gypsy, if indeed she existed, had not foreseen a wild card in Osiel's future.[40] Second Lieutenant Alejandro Lucio Morales Betancourt, an ex-Army General Staff intelligence officer who had befriended the capo and even served as his personal pilot, was apprehended on November 17, 2001. He provided information that enabled the military to capture Cárdenas Guillén on March 14, 2003, after a shoot-out at an all-night birthday party for one of his daughters. Reportedly, the mole alluded to as "Geraldine" by the government, scurried into a witness protection program.[41]

The DEA considered the arrest important: "[it] sends a message to traffickers that violence and intimidation will not protect them from law enforcement," authorities said. US Ambassador Tony Garza lauded the capture as "a great victory for law enforcement," adding that "there is no doubt that Americans and Mexicans will be a lot better off with him and his cohorts behind bars." The envoy also urged American and Mexican officials "not to let our guard down" and continue pursuing drug leaders.[42] Osiel's men, as it turned out, remained active, even with their commander behind bars.

On May 6, 2003, Los Zetas allegedly murdered Edelio "El Yeyo" López Falcón in a Guadalajara restaurant. An ally of the once-almighty Juárez Cartel, he had poached on Gulf Cartel territory after Osiel's takedown, testing the stability of the imprisoned drug lord's security apparatus by moving illicit loads through the syndicate's territory without permission.[43]

On April 1, 2003, state law-enforcement officials arrested the drug lord's confidant and possible successor, "El Memeloco" Vázquez. They found him drinking with friends in a Veracruz dive. The officer spearheading the arrest was named "Policeman of the Year" by the state government. A year later, authorities dismantled a cell of José Alfredo Cárdenas, Osiel's nephew, who kept in telephone contact with his uncle residing in comfortable accommodations in La Palma penitentiary. In mid-2004, the army seized Ramiro "El Matí" García Hernández, an Osiel subordinate, who specialized in money laundering. The arrest took place in the Ciudad Satélite suburb of the DF, where authorities found $2 million, 160 kilos of cocaine, and six accomplices in various safe houses.[44]

On October 24, 2004, the army captured the boyishly handsome Carlos Alberto "El Tísico" Mendoza Rosales in his luxurious residence in the Colonia Lomas de Santa Maria, in Morelia, the capital of Michoacán. Osiel's top operator in Pacific Coast states of Michoacán and Guerrero, El Tísico had hatched a plot to free Osiel from prison. *Reforma* reported that the criminal offered a prodigious bribe if he were released.

With these veterans out of the picture, Los Zetas' leadership devolved to El Kelín González Pizaña, Osiel's chief executioner, who had threatened the US agents at gunpoint in 1999. He ensured the transport of drugs from Colombia to Texas, which meant his name had registered on the radar of US law enforcement. By the time González Pizaña took over as head of Los Zetas, the United States had announced a $1 million reward for his detention.

El Kelín's leadership was short-lived. In late October 2004, police apprehended him and fifty-five revelers as they were celebrating at "La Covacha," a house of prostitution in Matamoros that the Zeta owned. The 1:00 a.m. arrest took four lives, including that of a bodyguard, who died instantly when a Vietnam-style hand grenade exploded in his hand.[45] El Kelín unsuccessfully sought to escape in an armored Volkswagen Passat, throwing grenades at pursuers who attempted to block his flight. On a lighter note, twenty-two *teiboleras* or strippers, who were taken into custody, complained that they had to spend one night in the slammer.[46]

Even after these reverses, Los Zetas continued to function, and The Executioner earned fame because of his appalling ferocity and derring-do during warfare against the Sinaloa Cartel. Born in 1974 in Apan, Hidalgo, famous for pulque and charrería, the Mexican rodeo, the ex-GAFE joined forces at the apex of Los Zetas' pyramid with former Reynosa policeman Miguel Ángel "El 40" Treviño Morales.

A native of Nuevo Laredo, where he was born on June 28, 1973, El 40 falsely claimed to have been a GAFE.[47] Indeed, the skinny young man called "Miguelito" washed cars, ran errands, and acted as an all-round gofer for Gulf Cartel chieftain García Abrego before becoming a Reynosa policeman. After apprehending him on drug charges, the Dallas Sheriff's Department released the young hoodlum. On August 1, 2000, the Federal Court of North Texas ordered his capture for the possession and intent to distribute drugs—charges that were dropped on May 16, 2008. The Federal District Court in the District of Columbia had issued a warrant for his arrest on March 13, 2008.[48]

The Executioner's ironfisted command of his mercenaries propelled him into the Gulf Cartel's hierarchy, which included Osiel's brother, Tony Tormenta Cárdenas Guillén, and their longtime confederate, El Coss Costilla Sánchez. The Gulf Cartel appeared vulnerable. Its overlord languished in prison, while many of his most valued comrades had been captured or killed. Its leaders seemed disoriented, and Gregorio "El Goyo" Sauceda Gamboa, a former detective, the organization's plaza chief in Reynosa and Matamoros, and a drug addict, was dying of cancer.

Under The Executioner's direction, the paramilitaries trafficked in small quantities of drugs and earned "black money" by vouchsafing protection to gambling halls, pirate taxi drivers, illicit massage parlors, table-dance bars, bordellos, and unlicensed nightclubs. They also derived income from used-car lots from which they took either a few thousand dollars or vehicles. The owners' inability to come up with extortion fees forced closure of some of these dealerships.[49] Local gangs gave a wide berth to Los Zetas because of the savagery employed against rivals. For example, in 2005 at the behest of El 40, the Nuevo Laredo police kidnapped thirty-four of his foes whom they took to a house in the city's Benito Juárez neighborhood. Treviño Morales strutted in, wearing a black Special Forces uniform. He ordered Felipe López, known as "El Güerillo," to be separated from the group, according to a former Zeta. When the seventeen-year-old resisted, "El Maco," an El 40 henchman, bound his wrists and neck. After the teenager was subdued, Treviño Morales asked the horror-stricken onlookers, "Which of you knows the location of the heart?" before plunging a knife into the chest of the Felipe López, who died immediately.

Next he turned to a hostage called "El Ruco," asking, "How old are you?" When the terrified victim answered "Fifty-two," Trevino Morales replied, "You have lived too long, and you are going to join the *muchacho.*" The psychopath's hit men crammed the two corpses into the truck of a compact car and disposed of them.[50]

Their tactics brought notoriety and enabled them to retain their small-time "clients" and to extort money from such legitimate businesses as automobile sellers, warehouses, hospitals, supermarkets, and clinics. The broadening of the customer base ensured higher earnings, though it wouldn't be long before the Gulf Cartel faced threatening competition from ambitious rivals.

A few days before his scheduled extradition to the United States, the infamous Joaquin "El Chapo" Guzmán[51] fled from the La Puente

Grande maximum-security prison in Jalisco State, where he had been serving a twenty-five-year sentence for conspiracy, bribery, and "crimes against health." Behind bars, the kingpin enjoyed a sybaritic lifestyle: conjugal visits, access to other women, alcohol, drugs, sumptuous meals, a computer, four cell phones, a television set, stereo, wild parties, and all the creature comfort that money could buy. Still, the capo was ready to resume his profession without pesky constraints.[52] Sinaloans such as the Beltrán Leyva brothers (BLO),[53] Mayel "El Mayo" Zambada García, Juan José "El Azul" Esparragoza Moreno, and dozens of other conspirators helped orchestrate this blatant escape, which made inventive use of a prison laundry basket after El Chapo's electronically controlled cell door inexplicably flew open during a period when video cameras went dark.

The feat became known as the "golden kilogram"—an allusion to the weight of the precious metal used to buy off those who helped the inmate gain his freedom.[54] El Chapo once boasted that he spent $5 million each month on bribes to police and other officials. His ability to finance the finely tuned operation became evident when *Forbes* magazine trumpeted him as the 701st richest person in the world in 2009.[55] A federal investigation led to the arrest of seventy-one prison officials, and comedians began lampooning the name of the prison *El Puente Grande* (the "Big Bridge"), calling it *La Puerta Grande*—(the "Big Door"). "He remains fairly safe in Mexico because of his influence and ability to corrupt," said one US official.[56]

In the wake of his 2001 escape, Guzmán Loera rendezvoused in Cuernavaca to map a strategy with allies "El Mayo" Zambada, Ignacio "El Nacho" Coronel Villarreal, "El Azul" Esparragoza Moreno, "El Barbas" Beltrán Leyva, and twenty other high-level gangsters—a group the DEA baptized as the "Blood Alliance."[57] The Beltrán Leyvas had become a potent component of the Sinaloa Cartel while El Chapo was incarcerated. They sought to vanquish the AFO in Tijuana, crush the Gulf Cartel, and exterminate Los Zetas. Above all, the ABOs and El Chapo coveted control of Nuevo Laredo and other valuable open sesames to the United States.

After leaving La Puente Grande, El Chapo repaired to his ranch near La Tuna, a five-hour drive from Badiraguato, Sinaloa, which served as his home base in the so-called Golden Triangle where Sinaloa, Durango, and Chihuahua converge. There, he worked out the details of projects against enemies even as he fortified his relationship to Colombian cocaine suppliers. El Chapo began implementing his blueprint by alerting authorities to the hiding place of the AFO's top figure, Benjamín Arellano Félix (arrested March 9, 2002, in Puebla), and orchestrating the murder of Rodolfo "Golden Baby" Carrillo Fuentes (killed with his wife on September 12, 2004, in Culiacán), the youngest brother of Amado and Vicente.[58] Like any good soap opera, the plot thickened when a hit man, allegedly commissioned by Vicente Carrillo Fuentes, who had broken with the Sinaloa Cartel, fired eight bullets into El Chapo's younger brother, Arturo "El Pollo"/"The Chicken" Gúzman Loera, inside La Palma in late 2004. Honor-bound by blood, El Chapo had to retaliate.

One of the most forceful advocates for attacking the northern cartel was Édgar "La Barbie" Valdez Villarreal, El Chapo's premier enforcer and, later, the chief hit man for Beltrán Leyvas and head of "Los Negros" death squad. The nickname of this Texas-born killer derived from his fair skin and cornflower-blue eyes that reminded some of "Ken," a Mattel toy introduced in 1961 as Barbie's plastic boyfriend. Trained as a bill collector for the Beltrán Leyvas, Valdez Villarreal relished the fast lane—designer clothes, fancy automobiles, chic nightclubs, gorgeous women, and lots and lots of alcohol—before his arrest in late August 2010. Even then, he was pictured in designer clothes. It should be noted that although La Barbie is a US citizen, the Calderón administration has dragged its feet on returning him to his native land, possibly because he is a walking encyclopedia on ties between public figures and the mobs.

Years before, the pretty hit man had incurred The Executioner's wrath for having tortured and killed dozens of Lazcano's comrades during nasty confrontations between the Sinaloa Cartel and the Gulf Cartel. Nevertheless, by 2007, leaders of the two syndicates recognized that raging conflict hurt business and entered into an uneasy entente. A close observer evaluated the truce as equal parts precarious and valuable—so much so that both the Mexican Justice Department and military were careful not to disrupt the pact.[59]

Nuevo Laredo, Reynosa, and Matamoros erupted into war zones, with the army synchronizing its actions with the Sinaloans against the Gulf Cartel and their Zeta allies. Though behind prison walls, Osiel continued to give marching orders to his troops in the field.

For upwards of fourteen months the Beltrán Leyva Organization (BLO), La Barbie, and El Chapo tried in vain to take possession of the North. So determined was El Chapo to overcome his foes that he allegedly recruited Colombian guerrillas and Mara Salvatrucha cutthroats to assist in the conflict.[60] Los Zetas fought hammer and tongs to keep their adversaries at bay. The turning point was the June 8, 2005, assassination of Nuevo Laredo's municipal police chief, Alejandro Domínguez Coello, after only hours on the job. On the same day, seven masked gunmen stormed into a hospital in Chihuahua and murdered a federal agent who was recovering from gunshot wounds. President Fox immediately dispatched additional federal, military, and police units to the northern city.[61] Under pressure from the government, and with no clear vision of victory, La Barbie and the Sinaloans reluctantly decided to seek a rapprochement with the Gulf Cartel. They concluded that continued warfare was bad for business. Their overtures and Osiel's eventual removal from Mexico impelled a polarization that eventually pulled Los Zetas away from the Gulf Cartel.

Meanwhile, The Executioner met with other Zeta leaders. During a lengthy social hour lubricated with strong drink, Lazcano warmly exchanged handshakes and abrazos with plaza bosses, whom he lauded as "division chiefs." Next came the business session when he asked whether Los Zetas should accept the Gulf–Sinaloa Cartel rapprochement. "Those in agreement with peace, raise your hands!" The Executioner said to the assembly. All but three participants raised their hands.[62] The dissenters had their own reasons for turning thumbs down on the pact: one had recently lost a brother to the enemy; a second worried that a truce would weaken Los Zetas, and the third simply did not trust the former adversaries, an opinion shared by The Executioner.

Next, the top boss called for a vote on the controversial question of whether Los Zetas should remain in bed with the Gulf Cartel or go their separate way. They chose the latter option. El Coss knew of the results but was incapable of crossing The Executioner and his stalwarts. To so do would require support from the Sinaloa Cartel and its allies.

El Lazca's 2007 decision to have Los Zetas cast ballots on peace with the Sinaloa Federation presaged the impending split with the Gulf Cartel, which is examined in chapter 11. The second omen appeared later in the year when, much to the chagrin of El Coss and Tony Tormenta, the militaristic organization formed situational alliances with the formidable BLO.

Their first assignment was to provide protection in Zacatecas against the Sinaloa Cartel, from which the Beltrán Leyvas had split, arising from a fallout between El Chapo and Arturo Beltrán Leyva. Arturo had taken over the family syndicate after the January 21, 2008, arrest of his elder brother, Alfredo. Beginning in mid-2007, the Zeta–BLO collaboration took place in one-third of the state, including Fresnillo, Jerez, Tepechitlán, Tlaltenango, Chachihuite, and Sombrere—municipalities that witnessed the fiercest conflict between the Beltrán Leyvas and El Chapo. Within two years, Los Zetas dominated the north-central state known for rich deposits of silver and other minerals, and its strategic trafficking routes. Although Governor Amalia García Medina (2004–10) denied their presence, the mercenaries made clear that "Zacatecas is written with a Z." Los Zetas also cooperated with the BLO in Quintana Roo and in the port of Manzanillo, Colima.

At their zenith, the Beltrán Leyvas presided over illegal commerce at the Cancún, Acapulco, Toluca, Mexico City, and Monterrey airports. In Quintana Roo, where Cancún is located, the cartel and Los Zetas infiltrated and corrupted local, state, and federal police. In addition, the Beltrán Leyvas penetrated the highest echelons of Mexico's security apparatus, and for hefty payoffs, officials leaked information about pending strikes against them and other syndicates.[63] Contributing to their power were large stocks of cocaine and the employment of brutal operators—notably, La Barbie, Sergio "El Grande" Villarreal Barragán, and Gerardo "El Indio" Álvarez Vázquez.

After marines killed Arturo Beltrán Leyva in Cuernavaca in late-2009, the BLO reeled from one blow after another. On August 30, 2010, authorities arrested La Barbie, who had established a separate criminal enterprise, La Compañía, and had gone on a rampage against his former masters. Other reversals included the arrest of José Jorge "JJ" Balderas Garza (January 18, 2010), Gerardo "El Indio" Álvarez Vázquez (April 21, 2010), José Francisco "El Contador" Barreto García (June 23, 2010), La Barbie's father-in-law Carlos "El Compadre"/"El Charro" Montemayor (November 24, 2010), and Colombian drug supplier, Harold Mauricio "El Conejo" Poveda (November 6, 2010).

The Executioner and El 40 also forged alliances with the Juárez Cartel and its brutal enforcement gang, La Línea, and the Arellano Felix organization in Tijuana.

Before his capture, confinement, and extradition, Osiel had imparted some of his skills, tactics, and possibly contacts related to the drug business. Observing Osiel's deal-making, The Executioner and El 40 became vaguely acquainted with Colombian cocaine suppliers and distributors in the United States. Juan Carlos "JC" de la Cruz Reyna, an Osiel confidant, was in charge of transshipping drugs arriving in Veracruz. Although generally associated with the Gulf Cartel, he may have transferred his trafficking knowledge to Los Zetas before the army arrested him on August 29, 2007. Luis Reyes Enríquez, who handled imports from Central and South America before his capture in mid-2006, also may have assisted Los Zetas' entrée into narco-activities.

Eventually, Los Zetas developed desultory contacts with Luis Carlos Cristancho Beltrán and several other Colombians, most of whom used pseudonyms, in Coatzocoalcos, Veracruz. Nonetheless, these contacts ebbed and flowed, and Los Zetas had to content themselves with relatively small shipments, the one exception being the October 2007 Altamira cargo, which is examined later. Only in 2010 and 2011 did Los Zetas become important traffickers, which put them at deadly odds with the Sinaloa Cartel and its janissaries.[64]

Meanwhile, Los Zetas continued to expand their criminal pursuits beyond narcotics, extortion, and protection. As examined later, they diversified into murder-for-hire, kidnapping, human smuggling, contraband, petroleum theft, auto robbery, loan-sharking, the sale of human body parts, and other ventures (their criminal feats are summarized in table 4).

For several years, Los Zetas steered clear of San Pedro Garza García, which borders Monterrey and is the nation's most affluent city, because its mercurial mayor Mauricio Fernández Garza, scion of a Croesus-rich family, had hammered out a mutually convenient arrangement with the BLO. As evidence of the turbulence of the drug panorama, a year earlier the Beltrán Leyvas had dispatched a unit known as "Los Matazetas" or "Zeta Killers" to eliminate the paramilitaries in Cancún.[65]

The Executioner and El 40 added to their territory along with their activities. By 2009, they called the shots in roughly 50 percent of Tamaulipas. The Gulf Cartel held sway throughout the Reynosa–Matamoros–San Fernando triangle, as well as in Ciudad Miguel Alemán, across from Roma, Texas. While launching periodic attacks against the Gulf Cartel in these municipalities, Los Zetas controlled the rest of the Tamaulipas' northern border, including Nuevo Laredo, once the Gulf's passageway into the United States, according to Will Glaspy, the DEA special agent in charge in McAllen. They also established a beachhead in Monterrey, a vital choke point for northbound commerce.[66] Los Zetas boast greater links to cocaine flowing through Central America; the Gulf Cartel maintains stronger connections to marijuana plantations farther south in Mexico, he added. Los Zetas' reach extends to most of the Gulf Coast, the Yucatán Peninsula, Aguascalientes, Morelos, Oaxaca, Zacatecas, an enclave in Michoacán, and

Central and South America. At the same time, they have worked with the Beltrán Leyvas in Guerrero, Puebla, and Quintana Roo.[67] As Los Zetas grew in size and strength, the criminal phalanx began to rely on superior organization and training to keep a step ahead of their growing list of adversaries, with whom they would clash in Tamaulipas, Veracruz, Sinaloa, and Jalisco.

Notes

1. An investigative journalist indicates that Osiel was undergoing liposuction and plastic surgery to change his appearance at the time; see Ricardo Ravelo, "Las entranos del ejército," *Proceso*, May 16, 2010.
2. Ravelo, *Osiel: vida y tragedia de un capo* (Mexico City: Grijalbo, 2009): 202.
3. Osiel had other brothers (Rafael, Ezequiel, and Homero) and a sister (Lilia). Besides Osiel and Mario, Homero was also involved with the Gulf Cartel, but never as a big shot.
4. "Los Cárdenas Guillén: narcomenudistas que llegaron a capos," "*M Semanal*," November 14, 2010.
5. Chris Eskridge, "Mexican Cartels and Their Integration into Mexican Socio-Political Culture." An earlier version of this paper was presented at the International Conference on Organized Crime: Myth, Power, Profit, October 1999, Lausanne, Switzerland, p. 10, www.customscorruption.com/mexican_cartels_integr.htm.
6. Peter Lupsha, "Transnational Narco-Corruption and Narco-Investment: A Focus on Mexico." *PBS Frontline*, www.pbs.org/wgbh/pages/frontline/shows/mexico/readings/lupsha.html.
7. See Terrance E. Poppa, *Drug Lord: The Life & Death of Mexican Kingpin: A True Story* (2nd ed., revised and updated; Seattle, WA: Demand Publications, 1998).
8. Jiménez, "Identifica el Ejército tres rutas de cárteles."
9. John J. Bailey and Roy Godson, *Organized Crime and Democratic Governability: Mexico and the U.S.–Mexican Borderlands* (Pittsburgh, PA: University of Pittsburgh Press, 2001): 48; and Mark Fineman, "Mexican Drug Cartel Chief Convicted in U.S.," *Los Angeles Times*, October 17, 1996.
10. Ravelo, *Osiel*, pp. 122 and 123.
11. Ibid., p. 172.
12. These GAFES were special forces assigned to military zones, not the elite GAFES who trained abroad; see Abel Barajas, "Muestran 'Los Zetas' poderío," *Reforma*, September 12, 2004.
13. Quoted in Ravelo, *Osiel*, p. 173.
14. The Mexican Army has several special forces units, including the regular GAFES, who are deployed in the twelve military regions; and the extremely select "High Command Special Forces Airmobile Group," whose cadres report directly to the secretary of defense.
15. Quoted in Mark Fineman, "General Goes High-Profile in Mexico," *Los Angeles Times*, December 5, 1996.
16. Ravelo, "Las entranos del ejército"; the Mexican Army suffered 99,849 desertions between 2001 and 2006, with most defections occurring during

soldiers' first year in uniform; see "Desertaron 100 mil militares con Fox," *Milenio*, July 20, 2007; most defections occur during soldiers' first year in uniform.

17. "'Invierten' sicarios en cartel," *El Nuevo Heraldo*, March 1, 2010.
18. "Official: Mexican Cartels Hiring Common Criminals," *The Monitor*, April 7, 2011.
19. Marco A. Rodríguez Martínez, "El poder de los 'zetas,'" www.monografías. com.
20. Lisa J. Campbell, "Los Zetas: Operational Assessment," in Robert J. Bunker (ed.), *Narcos Over the Border: Gangs, Cartels and Mercenaries* (New York, NY: Routledge, 2011): 56.
21. Barajas, "Muestran 'Los Zetas' poderío," *Reforma*, September 12, 2004.
22. Some believe that Guzmán Decena acquired the call sign "Z-1" because Federal Police used these symbols to identify the mercenaries' kingpin; another theory holds that "Z" was a code letter used by GAFE squads to communicate with each other; and a third explanation holds that the name derives from the "zeta azul," the color of uniforms worn by military officers; see "Ex militar, de 36 años: el cruel líder de 'Los Zetas,'" *Diario Despertar de Oaxaca*, January 3, 2011.
23. "Pagan Zetas en dólares a kaibiles," *Terra*, October 4, 2006.
24. Other "scorpions" killed in the shoot-out include Sergio Antonio "El Tyson"/"Escorpión 1" Fuentes, Sergio M. "Escorpión 18" Vázquez (or Raúl Marmolejo Gómez), Hugo "Escorpión "26" Lira, and Refugio Aldalberto "Escorpión 42" Vargas Cortes; see "New Details Released about Gulf Cartel Leader's Death," *ValleyCentral.com*, November 7, 2010.
25. José Réyez, "Las operaciones secretas del cártel del Golfo," *Voltairnet.org*, August 31, 2009.
26. *United States of America v. Juan Garcia Abrego*, United States Court of Appeals, *Fifth Circuit*, May 6, 1998, http://altlaw.org/v1/cases/1090088.
27. Library of Congress, *Organized Crime and Terrorist Activity in Mexico*, 1999–2002, February 2003; and "Ex militar de 36 años: el cruel líder de 'Los Zetas,'" *Diario Despertar de Oaxaca*, January 3, 2011.
28. Barajas, "Muestran 'Los Zetas' poderío," *Reforma*, September 12, 2004.
29. Ravelo, *Osiel*, pp. 201–202.
30. Ibid., p. 134.
31. María Idalia Gómez and Darío Fritz, "Cuando la prisión era una fiesta," *El Universal.com.mx*, May 16, 2005.
32. "Las operaciones secretas del cártel del Golfo," *Revista Contralinea*, August 30, 2009.
33. The material in this section profits greatly from Dane Schiller, "A *Houston Chronicle Exclusive* 'I Knew What They'd Do to Me,'" *Houston Chronicle*, March 14, 2010.
34. Quoted in Ravelo, *Osiel*, p. 185.
35. The conference room on the top floor of the DEA's Arlington headquarters bears martyr Camarena's name.
36. José Gabriel Coley Pérez, "El imperio del Lazca durante el foxismo," *Voltaire*, September 7, 2009, www.voltairenet.org/article1619.html.
37. Mark Stevenson, "Mexico Arrests Alleged Drug Lord Osiel Cardenas after Shootout near U.S. Border," *Associated Press*, March 15, 2003.

38. Ricardo Ravelo, *Los Capos* (Mexico City: Debolsillo, 2007): 248.
39. Two federal investigations of the state executive's ties to drug traffickers failed to turn up sufficient evidence to indict him; see "Reconoce PGR que tiene 2 averiguaciones en contra del gobernador Tomás Yarrington, pero aclara, "éstas se irán al 'archivo' por no encontrar delitos," *Es Mas*, October 20, 2004.
40. The Gypsy did warn of a "light-complexioned person is close to you and will talk much about your secrets." Osiel assumed she meant his longtime ally Francisco "Paquito" Vázquez Guzmán, whom he had assassinated; see Ravel, *Osiel*, p. 202.
41. Another version holds that Morales Betancourt was arrested on November 17, 2001, after which he shared information with his captors and, in return, was admitted to a witness protection program; see *Agencia Reforma*, "Amplia Lazcano alcance de 'Zetas,'" *McAllear.com*, March 1, 2010.
42. Quoted in Stevenson, "Mexico Arrests Alleged Drug Lord."
43. David Aponte, "Lideres narcos pactan el la Palma transiego de droga," *El Universal*, January 5, 2005.
44. "Fuerzas especiales del Ejército captural a 'El Mati,' lugarteniente de Osiel Cárdenas: Junto con el narco fueron capturados seis cómplices," *EsMas*, August 10, 2004.
45. Presidencia de la República, "Suma Cártel del Golfo 5 golpes en su contra," October 30, 2004.
46. Marco Antonio Rodríguez Martínez, "El Poder de los Zetas," *Monografías. com*, 2006.
47. Other certificates contain birth dates of November 18, 1970, January 25, 1973, and July 17, 1976; see "Un narco violento que está en la mira," *Reforma. com*, December 6, 2010.
48. Ibid.
49. "Security and Law Enforcement," *Frontera Norte Sur*, July 2003, www.nmsu. edu/~frontera/jul03/secr.html.
50. "Un narco violento que está en la mira," *Reforma.com*, December 6, 2010.
51. Close observers state that the five-foot six-inch Guzmán Loera prefers to be called "El Tío," the uncle, in lieu of "El Chapo," a nickname which means "shorty."
52. Héctor de Mauleón, *Marca de sangre, los años de la delincuencia organizada* (Mexico City: Editorial Planeta, 2010): 70–71.
53. This cartel was known as the Beltrán Leyva Organization (BLO) or the Arturo Beltrán Leyvas (ABLs), after its leader Arturo Beltrán Leyva, whom marines killed on December 16, 2010.
54. Guy Lawson, "The Making of a Narco State," *Rolling Stone Magazine*, March 4, 2009, www.rollingstone.com/politics.
55. "The World's Billionaires," *Forbes*, March 3, 2010.
56. Jack Riley, DEA special agent, interviewed on "All Things Considered," *National Public Radio*, July 15, 2008.
57. Mauleón, *Marca de sangre*, pp. 69–71.
58. Ricardo Ravelo, "El capo del panismo," *Proceso*, March 16, 2009.
59. Ricardo Ravelo, "Soy un 'trienta y cinco,'" *Proceso*, November 11, 2007.
60. "Se refuerza el cártel de Sinaloa," *EFE*, August 10, 2005.

61. Ginger Thompson, "Rival Drug Gangs Turn the Streets of Nuevo Laredo into a War Zone," *New York Times*, December 4, 2005; and "Gunmen Kill Police Chief on First Day on Job," *Associated Press*, June 9, 2005.

62. Ibid.

63. Francisco Gómez, "Operación Limpieza cimbra a la PGR," *El Universal*, December 27, 2008.

64. E. Eduardo Castillo, "Dumping of 35 Bodies Seen as Challenge to Zetas," *Associated Press*, September 21, 2011.

65. James C. McKinley Jr., "Keeping his Spies Close, and Maybe a Cartel Closer," *New York Times*, April 20, 2010; and "Fracturan cubanas nexo Zetas-Beltrán," *Reforma*, November 22, 2009.

66. "Controla crimen región fronteriza," *Reforma*, May 10, 2011.

67. Jared Taylor, "Cartel Split Boosts Pot Traffic through Valley," *The Monitor*, June 12, 2011.

2

Leadership, Organization, and Training

El 40 believed that his small-time drug sellers had pocketed money they were supposed to turn over to a cartel collection agent. Accompanied by several thugs, Los Zetas' number two commander paid a surprise visit to the shabby boarding house where the vendors lived. They barged into their quarters and lined the men up against the wall. Then, with a two-by-four, the Zeta strongman beat the first alleged cheat to death. The second experienced a ghastlier fate. Treviño Morales slashed his throat with a razor-sharp machete, drove his hand through the victim's bloody thorax, and yanked out his heart. Los Zetas demand every peso they believe owed to them. One observer stated, "The day of a drug capo is as pressure-filled as that of any executive in a large corporation. They have accountants watching every centavo."[1] At the core of Los Zetas' organizational structure runs an accounting system that registers the flow of dirty dollars generated from various revenue streams. Accounting and leadership stand out as enduring strengths—without one or the other, Osiel's former hit men never would have achieved the success and influence they eventually attained.

Leadership, Regional Bosses, and Estacas

Heriberto Lazcano and Treviño Morales are the undisputed leaders of Los Zetas, but they make an odd couple. For many years, Los Zetas' commander in chief, The Executioner, often hid in one of his several heavily guarded houses in Valle Hermoso, southwest of Matamoros. To avoid being killed or captured in 2012, he is believed to have moved to Saltillo or somewhere else in Coahuila. Congruent with Special Forces training, Lazcano maintains a much lower profile than El 40. He concentrates on such military priorities as purchasing arms, finding training facilities, supervising instruction, contriving tactics, formulating intelligence procedures, designing communications, and laying out the approach to conducting effective searches. In addition, he names plaza bosses and promotes an esprit de corps through rescuing the bodies of dead Zetas, compensating Zeta families for lost loved-ones, and organizing Christmas parties and other morale building events. The Executioner also pioneered the diversification of his organization's money-making ventures. Besides directing drug loads through Mexico to the United States, he is involved in southbound currency shipments.[2] El Lazca has transmitted his craftiness and caution to his entourage, relatively few of whom landed behind bars or in graves.

One major exception was his nephew, Roberto "El Beto"/"El Felino" Rivero Arana, whom Federal Ministerial Police captured in Tabasco in late March 2010. Authorities asserted that the young man was *jefe* of Los Zetas in Tabasco, Veracruz, Campeche, Chiapas, and Quintana Roo. Also arrested were the director of security for Ciudad del Carmen, Campeche, who reportedly protected El Beto for Mex$200,000 per month; and Clarissa Yamireth Zeleta Hernández. Like his uncle, Rivero Arana kept a stock of weapons, including 5 AK-47s, 5 AR-15s, 1 grenade, 4,600 cartridges, 13 loaders, and various pistols, as well as 800 bags of marijuana containing approximately 100 grams each. In keeping with Zeta practices, El Beto also had military boots, 26 police tee shirts, and 14 pairs of police-style pants.

El Lazca shuns the limelight and seeks to blend into the population. Nonetheless, the Mexican magazine *Details* heralded him one of the fifty most powerful people in the world in a ranking that also included golfer Tiger Woods, singer Eminem and Iraqi Shia leader Sayyid Muqtada al-Sadr.

El 40 reportedly haunts his native city, Nuevo Laredo, but travels to other parts of the country and to Guatemala. He directs the actions of the plaza bosses, takes charge of money generated by cartel operations, and supervises Los Zetas' initiatives in Guatemala and, probably, other Central American nations. Treviño Morales has an affinity for flashy gold chains, snakeskin boots, and expensive cars, favoring Porsches and Corvettes. He has developed a reputation for extreme brutality—a man who really "gets off" on delivering beastly coups de grâce, according to a law-enforcement official who asked to remain anonymous. Within Mexico's criminal netherworld, it is said that El 40 personally killed a father and mother before boiling their baby to death in an oil-filled cauldron designed for cooking pigs. This event may or may not have occurred, but it is believable in light of other atrocities committed by the sadist. His psychopathic behavior impelled his rise in the organization. The US State Department reported that, between 2006 and early 2007, Treviño Morales served as the Gulf Cartel's plaza boss in Nuevo Laredo and, following the March 3, 2007, death of Efraín Teodoro "Z-14"/"El Efra" Torres, became plaza boss in Veracruz. In addition, El 40 has used the alias "David Estrada Corado." Zeta-watchers also claim that he actuated the grenade attacks on the Televisa TV station in Monterrey (January 6, 2009), the Televisa TV station in Ciudad Victoria (August 26, 2010), and the US Consulate General in Monterrey (October 13, 2008; April 10, 2010).

The Executioner and El 40 might be analogized to Benjamín and Ramón Eduardo Arellano Félix of the Tijuana Cartel. The former, who was arrested in March 2002 and extradited to the United States in April 2011, provided the brains for the operations; the latter, killed in February 2002, coordinated the organization's ruthless *pistoleros* and thrived on violence.

The chieftains of Los Zetas keep in touch through intermediaries or by sophisticated Nextel cell phones, which they discard after each call. They are believed to meet once a month in Rio Bravo, Valle Hermoso, Saltillo, Monterrey, Sabinas, Nuevo León, or even in Hidalgo, Tamaulipas, where El 40 and The Executioner own a horse ranch. Both men have large bounties hanging over their heads: $5 million from the US government and $2.5 million from the Mexican government, a total of $15 million for information leading to the capture of both men.

Besides organized crime, their common interests include a lust for voluptuous blondes, fondness for fancy, bejeweled weapons, the thrill of hunting exotic creatures, and the excitement of racing Ferraris and other sports cars. An unpublished, perhaps telling photograph of The Executioner depicts him fondling and undressing a buxom young woman clad in whipped cream as if it were a bikini. Another law-enforcement officer asserted that The Executioner and his bodyguards once showed up at a Zeta social event in drag—a claim for which there is no independent verification.

These men relish shooting zebras, gazelles, and other imported animals at special game preserves in Coahuila and San Luis Potosí. They also share a passion for betting on their favorite steeds, often near Ramos Arizpe, Coahuila, outside of Monterrey. The Executioner sometimes watches races from his armored SUV, surrounded by bodyguards. One of his horses, worth several hundred thousand dollars, died after a race because he had overdosed the creature with cocaine—such is his lust for competition and winning.[3] Both men are íknown to have dispatched buyers to acquire thoroughbreds at auctions in Ruidoso, New Mexico, and in Oklahoma. Treviño Morales takes the sport of kings much more earnestly than The Executioner, and does not brook defeats graciously on the racetrack. In late 2009, his horse lost a race. Rather than pay off his debt, he murdered the owner of the winning steed. Then he dispatched hit men to his adversary's funeral, where they killed his cousin in front of dozens of mourners. A week later, he directed commandos to steal all of the family's cattle and horses.

Each leader has key Zetas who are especially loyal to him and whom he pays directly. In the case of The Executioner, they are such ex-GAFES as José Alberto "El Paisa" González Xalate, Iván "Z-50"/ "El Talibán" Velázquez Caballero, Jorge "El Chuta" López (Northeast), Gustavo "El Erótico" González Castro, Priciliano Ibarra Yepis, Peluchín, Jesús Enrique "Z-8"/"Mamito" Rejón Aguilar (captured on July 3, 2011), and Raúl Lucio "El Lucky"/"Z-16" Hernández Lechuga (captured December 12, 2011).

Among El 40's loyalists, who tend to come from Nuevo León, are his brother Omar, Eulalio "El Flaco" Juárez Cifuentes, Francisco "El Quemado" Medina Mejía (Monterrey), Salvador Alfonso "La Ardilla" Martínez Escobedo, and José "El Comandante Pepito 1" Sarabia Castro (former San Luis Potosí plaza boss, who was captured on January 11, 2012, and charged with the February 15, 2011, murder of Jaime Zapata, an agent with the US Immigration and Customs Enforcement Agency—ICE). On November 15, 2011, Special Forces captured another of Treviño Morales' devotees, Alfredo "Alfredo N"/"El Comandante Alemán" Alemán Narváez, a major figure in San Luis Potosí and collaborator of El Talibán.

The Zetas have organized the country into at least five regions. Regional chiefs implement commands issued by superiors in the regions for which they are responsible. Although subordinate to The Executioner and El 40, "The Veterans" ("El Viejos" or "Cobras Viejos") supposedly form the organization's second tier and are respectfully referred to as professional university degree holders ("los licenciados"), teachers ("los maestros"), or engineers ("los ingenieros"), according to the respected newspaper *El Universal*.[4] Of course, this analysis appeared in late 2008, and when their names appear in the media, Los Zetas change their structure to confuse their foes.

As indicated in Figure 1, in early 2012, the regional leaders or lieutenants were believed to be the following: Francisco "El Quemado" Medina Mejía (Monterrey); El 40's brother Omar "El 42" Treviño Morales (Piedras Negras); El Paisa González Xalate (Saltillo and nearby areas; La Ardilla Martinez Escobedo (Tamaulipas—although he may have moved south because of increased military pressure from Operation Northern Lynx); Jorge "El Chuta" López (Northeast); Gustavo "El Erótico" González Castro (Tamaulipas area, but has also operated in Veracruz, Michoacán, and Querétaro); BALU (San Luis Potosí); and José María Guizar Valencia (southern region).

Other important figures are Iván "Z-50"/"El Talibán" Velázquez Caballero (Zacatecas); Emilio "El TJ"/"El Tejón" Chamorro Almazán and Raúl "El Tavabo" de Aquino Saturnino (DF Mexico State region); Víctor Nazario Castrejón Peña (Guerrero); and an activist known only as "Z-200," possibly another nickname for Treviño Morales, who reportedly oversees operations in Guatemala and other Central American countries.

Rising stars in the organization include Eulalio "El Lalo"/"El Flaco" Juárez Sifuentes and a man known to authorities only by the sobriquet "El Peluso."

The lieutenants implement commands issued by superiors. This second tier oversees the work of individuals who are equivalent to sergeants—each is responsible for a half dozen or more separate *estacas* or cells whose five to seven members often do not know each other. Although all Zetas are trained killers, these grassroots units specialize in transportation, extortion, logistics, kidnapping, prostitution, storage, transportation, contraband, and operation of nightclubs, casinos, and other businesses. Sergeants are loath to share the names of their hit men with other sergeants, lest they try to recruit their underlings. Captured accountant Sergio "El Toto" Mora Cortés, mentioned below, said that one individual—called "El Tartas"—was in charge of all estacas in San Luis Potosí.

Discipline is swift and harsh. Once when a lowly member of Los Zetas guarded a stash house, he took a risk and began to sample the merchandise. For this dereliction of duty, he was beaten black-and-blue with a paddle. More serious transgressions precipitate more savage torture or even the death of the offender.

The Executioner and El 40 impose harsh discipline on their cadres. Alfredo "El Chicles" Rangel Buendía approached Lazcano, saying, "I want to open a *fayuca*, a small shop dealing in illegally imported electronics and other wares. If you help me with a loan, I will repay you in a month." When El Chicles failed to make good on his promise, The Executioner ordered him killed. He then relented and punished the transgression by holding the fellow Zeta prisoner for a month, during which he received only water and one meal a day. Rangel Buendía learned the importance of keeping his word.

So-called *zetacuaches* receive harsher treatment. When they fail to perform, Los Zetas will take the lives of these undisciplined punks, possibly by hanging them from bridges.

The Executioner and El 40 afford plaza bosses a great deal of leeway, provided they attain their financial quotas. If they achieve or exceed this dollar amount, they can aspire to bonuses and a more lucrative plaza, generally along the coast where drugs enter the country. Falling short, though, means they face demotion to a smaller plaza. Failure to meet their goals at the new post will find them relegated to such inferior posts as hit men or couriers—or they may pay in cash for their mistakes.

As long as they don't embarrass or endanger the organization, plaza bosses can supplement their revenue with nondrug-related activities. Nevertheless, they must not intrude on the domain of fellow plaza bosses. Jaime "El Hummer" González Durán, a Zeta big shot discussed below, clashed with El Mamito Rejón Aguilar, another original Zeta, for not shelling out a fee to cross his turf. A similar confrontation took place between El Hummer and Gregorio "El Goyo"/"El Caramuela" Sauceda Gamboa of the Gulf Cartel.

No longer can plaza bosses, as in the past, invest in narcotics shipments. They still may be rewarded for successfully completing a transaction. At the same time, they will have to pay The Executioner or El 40 for any losses sustained on their watches, as was the case of the Altamira seizure in 2007 examined later.

Familiarity with fellow Zetas is on a need-to-know basis for security reasons. Thus, when soldiers captured Alberto "El Tony"/"Comandante Castillo" Sánchez Hinjosa for receiving six tons of cocaine transported by a semisubmergible vessel off the coast of Oaxaca in late summer 2008, they could not destroy Los Zetas' segmented organization even though El Tony trafficked cocaine throughout the southern part of the country.

All plaza bosses emphasize security and permeate their areas of operation with lookouts called "The Windows" ("Las Ventanas") and "The Hawks" ("Los Halcones"). The police whom Los Zetas have corrupted provide eyes and ears, as do convenience store clerks, newspaper sellers, and the petty street vendors. Several other groups spy for the cartel, even hanging out on street corners to keep tabs on distribution zones. Bike-riding youngsters from ages twelve to seventeen immediately report the entry of strange individuals, groups, or vehicles into their neighborhoods. The Windows and the Hawks also help identify subjects whom their bosses seek to torture, kidnap, or murder. They may whistle warning or, in many cases, use cell phones. Authorities found eighty members, equipped with radio transmitters, in Matamoros alone. An important city like Reynosa, a Gulf Cartel center, may have upward of three hundred of these watchdogs. These sentinels also keep a close eye on air, bus, and railway terminals.

The other groups are as follows:

1. "The Hidden Ones" (*Los Tapados*) are poor people, often children, who are recruited (with cell phones, school supplies, backpacks, and other items) to hoist banners, chant slogans, and mobilize opposition to the presence of the military and Federal Police in their states.

2. "The Military Killers" (*Los Matamilitares*) form a cell devoted to executing members of the armed forces. This cell, which enjoyed the protection of Cancún Police Chief Velasco Delgado, is alleged to have executed General Tello Quiñones, who had been dispatched to Cancún to combat crime in Quintana Roo. Authorities arrested Octavio "El Gori 4" Almanza Morales for the assassination, and the army captured his brother Raymundo on May 20, 2009. The navy killed yet another sibling, Eduardo, on December 4, 2009. He was believed to be responsible for the early November 2009 murder of Brig. Gen. (ret.) Juan Arturo Esparza García, the newly appointed secretary of public safety in García, Nuevo León. Authorities are convinced that the Almanza Morales brothers authored numerous homicides and kidnappings in the Monterrey area, including the execution of nine Mexican soldiers in October 2008. They worked closely with Sigifredo "El Canicón" Najera Talamantes, the presumed mastermind of the October 2008 attack on the US Consulate General in Monterry, who was arrested in Saltillo in March 2009. The Defense Ministry has denounced Zeta propaganda that charges the military with "soldiers' crimes" against civilians. The military announced that 24.53 percent of its personnel are waging war on crime syndicates, which are responsible for the placards denouncing human rights abuses.[5]

3. Some members of Estacas may guard ranking Zetas or they may be dispatched to take care of problems that arise with competitors, according to Tomás Coronado Olmos, Jalisco's attorney general.[6]

In 2010, the Defense Ministry named other Zeta leaders, who include[7]

- José Alberto "El Paisa"/"El Paisano" González Chanate (lying low after reportedly ordering the killing of seventy-two illegal immigrants from Central and South America on August 24, 2010);
- "El Calaveras" (Ciudad Victoria, Tamaulipas);
- "El Mostachón" (Nuevo Laredo);
- "La Estrella" (top operative in villages of La Misión, Comales, and Santa Gertrudis);
- "El Puchini" (operative in San Fernando before the Gulf Cartel took control of the municipality);
- "El Karate" (top operative in Miguel Alemán and Ciudad Mier);
- brothers Matías "El Conejo I" and Beto "El Conejo II" (town of Guardias in China municipality);
- brothers Juan Pedro "El 27"/"El Orejón" and José Manuel "El 31" Saldivar Farías (believed responsible for the September 30, 2010, shooting death of David Hartley, thirty, a US citizen who was jet-skiing with his wife on the Mexican side of the Falcon Dam on the Río Grande);
- army deserter Juan "El Colmillo" Vera Ovando, Noé "El Tigre" Minez, and Juan Pedro "El 27"/"El Orejón" Saldívar Farías (commanders who are responsible for the plaza of Camargo and Comales and who ordered the massacre of the illegal aliens in Tamaulipas); and
- Orlando Monsivais Treviño, twenty-eight, a nephew of "El 40" Treviño Morales (believed to have organized the December 2010 escape of 140 Zetas from a Nuevo Laredo prison).

Of course, the syndicate, which may have included seven hundred to one thousand hard-core elements in early 2012, also needs as many cadres as possible to combat its ever-larger number of enemies. An increasing number of recruits for lookout and courier positions come from poor, rural areas and are no more than common criminals.[8] Los Zetas also seize domestic and foreign migrants whom they have placed in semiservitude as petty drug vendors, domestics, drivers, or errand-runners. Police report that no family member claims many of the bodies of those who die in the service of Los Zetas and other cartels—either because they have lost touch with these individuals or because they want to avoid association with the underworld.

Some small-time criminals identify themselves as "Los Zetas" as if it were a brand name like McDonald's. This tactic helps elevate the fear of targets and victims. "It's gotten to the point where you get drunk, shoot at some cans, and paint your face black, and that makes you a Zeta.... A lot of it is image and myth. No one even honks their horn in the streets here—you might anger the wrong person. And now, every thug with a pistol says he's a Zeta because he knows it terrifies people here,"

Figure 2-1: STRUCTURE OF LOS ZETAS

Heriberto "The Executioner"/"El Lazca"
Lazcano Lazcano

Miguel Ángel "El 40" Treviño Morales

Top Leaders	Chief Responsibilities	Background	Residence (moves often)	Mutual Interests of the two leaders	Contacts
Heriberto "The Executioner" Lazcano Lazcano	• Sets military strategy • Oversees arms purchases • Finds training facilities • Directs intelligence • Supervises communications • Names plaza bosses • Promotes esprit de corps	Born Dec. 25, 1974, Hidalgo; Joined Army on June 5, 1991 at age 17; promoted to corporal on July 5, 1993; selected for GAFES; resigned March 27, 1998	Several homes in Tamaulipas. Coahuila	• Buxom women • Ornate arms • Quality horses • Horse-racing • Hunting exotic animals on ranch in Coahuila • Racing Ferraris and other sports cars	The Executioner and El 40 meet approximately once a month; otherwise, they communicate through subordinates and Nextel cell phones, which are discarded after every call
Miguel Ángel "El 40" Treviño Morales	• Gives orders to Plaza bosses • Handles financial operations • Maintains contacts with Colombians • Controls operations in Central America	Born Nov. 18, 1972; Nuevo Laredo; did odd jobs for Gulf Cartel; and his cruelty vaulted him into a leadership post.	Nuevo Laredo	Although both men are brutal, "El 40" seems to get a thrill from performing sadistic acts. His brother "Omar" often calms him down	

KEY REGIONAL/LOCAL LEADERS

NORTHEAST & MONTERREY:	Francisco "El Quemado" Medina Mejía
NORTHEAST (Piedras Negras):	Omar "El 42" Treviño Morales
NORTHEAST (Saltillo):	Alberto José "El Paisa" González Xalate
NORTHEAST (Tamaulipas):	Salvador Alfonso "La Ardilla"/"The Squirrel" Martínez Escobar
	Jorge "El Chuta" López
	Gustavo "El Erótico" González Castro (has also operated in Veracruz, Michoacán, and Querétaro)
NORTH-CENTRAL (Durango):	José Luis "El Pepito 1" Sarabia (captured Jan.11, 2012)
ZACATECAS	Iván "El Talibán" Veláquez Caballos
SAN LUIS POTOSÍ	BALU (no other name)
HIDALGO	MEMO or MIMIN (no other name)

33

KEY REGIONAL/LOCAL LEADERS CONTINUED

MEXICO STATE	Raúl "El Tavabo" de Aquino Saturnino
MEXICO CITY AREA:	Emilio "El TJ"/"El Tejon Chamorro Almazán
SOUTH (Regional Leader)	José Maria Guizar Valencia
GUERRERO:	Victor Nazario Castrejón Peña
GUATEMALA:	"Z-200" (no other name); may be another pseudonym for "El 40"

THE EXECUTIONER'S MEN

BODY GUARDS (6 to 12)

PLAZA BOSSES

Plaza bosses are males—except for Verónica, "La Flaka"/"La Vero" Mireya Moreno Carreón, a former decorated cop who ran San Nicolás de los Garza, NL, before Marines captured her on Sept. 11, 2011

FINANCIAL OPERATORS

Reports NOT to plaza boss, but via intermediaries to "El 40" and his brother Omar "El 42;" a half-dozen auditors keep track of financial operators by making unannounced visits to their residences; and money is transmitted to "El 40" and "El 42" by messengers in the North; elsewhere couriers or "casas de cambio" may be used. Any deposits in banks are small to avoid attracting attention.

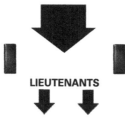

LIEUTENANTS

SERGEANTS

Operatives, whom the authors identify as "sergeants," supervise specialized cells of "estacas" composed of five to seven Zetas. Some estacas specialize in trafficking routes, extortion, prostitution, murder-for-hire, intelligence; others may serve as bodyguards for leaders. The sergeants may farm out work to local gangs in return for a 60%+ slice of revenue illegally generated; in these cases, the gangs may call themselves "Zetas" to increase their effectiveness.

This is roughly Los Zetas' structure in February 2012; plaza bosses are moving even more frequently because of increasing pressure after (1) the August 25, 2011 Casino Royale fire-bombing, (2) major attacks on the renegrades in Veracruz, and (3) hostilities erupted in Sinaloa and Jalisco.

Chart designed by Lucinda H. Baker
@ copyrighted, George W. Grayson, 2012.

a Nuevo León resident told a journalist. "I had my car spray-painted with graffiti recently—'Zeta 25.' It was some gangbangers. They're all little Zeta wannabes."

The prevalence of pseudo-Zetas and continual changes in the organization's assignments keep authorities guessing about who is in charge of a given plaza, city, or state, further complicating plans to track, corner, and capture midlevel figures. Although under orders from the top, plaza bosses in hot spots like Monterrey may live longer to enjoy life and the trappings of their criminal power in other venues. The twenty-day Operación Lince Norte (Northern Lynx Operation) carried out in mid-2011 pushed more Zetas into Veracruz, where they engaged in killings, kidnappings, and other crimes. Among their possible victims were four navy personnel—three marines and one cadet.[9] President Calderón blamed former PRI governor Fidel Herrera Beltrán (2004–10) for allowing the state to "fall into the hands of Los Zetas."

On a less chilling note, for years The Executioner and El 40 threw raucous Christmas parties, known as *narco-posadas*, for plaza bosses and other cartel operatives from the entire country who flaunted their Zeta insignias, an encircled "Z" on khaki shirts, or a "Z" tattoo on upper biceps. This Bacchanalian fete, which usually took place in Tamaulipas, featured sumptuous food, an abundance of alcoholic beverages, cocaine, marijuana, heroin, the conferral of bonuses, bawdy song fests, *corridos* performed by balladeers, and a plethora of high-end prostitutes. The festivities also featured raffles for houses and new automobiles. Most important of all, plaza bosses were assigned for the upcoming year. Lazcano and Treviño Morales were on hand, along with key leaders from around the country.[10]

A protected witness said that El Lazca used a *narco-posada* to place Luis Enrique "El Rex"/"Z-12" Reyes in charge of Mexico City before his late June 2007 apprehension in Hidalgo.[11] The absence of information about a 2011 gathering may mean that none was held or it took place in secret.

Latin Grammy winner Alejandra Guzmán reportedly performed for Los Zetas at their December 2006 Christmas party, which The Executioner hosted in "Las Liebres" sports complex in Río Bravo, Tamaulipas. Whether the "Queen of Rock" of the Hispanic world makes a return appearance may depend on whether plastic surgeons can repair a botched "butt job" performed in late 2009 to make her "more beautiful."[12]

Mexican weekly news magazine *Proceso* reported that authorities crashed a December party at the Real del Lago hotel in Villahermosa where Zeta big shots were handing out Christmas bonuses known as *aguinaldos*. The police arrested Coahuila natives Julio "El Compadre" Acosta Saucedo and his son Arturo "El Junior" Acosta Vargas, two of the four Zetas involved in killing Marine Third Petty Officer Ángulo Córdova. They also seized two lookouts, Yesenia "La Ximena" Hernández Valencia and Israel de Jesús "El Goten" García Reyes. In addition, the law-enforcement officials found two notebooks with information about the cartel's activities and operatives.[13]

Los Zetas are increasingly depending on green-as-grass teenagers to help track down targets for kidnapping and other crimes. This is especially true in Pachuca, Hidalgo—a plaza believed to have been headed by Alejandro "El Cepillo"/"The Brush" Segura Téllez until his early March 2009 arrest. There, Federal Police took into custody three youngsters from Nuevo Laredo—Mario "El Yodo" (aged thirteen), Julio "El Fede" (aged fourteen), and Raúl "El Rule" (aged sixteen)—who claimed to be selling clothing. Los Zetas also pay Mex$10,000 for executions to Eduardo "EL Lalito" González Trejo and other young criminals in the Tepito area of Mexico City. The youthful killers belong to such local gangs as El Rey de Tepito or El Vale.

Although he sent his own children out of the country for their safety, the growing allure of a life of crime prompted Sinaloa Governor Mario López Valdez to urge young people in his state to shun gangs and syndicates in favor of studying to form part of the Elite State Police. Like iron filings to a magnet, teenagers are attracted to the latest model cars, gorgeous women, fistfuls of money, and stylish clothing that many cartel members flaunt, even as they prize close ties to their own families, especially the women who bore them.[14] Even The Executioner does the bidding of his mother, who lives in his native Hidalgo and runs a restaurant in the state capital of Pachuca.[15] Los Zetas' top man provided manpower and funds in 2009 to construct the San Juan de los Lagos chapel in El Tezontle, a neighborhood of ten thousand residents who live south of Pachuca, three hundred meters from a base of the Eighteenth Military Zone. The Executioner's mother procured the contribution, and a plaque on the brightly colored, flower-filled building recognizes her son's generosity.[16] The marker reads, "Center of Evangelization and Catechism John Paul II. Donated by Heriberto Lazcano Lazcano." This tribute embarrassed the Roman Catholic Church. Domingo Díaz Martínez, the archbishop of Tulancingo, which embraces the chapel's venue, said hypocritically, "Of course, we knew of the aid [provided by Lazcano]. The error was having permitted the installation of a marker."[17]

A second Zeta mother gained attention when her devoted son, El Mamito, was apprehended in the small town of Atizapan de Zaragoza in Mexico State on his way to visit her in Campeche State.

Los Zetas depend on terrorizing the citizenry, the police, and the military. Much to the surprise of the residents of Ciudad Victoria on April 30, 2010, the paramilitaries staged a large Día del Niño or Children's Day fun fest in the city's Praxedis Balboa Stadium. The celebration had live music, clowns, inflatable bouncers, candy, and hundreds of high-end gifts, including bicycles and toys for those in attendance. Toward the end of the event, Los Zetas hung a banner from the stadium's roof that said presents were not enough, that parents should spend time with their children and give them their love; the banner was signed by "The Executioner" Lazcano and La Compañía Z. Just a few days later, in the same city, the Zetas sponsored a Mother's Day event on May 10, where those in attendance received such appliances as refrigerators, TVs, and irons. Local media didn't mention Los Zetas' patronage, but both of their events grabbed the spotlight away from state and municipal ceremonies that took place on the same day.

Another quasi-benevolent act attributed to them took place on November 2, 2008, when residents took pleasure in the annual "Day of the Dead" parade in Ojocaliente, Zacatecas, where a shrine honors la Santísima Muerte, the saint of death. Among masked marchers from neighborhoods and schools and appropriately decorated floats appeared a vehicle with figures and emblems of death. The driver directed the large truck into the town's central square, where riders tossed skull-shaped candy to children. Los Zetas had arrived dressed as soldiers and federal policemen. At 9.00 p.m., they abducted Roberto García Cárdenas, the town's usurious moneylender. After his family paid the Mex$600,000 ($50,000) ransom, they released the parasitic loan shark but immediately grabbed his wife and son. The fifty-member police force had resigned earlier, and the situation was resolved only when the state paid the bounty.

As mentioned, Governor Amalia García insisted that "outside groups" did not operate in her state. Her Panglossian statements aside, various Zacatecas municipalities, especially those near Durango and Jalisco, have suffered depredations at the hands of Los Zetas: beating

Ojocaliente's mayor (December 2007); a gun battle with the army in Villa de Cos (May 6, 2008); kidnapping and robbing three hundred residents at a horse race in Chalchiuites (July 13, 2008); wounding State Municipal Police chief (November 23, 2008); threatening reporter for *El Sol de México* (December 9, 2008); kidnapping ex-mayor of Villanueva and two wealthy businessmen (November 9 and 10, 2008); and killing two Ojocaliente policemen (November 10, 2009).[18]

Los Zetas were prolific and proficient at infiltrating police forces in many municipalities. The events surrounding the November 7, 2008, capture of Zeta big shot Jaime "El Hummer" González Durán in Reynosa illuminate this relationship. The Drug Enforcement Administration developed excellent intelligence about the whereabouts of El Hummer, an original Zeta who controlled narcotics exports to the United States and oversaw trafficking in Nuevo León, Michoacán, Hidalgo, Veracruz, Tabasco, Quintana Roo, and Mexico City. They determined that the thirty-two-year-old pudgy-faced native of San Luis Potosí was hiding in Reynosa, using the pseudonym Arturo Sánchez Fuentes.

They doubted that the Mexican Army had either the manpower or the commitment to capture the ex-GAFE whose counterinsurgency expertise was only surpassed by his cruelty. For instance, he supposedly masterminded the murder of balladeer Valentín Elizalde whose *corridos* offended Los Zetas.

As a result, DEA officials worked with a contingent of the Federal Police Support Forces, known as the Special Operations Group, an agency under the purview of the Public Security Ministry (SSP). Headed by Gen. (ret.) Rodolfo Cruz López, Los GOPES has approximately one hundred elements organized in eight- to twelve-member teams. Los GOPES' officers met with US agents in McAllen and showed eagerness to capture the man purported to be the ranking Zeta after The Executioner and El 40.

At 8:30 a.m.[19] on November 7, 2008, Los GOPES mobilized their forces in rented vehicles to minimize suspicion and waited for DEA agents to inform them whether El Hummer was in "House A" or "House B." Upon learning the precise location, Los GOPES crashed into the presumed safe house. They found an arsenal of weapons, but no González Durán. In a frantic exchange of telephone calls, Los GOPES informed the Americans that "we have searched the residence from top to bottom and there is no sign of him." DEA officials urged the Mexicans to continue ransacking the residence. "We know he's there. Look again!" they implored.

The second time was magic. Los GOPES discovered the culprit ensconced between two single beds that had been pulled together and covered with a blanket. They snatched the perp before he could pull his .38-caliber gold-plated pistol from his belt.

Realizing that his allies would try to prevent El Hummer's incarceration, authorities then dispatched an SSP convoy to the Reynosa airport two miles away; however, to elude the prisoner's comrades, Los GOPES spirited him out the back door in an unobtrusive rental car. All hell broke loose once the ruse was discovered. Local Zetas, who had thrown up roadblocks on the route to the airport in league with the Reynosa police, launched a no-holds-barred gun battle to gain their comrade's release. Army reserves were called in, and a prolonged gun battle ensued, while authorities awaited the arrival from Mexico City of a Grumman II jet to the take the fugitive to the capital.[20] A court convicted him of participating in organized crime and drug offenses. He was incarcerated in La Palma, where he is serving a twenty-one-year sentence.

Los Zetas abhor mimics, on whom they practice excruciating cruelty, invoking a level of fear that persuades many to avoid mention of the cartel's name among strangers. In areas where they are active, just referring to "Los Zetas" is like publicly talking about the plague in a medieval city. The fear gave birth to copycats, whom pundits label as "McZetas," inasmuch as they try to enrich themselves by taking advantage of a market-tested criminal brand. These pretenders made 689 extortion attempts in Mexico City alone in 2008.

Although the chances are zero that they will change their image, genuine Zetas do not abide amateurs who grab for a slice of their market. In addition, their imitators may not make good on threats, diminishing the organization's credibility. Some Zeta plaza bosses will leave a family alone after it cooperates and pays the ransom or extortion money demanded. In contrast, phony Zetas may take repeated actions against the same business or household.

The genuine Zetas take quick revenge on imitators who fall into their clutches. In October 2007, Zeta impostors demanded first $1 million and then Mex$1 million from a restaurant owner. After they shot up the façade of his home, the family quickly moved to another state. In May 2008, a thirty-five-year-old man was found in Monterrey. He had been tortured and an ice pick thrust through his throat. A note dangled from clenched fingers: "This is one of those who carried out extortions by telephone trying to pass for 'Z.'" In February 2009, the brigands executed two "false Zetas" in Reynosa, leaving behind a handwritten missive saying, "This is what will happen to those who attempt to pass themselves off as Zetas." In May 2010, Oaxacan authorities discovered a chopped-up body near Juchitán, with a note saying he had been executed for posing as a Zeta.

A gang of kidnappers who falsely called themselves Los Zetas to collect ransoms in Nuevo Laredo landed behind bars and were promptly murdered. A municipal official said the killings were "most likely carried out on orders from the Zetas." He added that "the Zetas don't like their names used in vain, plus they want to tell society, 'Hey, we've changed. We're not kidnappers or extortionists. We're one of you.'"[21]

Los Zetas are the only Mexican cartel with a major women's component—Las *Panteras* or "Panthers." These Panthers, who are concentrated in Nuevo León, have structures in other areas. Authorities captured their leader, believed to be Ashly "La Comandante Bombón"/"Commander Candy" Narro López, in Cancún on February 9, 2009, in connection with the murder of General Tello Quiñones. The brutality of the former employee of an insurance company made her "a female Treviño Morales," in the words of a former US law-enforcement agent. These skilled women negotiate deals with police, politicians, military officers, and others who can assist Los Zetas. Should talks break down, a *pantera* may kill her interlocutor. First identified at a party thrown by The Executioner in mid-December 2006, these women change their makeup and the color and style of their hair according to their assignment.

It's not known whether Carmen del Consuelo "La Contadora" Sáenz Manríquez belongs to Las Panteras, but she has facilitated kidnappings for Los Zetas on both sides of the border. Campeche's attorney general is also pursuing the thirty-one-year-old almond-eyed beauty for possible involvement in the murder of four law-enforcement agents in mid-2008. These murders constituted partial retaliation for the arrest of ninety-eight subjects linked to the paramilitaries. La Contadora also uses the aliases Ana Claudia Morante Villanueva and Karla Aracely Luna Bello.[22]

Los Zetas show no mercy to distaff foes. The wealth of capos attracts some women. In drug-infested Sinaloa, girlfriends of drug dealers now make up a subculture known as *buchonas* or "prostitutes," who enjoy diamond-studded finger bling, fake breasts, and expensive designer clothing. "What a shame that there are ladies who get dazzled by the false shine of that money, who only aspire to be the girlfriends or loved ones of these vulgar thugs," commented an anonymous local resident. Before he escaped, Chapo Guzmán had an affair with a statuesque armed robber, Zulema Hernández. After her release in 2008, Los Zetas kidnapped and murdered their rival's lover, carving the letter "Z" on her stomach, buttocks, and chest.[23]

The Gulf Cartel has created a female unit known as "Las Medusas." Although these women carry weapons, they appear more like girl-friends of hit men than killers. In contrast, the Internet publication *Borderland Beat* reported that La Línea, the powerful band that works with the Juárez Cartel in Juárez and El Paso, has recruited and trained as commandos dozens of "pretty" women. "They are beautiful teenag-ers to deceive the enemy [Sinaloa Cartel] even more," a suspected gang member told an SSP investigative team.

Financial Operations

El 40 and his brother Omar manage the cartel's finances, which constitute a parallel structure to the organization's criminal activities. A protected witness claimed that he disbursed large sums to law-enforcement agencies: $150,000 a month to the Federal Police, $100,000 to the Ecatepec police, and $100,000 to the DF's Ministerial Police. The informant swore that "Manuelito," the owner of a large chain of meat stores in Monterrey and elsewhere in the north, performed the role of intermediary in the distribution of bribes.[24]

Women sometimes function as financial agents for Los Zetas. They live in well-protected homes or apartments and report not to the plaza boss but directly to higher-ups in the organization. The females receive and meticulously count the cash collected each day; they demand that the subordinates who work under the plaza boss provide receipts for their outlays on vehicles, apartments, weapons, or other major items, diminishing the chance that money disappears from the take. The func-tionaries either turn over the proceeds on a regular basis to a courier or deposit them in a local bank account to which cartel's leaders have access. Three or more floating auditors make unannounced visits to the accoun-tants to ensure that finances are in order (Table 2 indicates the Monter-rey plaza's nine-month expenditure in 2007). Yaneth Deyanira García Cruz, who was captured carrying Mex$10 million and $900 on March 20, 2009, is believed to have served as a financial operator before her March 2009 arrest.[25] She had worked in the credit card department of a legitimate bank. Strict accountability reduces the overhead of Los Zetas and contributes to its reputation as a cost-effective organization.

After the army captured and extradited to the United States Rubén Sauceda Rivera, the Gulf Cartel's financial guru, his successor was "Comandante Sol," whose real name remains a mystery. He handles or handled Los Zetas' funds and reports or reported directly to Treviño Morales or his brother Omar.

On May 29, 2010, the navy took into custody Hipólito Bonilla Céspedes, fifty-two, who was considered the accountant for El Lazca. He was caught with two aides and a policeman, a suitcase containing Mex$3.4 million and $380,000, and various weapons.[26]

The following month, the navy captured Raúl Amberto Padilla Gómez, thirty-two, a native of San Fernando, Tamaulipas, who was believed to be Los Zetas' accountant in San Pedro Garza García.

Also arrested at the scene were Omar Melesio Bejarano Lescas (thirty-five), Enrique Padillo Mendoza (forty), and Erick Humberto "El Erick" Gómez Méndez. In addition, two vehicles, firearms, communications equipment, marijuana, and cash were found.[27]

On February 27, 2011, the navy took into custody Sergio Mora "El Toto" Cortés, the self-described administrative supervisor and "financial advisor" for the San Luis Potosí plaza. He revealed that a Nuevo Laredo–based individual referred to as Zamudio, with the aliases of "El Samurai" or "El Samy," coordinated financial operators and their supervisors nationwide.

In early March, Federal Police seized Mario "Mayito" Jiménez Pérez, a financial operative who was accused of participating in the February 15, 2011, murder of Jaime Zapata, an agent with the US ICE.

Table 2   January–September 2007 Expenditures by Zetas'
　　　　　 Monterrey Plaza

Expenditure	Amount (in dollars)	Percentage of total
Administration and lookouts	18,400	2.85
Security	1,100	.17
Gifts	50,000	7.73
Raffles (five Rolex watches)	25,000	3.86
Payoffs to police	552,350	85.39
Total	*646,850*	*100.00*

Source: Confidential.

The following month, the army apprehended Hugo "El Maza" Martínez Morales, who allegedly handled the proceeds from street sales of drugs in Nuevo León. He had in his possession Mex$10 million, three firearms, eight vehicles, drugs, and communications equipment.[28]

In mid-2010, the Federal Police apprehended Jorge Alberto Jiménez González, considered another Zeta moneyman. Law-enforcement personnel took the twenty-seven-year-old into custody in Veracruz after he tried to outrun them in his sleek BMW. Accompanying the presumed accountant was Mónica Carolina Castro Peón, twenty-six, a certified teacher. Jiménez González claimed to have been recruited by Rolando "El Manitas" Veytia Bravo, who was a ranking Zeta in Veracruz before the army killed him along with four confederates in May 2011.[29]

In August 2011, the army arrested Valdemar "El Adal" Quintanillo Soriano, the highest Los Zetas financial operative taken into custody, and his assistants in Saltillo (José Guadalupe Yañez Martínez) and San Luis Potosí (José Ángel Zapata Pantoja).[30]

Table 3 presents some of the major money-movers in the cartel.

The organization keeps close tabs of its personnel. They compile records on its thousands of members, complicit policemen, and other employees on its payroll, their time in service, the period they have spent at plazas, and the date when they are due to be rotated to another plaza in the fourteen states in which they have a presence.[31] They also have data on the families of their cadres. Although El Hummer Durán and El Cachetes Pérez Rojas are in prison and Braulio "El Gonzo"/ "Z-20" Arellano Domínguez[32] is dead, their loved ones receive $1,000 every two weeks from the cartel. Of course, any Zeta who deserts can be certain that The Executioner and El 40 will take reprisals against him or his family.

An intrepid journalist for the *Brownsville Herald* managed to interview an ex-Zeta who goes by the pseudonym Antonio. His exodus required turning over cars, money, weapons, and deeds to his property to the syndicate. A cartel leader advised him "to leave the region and go somewhere else. Then he took me to the woods, to the area where we carried out our executions.

"I asked him, 'Hey, what's going on?' He just told me to get out of the vehicle. And I did, because he was the boss. Once I was out, I put my hand behind my back and gripped my gun, thinking that if I went down, I was taking one or two with me." Next, his handler mimed placing a gun to someone's head and pulling the trigger—"boom." Then,

Table 3 A Sampling of Los Zetas' Financial Operators

Zeta financial operator	Area of activity	Comment	Capture
Sáenz, Carmen del Consuelo (and various pseudonyms: Ana Claudia Morante Villanueva, Sonia Abigail Gutiérrez Mendoza, and Karla Araceli Luna Bellow	Responsible for southern region: Six municipalities in Veracruz (Veracruz, Poza Rica, Jalapa, Cosamaloapan, Coatzacoalco, and Córdoba); Oaxaca, Oaxaca; Tabasco; Cancún	Regional operator who worked under El Luky/El Lucky	Navy captured her in Córdoba, Veracruz, October 26, 2011
Valdemar "El Adal" Quintanillo Soriano	Monterrey, Saltillo, and Monclova (formerly in charge of Veracruz, San Luis Potosí, and Coahuila)	Major figure	Army captured him in Saltillo, August 4, 2011
Sergio "El Toto" Mora Cortés	San Luis Potosí	Administrative supervisor and financial advisor to then plaza boss José Luis "El Comandante Pepito" Sarabia	Navy captured him in Saltillo, May 27, 2011
Víctor Hugo "El 'Maza" Martínez Morales	Nuevo León	Handled street sales	Army captured him in Nuevo León, April 13, 2011
Mario "Mayito" Jiménez Pérez, 41	San Luis Potosí		Federal Police captured him in San Luis Potosí, March 5, 2011
Raúl Amberto Padilla Gómez, 32	Monterrey area, probably San Pedro Garza García	Also arrested were Omar Milesio Bejarano Lescas, 35; Enrique Padilla Mendoza, 40; Erick Humberto "El Erick" Gómez Méndez, 21	Navy captured this group in San Pedro Garza García, NL, June 4, 2010

Name	Location	Notes	Capture
Hipólito Bonilla Céspedes, 52		Believed to be The Hangman's accountant	Navy captured him in Monterrey, May 29, 2010
Jorge Alberto Jiménez González, 27	Veracruz	Accompanied by Mónica Carolina Castro Peón, 26, a certified teacher	Federal Police captured the pair in Veracruz, mid-2010
Yaneth Deyanira García Cruz		She had worked in the credit card department of a bank	March 20, 2009
Pedro Morquecho Morales	Unknown	Brother-in-law of The Executioner	Federal Police captured him in a Mexico City restaurant, October 1, 2008.
"Comandante Sol"	Unknown	Supposedly reported directly to El 40 or his brother Omar	NA
Rubén Sauceda Rivera	Tamaulipas	Known as "El Cacahuate," he managed the Gulf Cartel's finances, payroll, and vast real estate holdings throughout the late 1990s	Army captured him in Reynosa, January 14, 2002

Source: "Revelan creación del grupo de sicarias 'Las Panteras,'" *El Norte*, March 27, 2009; Lemic Madrid, "Detienen a Presunto Contador de Los Zetas," *Excélsior*, July 28, 2009; "Marineros detienen a presunto contador del líder de 'Los Zetas,'" *esmas*, May 30, 2010; "Capturan a contador de los Zetas en NL," *Milenio.com*, June 4, 2010; "Cae el Mayito, operador Zeta ligado a muerte de agente de EU," *Terra*, March 9, 2011; "Detienen a presunto contador de 'Los Zetas' en NL," *El Siglo* (Durango), April 13, 2011; "Detienen a El Maza, contador de Los Zetas in Nuevo León," *Excélsior*, April 13, 2011; and Rubén Mosso, "Captura Ejército en Saltillo a operator financiero," *Milenio*, August 4, 2011.

he "hugged me, and then smacked me on the head and said, 'let's go.' And he climbed back into the truck. I simply said, 'Thank you, sir,' and got back into the truck. I took a swig of Buchanan's, did some blow, and said to myself, 'I did it.'"[33]

Training

Exceptional leadership represents one of Los Zetas' strongest assets. Yet much of their initial success sprang from rigorous training. The original Zetas profited from Green Beret–style instruction in the army before defecting to the underworld. France's National Police Intervention Group prepared a "Mexican Rapid Intervention Force" to provide security for the 1986 World Cup matches held in Mexico City amid difficult economic conditions exacerbated by September 1985 earthquakes. The training emphasized the use of special weapons and counterterrorism tactics. On June 1, 1990, the group adopted its current name, Special Forces Airmobile Group. Eight years later, the GAFES saw action against the Zapatista National Liberation Army (EZLN), a rebel force in the southern state of Chiapas. They also began to participate in the war against drug cartels—distinguishing themselves by capturing Benjamin Arellano Félix of the Tijuana Cartel and, of course, Osiel Cárdenas. It is ironic that loyal GAFES helped to apprehend Osiel whom the renegade GAFES-turned-Zetas had been hired to safeguard.

American and Israeli experts also instructed members of this elite unit in rapid deployment, aerial assaults, marksmanship, ambushes, intelligence collection, countersurveillance techniques, prisoner rescues, sophisticated communications, and the art of intimidation. Beginning in 2005, four cashiered members of Colombia's Special Forces—two captains and two noncommissioned officers—provided training in command and intelligence operations, according to the Bogota daily *El Tiempo*. El Lazca recruited Germán "El Tatanka" Torres Jiménez, who began his criminal career in Veracruz as an instructor. The burly original Zeta, also known as "Z-25," displayed expertise in logistics, tactical combat, abduction, and the transfer of drugs.

El Tatanka also executed five members of La Familia Michoacana before the Federal Police arrested him in Poza Rica, Veracruz, in late April 2009. The army apostates have set up at least six camps to train fifteen- to eighteen-year olds and men in their early twenties, as well as ex-federal, state, and local police officers. The US State Department had adamantly denied that the United States had provided instruction to any Zeta.[34] According to *WikiLeaks* (cable 221688/2009), however,

Rogelio López Villafana, received antidrug training at Ft. Bragg, North Carolina, and after completing more than twenty years in the Mexican Army, he joined Los Zetas in 2007. Still, there is no evidence that any original Zetas underwent instruction in the United States.

Los Zetas allegedly conduct courses, usually for six months, at locations southwest of Matamoros, across the border from Brownsville; just north of the Nuevo Laredo airport; near the town of Abasolo, between Matamoros and Ciudad Victoria; and the "Rancho Las Amarillas," outside the rural community of China, which lies near the Nuevo León–Tamaulipas frontier. To the degree that the Mexican administration achieves more triumphs, the paramilitaries—some observers claim—could move their boot camps into the United States or establish others in Central America. In fact, the FBI has reported a Zeta cell's acquisition of a ranch in an isolated Texas county that is used for both training and "neutralizing" their competitors. On November 25, 2009, Salvadoran Federal Police Intelligence reported that no fewer than forty gang members from several countries in Central America were trained at a Zeta camp alongside Laguna El Tigre in Guatemala across the border from Tabasco.[35]

According to a protected witness, Guzmán Decena organized Los Zetas' first course in Matamoros, with instruction conducted by Luis Alberto "Z-5" Guerrero Reyes and ex-Lt. Carlos Hau Castañeda. These converted farms provide a site for instruction in AK-47 assault rifles, AR-15 rifles with grenade launchers, and .50-caliber machine guns, rapid deployment, aerial assaults, marksmanship, ambushes, surveillance techniques, sophisticated communications, physical fitness, and the art of intimidation. Many of these young men have also received training in counterinsurgency, intelligence gathering, and prisoner rescues. The group is extremely well armed, they wear body armor, and some wear Kevlar ballistic helmets; their arsenal includes AR-15 and AK-47 assault rifles, MP5 submachine guns, .50-caliber machine guns, grenade launchers, ground-to-air missiles, dynamite, and helicopters. They operate with modern wiretapping equipment and purchase the cellular phone codes of intended targets directly from the phone companies and providers. GOPES chief Cruz López and army officers have complained that the renegades often have firepower that is superior to that of the military and police.

In addition, the compounds provide a venue to dispose of corpses. "Traffickers go to great lengths to prepare themselves for battle," a senior US official said. "Part of that preparation is the use of firing ranges and combat training courses . . . And that's not something that we have seen before." Two of the facilities in Tamaulipas have airstrips. The training that Lazcano received as a GAFE alerted him to the imperative of intimidation. Thanks to this element, Los Zetas emerged as the most lethal and successful providers of protection when compared with gangs that competed for the same clients. The Texas-based trainees are reportedly schooled in home robberies, firearm use, and skills in running cars off the road to accomplish abductions.[36]

Notes

1. Quoted in "Las bandas de narcos son empresas en México," *El Universal* (Caracas), January 16, 2010.
2. Ignacio Alvarado "Alvarez, "Narcotráfico Heriberto Lazcano: Un poder tras las Sombra," *El Día Siete*, December 2005; "Sources: Zetas Head Lazcano Killed in Matamoros," *The Monitor*, June 17, 2011.
3. "Quien es Heriberto Lazcano Lazcano, alias 'El Lazca,' 'El Verdugo' o 'Z-3,'" *El Blog de Terror*, July 25, 2010, http://www.diariodelnarco.com/2011/04/insignias-y-uniformes-del-narco.html.
4. Francisco Gómez, "Los Zetas por dentro," *El Universal*, December 31, 2008.
5. María de la Luz González, "La Sedena denucia campaña en su contra," *El Universal.com*, April 4, 2011.
6. "Zetas denidos eran estacas," *Blog del Narco*, May 26, 2011.
7. "Sedena Identifies the Heads of Los Zetas," *Borderland Beat*, April 21, 2010; and "Controla crimen region fronteriza," *Reforma*, May 10, 2011.
8. "Official: Mexican Cartels Hiring Common Criminals," *The Monitor*, April 7, 2011.
9. "La Marina denuncia la desaparación de cuatro agentes en Veracruz," *CNN México*, August 15, 2011.
10. "Reclutan 'Zetas' mujeres para integrar célula: Las Panteras,'" *Terra*, March 27, 2009.
11. Carlos Avilés Allende, "Capturan a uno de los fundadores de Los Zetas," *El Universal.com.mx*, June 25, 2007.
12. "Alejandra Guzmán amenizó fiesta de Los Zetas," *El Economista*, January 11, 2011; and Istra Pacheco, "Mexican Rocker Alejandra Guzman's Flight Reversed," *SignonSandiego*, January 4, 2010.
13. "Los Zetas pagan aguinaldo a 'sicarios' en Tabasco," *Proceso*, December 24, 2009.
14. Javier Cabrera, "Malova pide a los niños no imitar a los narcos," *El Universal*, May 1, 2011.
15. The Mexican military does not allow its soldiers to patronize this eatery lest they fall prey to Zeta spies.
16. Marcos Muedano, "Festejan 2 años de temple construido por 'El Lazca,'" *El Universal.com.mx*, February 3, 2011; and "Fetejan 2 aniversario del templo donado por el Lazca," *AlertaPeriodista*, February 4, 2011.

17. Susana Moraga, "Sabían en Hidalgo de 'limosna': CEM," *El Diario.mx*, October 24, 2010.
18. José Gil Olmos, "Se escribe con Zeta," *Proceso* (special edition no. 28), *La Guerra del Narco*, 2010; and Sam Dillon, "Kidnappings in Mexico Send Shivers across Border," *New York Times*, January 5, 2009.
19. Anticartel operations usually take place in predawn hours when capos and their underlings, who frequently keep late hours, are just getting to sleep.
20. The explanation for not having the plane on hand may have been that its takeoff from Mexico City or its earlier presence in Reynosa would have alerted Los Zetas to the operation against "El Hummer."
21. Quoted in Alfredo Corchado, "Mexico's Zetas Gang Buys Businesses along Border in Move to Increase Legitimacy," *Dallas Morning News*, December 7, 2009.
22. "Mujer opera secuestros de *Los Zetas* fuera del país: PGR," *Milenio.com*, March 8, 2010.
23. Ioan Grillo, "Mexico's Female Narcos," *Globalpost*, December 19, 2010.
24. "Un narco violento que está en la mira," *Reforma.com*, December 6, 2010.
25. "Revelan creación del grupo de sicarias 'Las Panteras,'" *El Norte*, March 27, 2009.
26. "Marineros detienen a presunto contador del líder de 'Los Zetas,'" *esmas*, May 30, 2010.
27. "Capturan a contador de los Zetas en NL," *Milenio.com*, June 4, 2010; and "Aniquilar se escribe con Z," Estrictamente Personal column, *EjeCentral*, August 19, 2011.
28. "Detienen a presunto contador de 'Los Zetas' en NL," *El Siglo* (Durango), April 13, 2011.
29. "Identifican a presunto agresor de militares en Veracruz," *El Universal*, May 22, 2011.
30. Rubén Mosso, "Captura! Ejército en Saltillo a operator financiero," *Milenio*, August 4, 2011; and EFE, "Cae el operador financiero de los Zetas," *Diario Las Américas.com*, September 3, 2011.
31. These states are Coahuila, Nuevo León, Zacatecas, San Luis Potosí, Nayarit, Colima, Guanajuato, Hidalgo, Puebla, Tlaxcala, Veracruz, Oaxaca, Tabasco, Campeche, Yucatán, Mexico, Chihuahua, Chiapas, Quintana Roo, Mexico City, Tamaulipas, and Guerrero; see Benito Jiménez, "Ubica reporte de PF expansión de 'Zetas,'" *Reforma.com*, February 27, 2011.
32. The navy killed El Gonzo, plaza boss in Veracruz, on November 3, 2009; see "Muere en Veracruz líder 'Zeta' en tiroteo," *Reforma*, November 4, 2009.
33. "Zeta Recalls His Life, Warns against It," *Brownsville Herald*, February 17, 2011.
34. Statement by department spokesman Sean McCormack; see "Niega EU haber entrenado 'Zetas,'" *Excélsior*, May 20, 2008.
35. "Blowback Still Blows—Zetas, Kaibiles and MS-13," *NarcoGuerra Times*, November 26, 2009.
36. Lisa J. Campbell, "Los Zetas: Operational Assessment," in Robert J. Bunker (ed.), *Narcos Over the Border: Gangs, Cartels and Mercenaries* (New York, NY: Routledge, 2011): 69.

3

Resources

As indicated in Table 4, Los Zetas were the first major crime syndicate to broadly diversify their activities.

Table 4   Diversification of Los Zetas' Criminal Activities

Illegal activities	Examples
Drug smuggling	Cocaine, marijuana, methamphetamines, and some heroin.
Extortion	Even when behind bars, Los Zetas, who have detailed information about a family, demand money to prevent the kidnapping of a loved one.
Kidnapping	Illegal immigrants passing through Mexico; cells in most plazas are dedicated to this crime. If they cannot squeeze ransoms out of their families, Los Zetas may require captives to perform menial or low-skilled jobs in what amounts to semiservitude.
Human smuggling	The Mexican Human Rights Commission reported that in 6 months of 2009, 9,758 illegal aliens crossing Mexico were kidnapped and 13 assassinated. Of these victims, 91 reported complicity by "agents of the state," usually functionaries of the Mexican Migration Institute (INM).
Contraband	US officials and representatives of film studios and software manufacturers claim that Los Zetas and other cartels take a big cut out of the hundreds of millions of dollars in bootleg disks sold each year in Mexico.
Petroleum rustling	PEMEX revealed that during the first quarter of 2011, 264 illegal connections siphoned a total of 773,000 barrels from the monopoly—81.3% higher than in the first three months of 2010.

(Continued)

Table 4 (*Continued*)

Sale of body parts	A Zeta commander allegedly kidnapped 100 illegal Guatemalans working in a shirt factory in Coatzacoalcos, Veracruz. According to an escapee, the women would be turned into prostitutes, older men would become lookouts or small-time drug sellers, and the bodies of some healthier young men would be harvested for kidneys and other body parts.
Money laundering	Purchase of hotels, resorts, casinos, real estate, restaurants, and pharmacies.
Businesses	Calling themselves "The Company," Los Zetas have acquired businesses along the border, such as used-car dealerships, restaurants, casinos, liquor stores, and discotheques.
Prostitution	Cuban prostitutes in Cancún; "buying" Central American women from an immigrant smuggler and exploiting them as whores in bars and hotels in Reynosa; a refugee group asserts that 47 prostitution networks exist in Mexico.
Selling the right to cross its territory (*Derecho de Piso*)	Threatened gas producers in the Burgos basin in Tamaulipas and Nuevo León with death if they did not pay for the right to operate.
Murder for hire	Los Zetas allegedly gave Eduardo González Trejo (or Eduardo Trejo Ponce), El Lalito, Mex$40,000 to murder PJF Commander Víctor Hugo Moneda Rangel.
Providing protection	To the BLO and to Cuban gangs in Cancún.
Theft of automobiles and trucks	Especially in Tamaulipas and Nuevo León along the US border.
Paying small farmers to grow poppies and move contraband into Mexico	Notably in Guatemala, but also in areas of the Tierra Caliente.
Arson	Just after Christmas 2010, in a battle with the Sinaloa Cartel, Zetas set fire to houses in Tierras Coloradas, Durango, leaving homeless 150 Tepehuan Indians who speak Spanish as a second language and have neither electricity nor running water; the victims had already fled into the woods, sleeping under trees or hiding in caves after a raid by feared drug gangs on December 26; residents experienced cold winter weather, and the crops of farmers who refused to cooperate were burned.

Table 4 (*Continued*)

Roadblocks	Notably in Monterrey, its satellite cities, Reynosa and Guadalajara.

Sources: William & Mary student Lindsey C. Nicolai; and Lisa J. Campbell, "Los Zetas: Operational Assessment," in Robert J. Bunker (ed.), *Narcos Over the Border: Gangs, Cartels and Mercenaries* (New York, NY: Routledge, 2011): 70–71; "Los Zetas, tras ejecución del comandante Monteda," *Milenio.com*, March 18, 2009; "Cancún: las cubanas secuestradas, en red de prostitución de los Zetas," *Cubadebate*, September 17, 2009; Alfredo Corchado, "Mexico's Zetas Gang Buys Businesses along Border in Move to Increase Legitimacy, *Dallas Morning News*, December 7, 2009; "Bloquean sicarios carreteras en NL," *Reforma*, March 19, 2010; "Cobran zetas 'derecho de piso' a gaseras en el norte del país," *Noticias Durango Hoy*, February 16, 2011; Antonio Baranda, "Perfeccionan reos táctica de extorsíon," *Reforma.com*, June 1, 2010; Mica Rosenberg, "Mexico's Refugees: A Hidden Cost of Drugs War," *Reuters*, February 17, 2011 (arson); "Zetas' incendian pueblo en Durango," *El Economista*, February 18, 2011; Samuel Logan, "Networked Intelligence: Southern Pulse," May 10, 2011 (petroleum rustling); Verónica Sánchez, "Registrar desde 2009 liga entre INM-narco," *Reforma*, May 11, 2011 (abuse of illegal aliens); William Booth, "Mexico's Thriving Piracy Business Funds Cartels," *Washington Post*, May 30, 2011; Anne-Marie O'Connor, "Mexico's 'Inferno' of Exploitation," *Washington Post*, July 28, 2011; and Ana Laura Vásquez, "Ubican en México 47 redes de trata," *Reforma*, August 4, 2011.

Drug Revenues

In contrast to the Gulf Cartel, which concentrates on drugs, Los Zetas make money through multiple endeavors. Cocaine constitutes approximately 50 percent of the organization's revenue. Speaking off the record, analysts believe that extortion (10–15 percent), meth-amphetamines and heroin (5–10 percent), immigrant smuggling (5 percent), contraband (5 percent), and miscellaneous activities (10–15 percent) generate far less gross income.

Nicola Gratteri, Italy's antidrug prosecutor, claimed that Los Zetas have had ties with the Calabrian Mafia, N'drangheta, for at least two years. These links spring from the cheaper prices for cocaine offered by Los Zetas and the Gulf Cartel, which the Mexicans delivered for $25,000 per kilogram and the Italians sold to European consumers for $45,000 per kilogram.[1]

Specific Zeta leaders invested in shipments. A portion of the 11.7-ton shipment of cocaine captured in Altamira, Tamaulipas, on October 5, 2007, was earmarked for El 40. Although seven of his heavily armed cohorts were apprehended, Morales Treviño fled when he realized that law-enforcement officials had commandeered the scene.[2] None-theless, he exacted payment for the loss from Los Zetas' local plaza boss. Meanwhile, US Ambassador Antonio O. Garza "praised the Mexican government and President Calderón for another victory in the battle against narco-traffickers and criminals . . ." The envoy went out of his way to laud the Mexican armed forces and police who "risk their lives daily in the struggle against those who kill with impunity and poison the lives of innocent people in their quest for money."[3]

So abundant are their resources that in many areas law-enforcement officers, once rivals, now protect Los Zetas. Ministry of Public Security coordinator of intelligence, Luis Cárdenas Palomino, and the head of the Federal Support Forces, Gen. Cruz López, found that in early 2007 the cartel paid uniformed policemen in Hidalgo Mex$3,000 every fifteen days for their cooperation. The SSP accused ninety-two officers of working with Los Zetas.[4] In September 2009, another 123 law-enforcement officers in the state were apprehended. Those taken into custody belonged to the municipal police, the metropolitan police, and the state police. They were accused of receiving funds from Los Zetas in return for information, protection, and participation in kidnappings, extortion plots, and executions.[5] In the wake of the April 2010 massacre of 126 people in San Fernando, Tamaulipas, authorities arrested sixteen officers suspected of protecting Los Zetas who are believed to have carried out the atrocity.[6] The ubiquity of corrupt cops, who absorb upwards of 15 percent of the cartel's resources, has hatched the term *Zeta-policía* or *polizeta* to describe them.[7]

Kidnapping

At the same time, the cartel has diversified its activities, with kidnapping serving as another profit center. The paramilitaries' primary targets are wealthy professionals and businessmen. Once they grab a subject, they secrete him in a nearby safe house. The ransom negotiations resemble a minuet that takes several days to perform. The abductors dictate the price and the rules of the transaction, but arrangements have to be made for opening lines of communication, obtaining the money, and returning the victim, provided that the requested amount has been raised and authorities have not been alerted to the crime.

In late September 2009, a prosperous, middle-aged businessman in Monterrey went through roughly the same experience. This time, however, Los Zetas wanted the payment as fast as possible because they were husbanding cash amid escalating friction with the Gulf Cartel.[8]

Neither the lawyer nor the businessman lived ostentatiously. However, Los Zetas are on the lookout for individuals who may have made money by either cutting legal corners or through blatantly crooked deals. The nouveaux riches are especially vulnerable if they flaunt their recently acquired wealth by sporting bejeweled Rolex watches, wearing tailor-made clothing, owning expensive automobiles, and living in gaudy mansions.

At 3:00 a.m. in September 2010, Jesús López and several companions were driving on the toll road between Atlacomulco, Mexico State, and Morelia, Michoacán. Suddenly, a black Dodge Charger with flashing lights roared up behind them, pulled them over, and ordered the men out of their vehicle. López and his friends insisted, "We haven't committed a crime." After ransacking the car, the "police," who turned out to be Zetas, bound and gagged their prisoners before whisking them to a secluded wooded area about fifteen minutes away. After being commanded to lie down side by side, López believed that the end had come and that, at least, he would not have to pay off his staggering debts. Finally, Los Zetas drove away, apparently wanting only to steal the car. López imagined that "God thought 'I want you here [on earth] to endure more sacrifices.'"[9]

Less likely to be abducted are members of families with "old money." These men and women are threaded into a thick social network in their community, behave discreetly, and enjoy ties to the local, state, and, possibly, the national power structure.

In Zeta-infested Tabasco, for example, 164 kidnappings took place between 2008 and 2011, generating upwards of $7 million for organized crime; however, only sixty-five abductees were freed even though ransoms had been paid in most cases.[10]

Plaza chiefs—or even hit men—may engage in kidnappings on their own either to meet the monetary target assigned to them by Los Zetas' leaders or to increase their personal earnings.

Contraband

Los Zetas have cells devoted to hawking smuggled goods in Nuevo León, Tamaulipas, Veracruz, Quintana Roo, and other states. The Zeta subsidiary, Los Únicos, also copies movies, music DVDs, and similar digital entertainment products. In mid-2009, authorities mounted a drive against this illegal merchandise in Coahuila, San Luis Potosí, Veracruz, and Nuevo León. On June 21, the army arrested a high-level operator within Los Únicos, Gabriel "Don Gaby" Ayala Romero, known as "The Czar of Contraband," for allegedly extorting $1.8 million each month from hucksters in the Monterrey areas. At the time of his capture, Gabriel had in his possession quemadores (burners), a "plotter" (reproduction machine), thousands of audio and video disks, blank CDs, firearms, ammunition magazines, bullets, and a personal supply of marijuana. To ensure the vendors were marketing Los Zetas' products and not those of competitors, Gabriel and his cohorts affixed a small sticker on each item, showing a neighing black stallion imprinted on the letter "Z." In early 2011, an assassin killed the czar in the Topo Chico prison in Nuevo León.

Northeast of Monterrey in Tamaulipas, the organization also demanded that sellers peddle only merchandise provided by Los Zetas by December 1, 2008. To verify the source of the merchandise, they require the retailer to affix a stamp with the image of a Hummer vehicle on the upper right-hand side of packages. In addition, they forced theater managers to copy first-run films, which the criminals sold in the informal economy. Los Únicos threatened to kill peddlers who, according to the size of their operation, failed to pay Mex$500 to Mex$5,000 monthly for "rent" or "protection." Americans assigned to the US Consulate General in Monterrey purchased, as a joke, a wrestler's mask for a visiting colleague. The street seller thanked them profusely, saying, "Now I will be able to pay the five hundred pesos that Los Zetas demand each week." In some cases, Los Zetas resell imitation Adidas or Nike tennis shoes, Abercrombie clothing, and DVDs from China that passed through the ports of Lázaro Cárdenas, Manzanillo, or Long Beach, California, en route to the point of distribution. The criminal organization creates dummy import corporations to mask their activities.

In some cases, Los Zetas exact a monthly "war tax"—so named because they are in conflict with other underground groups—of tens of thousands of dollars on businesses, especially those with a fixed site such as hospitals, merchandise-laden warehouses, posh restaurants, fancy hotels, gambling parlors, supermarkets, and automobile dealerships. Even teachers have been forced to pay or submit to the consequences. In Veracruz, where they are increasingly active and under fire, Los Zetas call themselves "La Compañía." As in Tamaulipas, they took control of the black market with their well-known savagery, torturing and executing leaders of street hucksters who denounced their activities. As a result, informal sellers in Acauyucan, Xalapa, Coatzacoalcos, Minatitlán, and the port of Veracruz only handled DVDs, videos, and other articles provided by La Compañía. Moreover, the desperados' henchmen hijacked tractor-trailers and livestock trucks to resell stolen agricultural products and cattle on the black market in Veracruz while simultaneously expanding their extortion networks to table-dance cafes, brothels, bars, and discotheques. "Veracruz is like Chicago in the 1920s," reported the Mexican daily *La Reforma.*

Human Smuggling

Los Zetas have helped foreigners reach the United States illegally via Tabasco, Yucatán, Quintana Roo, and other southern coastal states. They charge the families of Cuban aliens up to $15,000 per person in an operation allegedly run by an ex-member of Fidel Castro's military, Iván Gregorio "El Tigre"/"El Talibán" Blanco, a naturalized Mexican citizen and Cancún resident shielded by Los Zetas. Each *pollo* (chicken) or migrant had to pay $350 to the Federal Police in Cancún, $300 to law-enforcement agents of the National Migration Institute (INM), $300 to Los Zetas, $200 for the airfare to Monterrey, $800 to a federal official in Monterrey, and $260 for a *coyote* to sneak him to the border.

When the Beltrán Leyvas learned that the Cubans were also involved in cocaine trafficking without their permission, they dispatched Los Matazetas, a squad of hit men then led by former Federal Police agent, Rubén "El Terri" Rivera Ramírez, to wipe out the intruders. On June 18, 2009, the bodies of Blanco and two of his accomplices, all of whom had been suffocated to death, were found. It was reported that Ulises de Jesús "El Bárbaro" Gutiérrez assumed the number one spot in the Cuban-American Mafia in the Mayan Riviera.[11]

Such criminality took place with impunity thanks to Cancún's police chief, Francisco "El Viking" Velasco Delgado, who was arrested on February 9, 2009, in connection with the brutal slaying of General Mauricio Enrique Tello Quiñones. The brigadier general was about to assume a top security post in the cartel-suffused resort city.[12] Los Zetas also protected the *polleros* who charged $6,000 a person to smuggle Chinese aliens into Mexico. For these activities, the paramilitaries paid Federal Police and immigration police and other INM agents between $300 and $800.[13]

The United Nations reported that Los Zetas also had a major stake in the trafficking of unlawful Central American migrants, who often needed protection from gangs to pass through Mexico. Those illegals who either refuse to join Los Zetas or cannot pay the fees demanded by the paramilitaries may be held hostage until their families scrape together the money. Although not providing a cartel-by-cartel breakdown, the UN estimates that the $1.6 billion that the Mexican syndicates derived from trafficking in illegal aliens surpassed their earnings from drug-related dealings.[14]

Sale of Body Parts

Unconfirmed reports indicate that Zeta cadres in Coatzacoalcos, Veracruz, came upon a factory in which a hundred illegal Guatemalans were turning out shirts. The commander offered the owner Mex$500 per worker. When the proprietor refused to sell his employees, the paramilitaries herded them into a truck and drove off. An escapee claimed that the captors planned to use the older men as street vendors and the women as prostitutes. Meanwhile, they planned to harvest the younger men's kidneys and other body parts to sell to unscrupulous middlemen, hospitals, physicians, and families.

Petroleum Rustling

In mid-May 2009, the PGR reported that, for the past two years, Los Zetas had siphoned some eighty thousand gallons of diesel oil weekly from the pipelines of Petróleos Mexicanos (PEMEX), Mexico's incurably corrupt oil monopoly, which provides nearly 40 percent of the national budget. It was later announced that the cartel had stolen more than $1 billion worth of oil. They "taxed the pipelines" by using powerful state-of-the-art drills to puncture pipelines, long rubber hoses to transport the purloined petroleum, and a fleet of tanker trucks to carry the substance to buyers. The criminals colluded with active or retired members of the Petroleum Workers' Union, who "are highly skilled people who have the technical knowledge to extract oil from the pipelines. They are now under the control of the Zetas."[15] "They practically own vast stretches of the pipelines, from the highway to the very door of the oil companies," stated a federal lawmaker.[16] The criminals went so far as to create spurious firms to hide their activities—a tactic observed in Texas, where the group resold to businessmen petroleum products stolen from Mexico's state-owned oil company PEMEX.

This siphoning of black gold began in 2006 and involved thefts in the states of Tamaulipas, Mexico State, Oaxaca, Tabasco, and the rugged hills around Veracruz.[17] They then sold the fuel to seventy distributors in central Mexico through a company called Auto Express Especializados Teoloyucan (AETSA).[18] In 2009, executives of two American energy companies—Y Gas & Oil and Trammo Petroleum—pled guilty to buying the pilfered hydrocarbons.[19]

Mexican federal authorities froze the bank accounts of a Zeta cell that used the illegal sale of oil and gas to launder money. The PGR indicated that between 2007 and 2008, the criminals had garnered more than $42 million by these unlawful transactions. Thirteen presumed Zetas were taken into custody.[20] Through mid-2011, the giant firm had detected thirty-two clandestine thefts in its liquid petroleum lines, each of which cost between Mex$60,000 and Mex$1 million.[21]

In mid-June 2010, the Federal Police arrested Francisco Guízar Pavón. The so-called King of Gasoline, a former PEMEX employee, reportedly had been stealing and reselling the fuel since the 1990s, if not earlier. In recent years, he had enjoyed the protection of Los Zetas in Veracruz and La Familia Michoacana in Michoacán.[22] According to *The Monitor*, a newspaper in McAllen, Texas, a large explosion generating plumes of black smoke that took place near a gas station in Nuevo Progreso, Tamaulipas, in April 2011 was in fact caused by illegal siphoning of gas. Reporters for the daily claimed to have been chased off by Zeta estacas when they arrived to document the fire. The estacas were apparently directing the firefighting efforts.[23]

Businesses

As cited in Table 4, Los Zetas operate on both sides of the US–Mexican border. "They own used-car lots, restaurants, discotheques, liquor stores," said Robert Garcia, a detective with the Laredo Police Department and a specialist on this cartel. "Basically, anything anywhere that moves to and from the border, or anything and anywhere they can launder large amounts of money, the Zetas have a hand in. They even own a dog-racing track," he noted.[24]

Money Laundering

The syndicate has a sophisticated money laundering capability. It uses dozens of seemingly innocuous businesses such as an auto wash in Guadalajara, the "Silueta Perfecta" spa in Mexico City, the Niño Féliz day care center in Culiacán, the Biosport de Hermosillo gymnasium in Hermosillo, as well as nightclubs, casinos, houses of ill repute, and properties abroad.[25]

Prostitution

Diplomats report that Los Zetas, who used to supply women to organized networks, have initiated their own prostitution ventures. "They're starting to change their business model and branching out into things like sex trafficking," a US official in Mexico City told a reporter. "They realize it is a lucrative way to generate revenue, and it is low risk," he added. A single mother from El Salvador was kidnapped and turned over to Los Zetas. She claimed they brought her to a house, presided over by the "The Butcher," where brutality reigned. Dozens of women passed through this building during the three months she was held captive. "Zetas from nine safe houses met to inspect the female arrivals. They raped a few right there. Others they took to hotel rooms. When the women returned, 'they cried a lot,'" she said. "They had bruises."[26] Los Zetas have forced young Mexican women, as well as those from Central America and Cuba, into prostitution rings that they operate throughout the country. A highly publicized case involved Taimy González, a young Cuban whose relatives had paid $12,000 for returning her to her family in Miami. When the time came for the exchange, Los Zetas, who has knitted ties with the Cuban Mafia, demanded an additional Mex$1 million before releasing their hostage.[27]

Attorneys

Los Zetas have the wealth to hire the best lawyers available to defend their cadres. For example, in August 2008, two NGOs—the Citizens' Council for Public Safety and Legal Justice and the Better Society Better Government—presented taped conversations to indicate that Attorney Francisco Javier Estrada Sánchez belonged to Los Zetas whose members he had defended in Tabasco and Veracruz. Estrada Sánchez was the first attorney convicted during the Calderón administration. The charges against him were as follows: corrupting members of the armed forces and police, serving as a go-between for convicts and narco-traffickers outside of prison, and involvement in organized crime.

On December 5, 2008, Baja California Governor José Guadalupe Osuna Millán urged lawyers not to take clients accused of organized crime. This admonition fell on deaf ears. During the last week in March 2009, forty-four lawyers registered to defend twenty-three policemen charged in Tijuana with crimes by the Assistant Attorney General for the Special Investigation of Organized Crime (SIEDO). The president of the Tijuana Bar Association emphasized that "we are accomplices to the crime if we defend individuals known to be guilty and permit or use false evidence, witnesses, and documents in his trial . . . ." Osiel Cárdenas had no fewer than thirty-nine lawyers registered to protect him, with Leonardo Oceguera Jiménez, who was later assassinated, being one of the most prominent. Another well-known litigator is Marisela Hernández, who defended Zeta Rogelio "El Kelin" González Pizaña; in addition to her legal duties, she also encouraged his family members to stage demonstrations outside the prison where he was confined.

Texas attorneys who represented Imurias "Comandante Tomate" Machado Treviño and other kidnappers allegedly working for El Hummer González Durán included the following: Gocha Allen Ramirez, Hugo Piña, Carlos Quintana, Marcus C. Barrera, James Scott Sullivan, José Luis Ramos, Gilberto Falcón, Crispin C. J. Quintanilla III, Manuel Guerra III.[28] Al Alvarez (McAllen) and Ernesto "Neto" Gamez Jr. (Brownsville) also have reputations as sharp barristers.

Thefts

Los Zetas were described as birds of prey for looting and robbing grocery stores, gas stations, convenience stores, and restaurants and for charging fees (*cuotas or pisos*) to shopkeepers and street vendors, under the threat of murdering them and their families unless, of course, they paid. Observers have also attributed to these criminals responsibility for the mass killing of cattle and the robbery of ranches along the border. They steal latest model trucks or SUVs from individuals or businesses, as was the case with the company of Schulemberg and Ticsa where they stole thirty trucks, as well as taking ten vehicles from the Chevrolet dealership in Miguel Alemán.

Armaments

Los Zetas have stocked safe houses with grenades, antitank weapons, assault rifles, and other heavy armaments.[29]

Below are several examples of discovered caches through January 2012:

> September 11, 2011: The navy reported that, in connection with the capture of Verónica "La Vero"/"La Flaca" Mireya Moreno Carreón, plaza boss in San Nicolás de Los Garza, Nuevo León, it discovered a .38-caliber pistol, ammunition, six cell phones, a stolen vehicle, hundred doses of what appeared to be cocaine, fifty doses of meth, and two packages of marijuana.[30]

> Mid-July to August 2, 2011: During *Operación Lince Norte* (Northern Lynx Operation), the army dispatched some 4,000 soldiers, 722 vehicles, and 23 airplanes to fight Los Zetas in the North. In addition to killing or capturing 200 paramilitaries, the military seized

Mex$6.5 million, about $540,000, in a Nuevo León city, 1,217 weapons, 3 tons of marijuana, $39,700 in US currency, and more than 260 vehicles, according to the military; soldiers also rescued 12 people who had been kidnapped.[31]

June 9, 2011: The navy announced finding weapons in Coahuila and Nuevo León. These included 215 firearms, most of which were high-powered, 500 military uniforms, and 5 suspects (Coahuila), as well as various pistols, grenade launchers, explosives, fragmentation grenades, thousands of cartridges, and 200 kilograms of cocaine (Nuevo León).[32]

June 6, 2011: The navy announced the seizure of weapons near Monclova, Nuevo León. They found 80 long firearms, 20 short firearms, 3 grenade launchers, 150 cartridges, 880 ammunition magazines, 3 kilograms of Emulgel and other explosives, 4 fragmentation grenades, and 8 stolen vehicles.[33]

June 1, 2011: Army discovered a subterranean deposit of arms and ammunition in the municipality of San Buenaventura, in northern Coahuila, 620 miles north of Mexico City. Soldiers seized 154 long firearms, including AK-47s and AR-15s, and 7 short firearms; 92,039 ammunition rounds of different calibers; an RPG rocket-launcher and 2 rockets; and 4 mortar grenades, a crossbow, 1 vehicle, and 435 gun belts.[34]

May 2011: In Higueras, 28 miles from Monterrey, soldiers of the Seventh Military Zone swarmed into a Zeta camp and captured 83 firearms, 60 grenades, 3 grenade launchers, 18,000 ammunition rounds, 230 AR-15 assault rifles, 19 SUVs, 22 cell phones, 52 two-way radios, and sand uniforms bearing the Zeta insignia.[35]

March 27–April 2, 2011: In northern Tamaulipas, the military commandeered 113 handguns, 12,167 ammunition rounds, 391 magazines, 2 magazine carriers, 2 rifle scopes, 3 grenade launchers, 77 grenades, 1 rocket launcher, a rocket, a crossbow, 2 tripods, 36 electric detonators, 12 meters of detonating cord, 2 detonator starters, $60,000 in dollars and pesos, 7 cell phones, 4 radios, 70 cars, a motorcycle, a camper trailer, military uniforms, 17 caps with "CDG" emblem (acronym for Gulf Cartel), and 1 cap with the letter "Z."[36]

October 22, 2010: Federal agents in Cárdenas, Tabasco, captured 72 long firearms, including 34 AK-47s, 13 AR-15s, 5 machine guns, 10 fragmentation grenades, 2,275 ammunition rounds, 4 cell phones, 2 vehicles, and 2 kilograms of cocaine; also apprehended were two Zetas—Margarito Mendoza López, forty, and Carmen Zúñiga Arcia, twenty-seven.[37]

September 26, 2010: Acting on information from a citizen, military personnel found a cache of arms in Fresnillo, Zacatecas. They discovered 3 long firearms, 4 pistols, 32 loaders, 1,063 cartridges, four 40 mm grenades, radio equipment, cell phones, 2 Federal Police license tags, 1 military identity card, and 3 gun belts.[38]

May 11, 2010: Sixty soldiers from the Seventh Military Zone raided a training camp hidden by trees five hundred meters from the Marín–Higueras highway near Higueras, Nuevo León. Although they killed one Zeta and wounded others, most of the paramilitaries fled into the nearby mountains. The army seized twelve vehicles (pickup trucks, SUVs, and vans), 3 grenade launchers, 109 grenades (including 29 40-mm grenades and 39 hand grenades), 2 rocket launchers, 3 anti-tank rockets, 2 Barett rifles, .50-caliber sniper rifles, more than 124 AK-47s and AR-15s, 15 handguns, 1,375 ammunition magazines, 55,000 rounds of ammunition of various calibers, military-style helmets, 20 communications radios, and uniforms and equipment bearing the shield-shaped patch of Los Zetas.[39]

November 7, 2008: The army and federal agents announced the largest seizure of arms in Mexico (to date). In Reynosa, they seized 7 Barett .50-caliber rifles, 287 grenades, AK-47s among 278 long firearms, 126 pistols, 2 grenade launchers, 500,000 bullets of various calibers, 14 dynamite caps, 67 bulletproof vests, and Mex$970,300 ($75,000), and $86,740 in cash. This raid included the capture of Jaime "El Hummer" González Durán.[40]

In light of this modern weaponry, Los Zetas have not resorted to medieval technology as did one cartel that used a metal-framed catapult, powered by heavy-duty elastic and mounted on a trailer, to hurl 45 pounds of marijuana into Naco, Arizona.[41]

However, they have built "Mad Max" style vehicles, made of cast iron or other robust bulletproof metals. These menacing behemoths transport troops and allow Zetas to fire through portals at their enemies. Deployment of earlier versions of this armored transport, known *El Monstruo* or The Monster, has led the Mexican military to purchase armored vehicles—another example of how the government is adapting its strategy to cope with Los Zetas as the organization efficiently spawns "shadow governments" in the territory where it operates with impunity buoyed by widespread corruption.[42]

Notes

1. Irene Savio, "Confirman nexo 'Zetas' e italianos," *Reforma*, September 19, 2008.
2. "Dictan prisón contra Zetas," *Terra*, December 10, 2007.
3. "Declaración del Embajador Antonio O. Garza," *Comunicado de Prensa*, US Embassy, October 5, 2007.

4. Benito Jiménez, "Acusan a mandos de proteger a 'Zetas,'" *Reforma.com*, June 29, 2009.
5. "México: arrestan a 124 policías por vínculos con Los Zetas," *Adnmundo.com*, September 15, 2009.
6. "Mexican Police under Suspicion in Mass Grave Case," *Australian News.Net*, April 14, 2011, www.australiannews.net/story/769368/ht/Mexican-police-under-suspicion-in-mass-graves-case.
7. Lisa J. Campbell, "Los Zetas: Operational Assessment," 68.
8. Coauthor's (Grayson) interview with abductee's family and business partner, who asked to remain anonymous.
9. Jesús López, interview with co-author (Grayson), Toluca, Mexico State, September 17, 2011.
10. José Ángel Castro, "99 ejecutados pese al pago de rescate," *Tabasco Hoy*, June 7, 2011.
11. "Pelean Cancún mafia cubana," *Reforma.com*, November 22, 2009; and "Identifican a los tres ejectados en Cancún; investan nexos con tráfico de cubanos," *Noticaribe*, June 19, 2009.
12. The source of this information is "Pitufo," an ex-Zeta now in a witness protection program; see "Tenía ex militar negocio con 'Zetas,'" *Reforma*, April 5, 2009.
13. Antonio Baranda, "Detallan 'Zetas' cobro a chinos," *Reforma*, January 10, 2010.
14. Silvia Garduño, "Controlan Zetas tráfico de migrantes," *Reforma*, June 19, 2010; and "El tráfico de migrantes da en México más ganancias que narco: ONU," *Excélsior*, March 28, 2011.
15. Quoted in Steve Fainaru and William Booth, "Mexico's Drug Cartels Siphon Liquid Gold," *Washington Post*, December 13, 2009.
16. Eduardo Mendoza Arellano quoted in Steve Fainaru and William Booth, "Mexico's Drug Cartels Siphon Liquid Gold," *Washington Post*, December 13, 2009.
17. "Los Zetas ordeñan ductos de Pemex," *Yahoo! Noticias*, August 7, 2009.
18. *NarcoGuerra Times*, May 25, 2009, http://narcoguerratimes.wordpress.com/2009/05/25/.
19. Fainaru and Booth, "Mexico's Drug Cartels Siphon Liquid Gold."
20. "México decomisa a Los Zetas cuentas para lavar dinero," *AOL Noticias*, February 16, 2011.
21. "Gasta Pemex hasta un mpd por toma illegal," *Reforma*, August 23, 2011.
22. "Cae en Monterrey 'rey de gasolinas,'" *Reforma*, June 14, 2010.
23. "No Injuries after Tanker Trucks Explode in Nuevo Progreso," *The Monitor*, April 22, 2011.
24. Alfredo Corchado, "Mexico's Zetas Gang Buys Businesses along Border in Move to Increase Legitimacy," *Dallas Morning News*, December 7, 2009.
25. "El dinero del narco, sin fronteras," *Diario de Yucatán*, December 26, 2009.
26. Quoted in Anne-Marie O'Connor, "Mexico's 'Inferno' of Exploitation," *Washington Post*, July 28, 2011.
27. Jean-Guy Allard, "Cancún: las cubanas secuestradas, en red de prostitución de los Zetas," *CubaDebate*, September 17, 2009.

28. Jared Taylor, "Lawyers' Names," e-mail to author, June 13, 2011; the information came from Texas Southern District Court, federal case no. 7:08-CR-01751.
29. Roig-Franzia, "Drug Trade Tyranny on the Border," p. A16.
30. Secretaría de la Marina, "Presunta Jefe de La Plaza de San Nicolás de los Garza, Nuevo León," *Press Communication* 283/2011, September 11, 2011.
31. The military captured financial operative Valdemar "Adal" Quintanilla Soriano and killed Jorge Luis "Pompín" de la Peña Brizuela, allegedly the Nuevo Laredo plaza boss; see Jason Buch, "Nuevo Laredo Zeta Boss Killed," *San Antonio Express-News*, August 7, 2011.
32. "Aseguran Marina más de 215 armas y uniformes de Los Zetas," *Notimex*, June 9, 2011.
33. Secretaría de la Marina, "Personal de la Armada de México asegura en Coahuila arsenal pertenciente presuntamente al grupo delictivo de los zetas, asi como más de una tonelada de marihuana en Nuevo León," *Comunicado de Prensa* 187/2011, June 6, 2011.
34. E. Eduardo Castillo, "Decomisan arsenal en México a cartel de Los Zetas," *Associated Press*, June 6, 2011.
35. "Mexican Troops Raid Camp Belonging to Los Zetas Gang," *Latin American Herald Tribune*, June 6, 2011.
36. Naxiely Lopez, "Report Details Drugs, Weapons and Explosives Seized by Mexican Military," *The Monitor*, April 5, 2011.
37. "México: Incautan arsenal a cártel de los Zetas," *La Prensa.hn_internacionales*, October 22, 2010; and "Presentan a Zetas detenidos con arsenal en Cárdenas," *El Heroico.com*, October 23, 2010.
38. "Militares arrestan a presuntos 'Zetas' en posesión de armas y municiones en Fresnillo (Galería)," *Universidad Tecnológica del Estado de Zacatecas*, September 26, 2010.
39. Samuel Logan, "Soldiers Raid Los Zetas Training Camp near Higueras, Nuevo León—May 11, 2010," *Southern Pulse*, May 16, 2010.
40. Dudley Althaus, "Mexican Officials Seize Arsenal, Arrest Gang Leader," *Houston Chronicle*, November 7, 2008.
41. "Mexico: Smugglers Try Medieval Tech," *New York Times*, January 28, 2011.
42. Mario Andrade, "Mad Mex—Los Zetas Use Road Warrior-Style Vehicles to Battle Other Cartels, Military," *The Intel Hub*, May 25, 2011.

4

A "Shadow Government": Dual Sovereignty

The well-coiffured, miniskirt-wearing secretary buzzed her boss, one of the state's most affluent businessmen, saying that he had a caller on the line.

"Who is it?" barked the harried CEO.

"He won't give me his name, but says it's extremely urgent," she replied.

Reluctantly, the multimillionaire, owner of a hugely successful chain of stores, snatched the phone and brusquely asked, "What is it?"

An eerie voice, who identified himself only as "a Zeta," commanded the executive to listen and listen carefully. "We have your son," rasped the caller, "and we will torture and execute him unless you pay one million dollars."

After saying he would be back in touch with the time and place of the exchange, the line went dead. The businessman suffered a parent's worst nightmare: his child whom he could not locate might be in the clutches of the opaque, beastly Los Zetas. He didn't even think about calling the police or the army. There was a real possibility that they had participated in—or acquiesced to—the kidnapping. Instead, the no-nonsense executive hurriedly riffled through his personal phone book until he found the private number of the governor, a personal acquaintance and a PRI stalwart, who was widely believed to work hand-in-glove with the underworld.

The politician took the call at once—only to hear the icy tones of the entrepreneur. "The Zetas have captured my son," he said. The state executive began to express sympathy and vaguely replied that he knew nothing of the abduction. "Shut up," thundered the entrepreneur. "Unless my boy is returned unharmed tomorrow, I am personally coming to your office and kill you!"

Needless to say, the governor could easily have protected himself. Yet there was such venom infused in the magnate's words that contacts were made and the youngster showed up at his home within twenty-four hours—not a hair on his head disturbed.

A mid-level intelligence analyst told this story to the senior coauthor. Even if apocryphal—and it may be—it demonstrates what the late Harvard historian described as "dual sovereignty." In his 1938 classic *The Anatomy of Revolution*, Crane Brinton analyzed situations in which aspirants for power configured an array of institutions—courts, tax offices, police, armies, etc.—that paralleled those of the ancient regime they sought to overthrow.[1] Robespierre's Jacobin Clubs erected their political scaffolding around the embattled Louis XVI on the eve of the 1789 revolution. Zealous Puritan Oliver Cromwell forged his New Model Army that purged England's Long Parliament before the 1649 predawn beheading of King Charles I, who wore two shirts to prevent the cold weather causing any noticeable shivers that the crowd could have mistaken for fear or weakness. And Lenin and his Bolsheviks founded their own ministate as they successfully swept the Romanovs from power in 1917.

Brinton described the setting as follows:[2]

> When another and conflicting chain of institutions provides another and conflicting set of decisions, then you have a dual sovereignty. Within the same society, two sets of institutions, leaders, and laws demand obedience, not in one single respect, but in the whole interwoven series of actions which make up life for the average man.

Latter-day examples of dual sovereignty involve the Basque nationalists and the Spanish government, Darfur separatist in the Sudan, the Kurds' élan to create their own state in the Mideast, and even the EZLN seeking to form autonomous indigenous enclaves within southern Mexico.

These conflicts and those described by Brinton focus on the move from one stage to the next in a revolutionary dance of violence. Los Zetas, however, show no interest in overthrowing Mexico's establishment. Indeed, such a gambit would be counterproductive: it would broaden the mobilization of the Mexicans armed against them, alienate powerful economic groups, outrage the middle class, and invite military intervention by the United States. Instead, these erstwhile Special

Forces seek to enhance their power through a shadow regime—some would say "shadowy"—to the point that they can conduct a plethora of profitable and illegal schemes with complete impunity, if not outright cooperation, from regularly constituted authorities. Table 5 presents some of the quasi-official functions performed by Los Zetas that, at least in textbooks, governments typically carry out.

Table 5   Elements of Dual Sovereignty

Function	Elected government	Narco government/cartels
Leadership	Mayor or governor	Plaza chief
Security	Legally appointed police chief	Killers who work for plaza chiefs and may even wear uniforms that they make or steal from the army or federal, state, and local police
Collection of resources	Taxation	"War Taxes" or extortion
Prisons	Federal, state, and local	Control by Los Zetas who exact bribes from other inmates
Economic activities	Economic development promoter	Creation of jobs for those growing and transporting drugs, as well as the employment of couriers, lookouts, and gunmen
Cultural affairs	Museums, art exhibitions, musical presentations	Sponsorship of *corridos* that extol the virtue of the capos; kill and/or intimidate singers who perform anti-Zeta ballads
Mass media	Director of communication and advertising in local newspapers, magazines, and electronic media	Narco-banners, presence on *YouTube*; a person called an *enlace* or "link" acts as a liaison between the media and the cartel. The organization also threatens to kill journalists who expose their activities, while bribing members of the Fourth Estate to cooperate with them through the *enlace*
Street propaganda	Mobilize support for government-supported events	Employ young people and street vendors to disseminate propaganda adverse to the Federal Police and armed forces

(Continued)

Table 5 (*Continued*)

Judiciary	Selected by legal procedures	Corrupt and intimidate judges, and even hold their own tribunals and exact penalties, including capital punishment, on those whom they find guilty
Elections	Organized in accordance with state and federal electoral laws and supervised by appropriate electoral institutes	Provide resources to their favorite candidates, regardless of party affiliation, while intimidating backers of their foes; concentrate on municipal and state office holders who can facilitate their growing, importing, storing, and moving drugs through their established routes
Credentials	Issued by federal, state, and municipal governments	Los Zetas have produced a prodigious number of drivers' licenses, voter credentials, travelers' checks, "vales" for supermarkets, and other documents in Ciudad Valles, San Luis Potosí, in a printing facility the size of four basketball courts

Protection

From Thomas Hobbes to John Locke to Jean-Jacques Rousseau, philosophers have agreed that the most important role of organized society is to ensure the safety of its citizens in their homes, streets, schools, and workplaces. Much to the chagrin of President Calderón, the federal, state, and local governments cannot fulfill this obligation. Evidence of this breakdown in law and order appears in Table 6, which illustrates the number of drug-related deaths since the Partido Acción Nacional (PAN) chief executive swore the presidential oath on December 1, 2006.

Los Zetas thrive on torture: plunging foes into vats of acid, be-headings, castrations, and the dismemberment of victims before they die. Of the 6,587 murders committed in 2009, 270 involved torture and 123 were beheadings. Twenty-six members of the armed forces perished, along with 234 law-enforcement agents. Although a hardware store magnate once yanked political strings enough to persuade a corrupt governor to secure the release of his son, families

Table 6   Executions in Border States from 2006 through 2011

State	2011	2010	2009	2008	2007	2006	Total
Tamaulipas	675	725	49	110	89	181	1,320
Nuevo León	1,789	610	99	79	107	50	2,182
Coahuila	595	199	151	53	29	17	852
Chihuahua	1,940	3,185	2,082	1,652	147	130	6,931
Sonora	142	249	152	137	125	61	728
Baja California	142	315	320	617	154	163	1,528
Northern States	5,283	5,283	2,853	2,648	651	602	13,541
Nationwide	12,366	11,583	6,587	5,207	2,275	2,119	39,365

Source: *Reforma*.

of most targets succumb to the proverbial "offer they can't refuse." They pay the ransom.

In the past, the low number of drug-related murders when compared with that in other states along the US border testified to the success the paramilitaries had in forging pacts with local politicians to consolidate their strength in Tamaulipas, a state governed by the PRI since the party's founding in 1929. However, a conflict in which three anti-Zeta organizations—the Gulf Cartel, the Sinaloa Cartel, and La Familia Michoacana/Knights Templars—waged war on the paramilitaries ignited increased killings in 2010, especially in Tamaulipas and Nuevo León.

Warranties

In 2009, Los Zetas demanded $300,000 for the return of a prominent lawyer who lived near Veracruz. Once his family had paid the bounty and his loved one was safe, a brother asked his criminal interlocutor, "How do we know that you won't seize my brother again or grab another of our relatives?" The Zeta overseeing the operation said, in effect, "You followed our orders, you kept quiet, and you paid in full. Not only will we not bother your family again, we will protect you from aggressive acts by other cartels."

After state leaders learned of the transaction, they beseeched the attorney and his family to keep mum about the incident, lest its revelation cast negative publicity on Veracruz, whose governor—like so many of his colleagues—aspired to become Mexico's president. Even worse, the state executive allegedly was closely associated with Los Zetas, according to former members of his administration who are now ensconced in a witness protection program.[3] The problem with the "warranty" concept lies in changes of plaza bosses. A new chief, who has financial goals to meet, may not adhere to his predecessor's promises.

Prisons

The government euphemistically calls many of its prisons "Centers of Social Readaptation" or CERESOs. Wardens, their subordinates, and guards nominally control these penal institutions, especially the nine high-security federal facilities. In reality, payoffs by inmates to their keepers, combined with the proliferation of organized gangs behind bars, give well-heeled convicts unparalleled influence. Wealthy "deluxe prisoners" grease the palms of guards, who—for the right price—will permit them to exit the facility for a few hours to conduct business, lovemaking, or criminal ventures. They will use every tactic including fear, intimidation, money, sex, etc., to compromise the prison staff and the administration.[4]

Inmates sometimes settle scores with adversaries behind bars—most notoriously exemplified in the 2004 murders of El Chapo's brother Arturo "El Pollo"/"The Chicken" Guzmán Loera (December 31) and his associate Miguel Ángel "Ceja Güera"/"White Eyebrow" Beltrán Lugo (October 6) inside La Palma prison. At the same time, drug lords carry on negotiations behind bars. The late Assistant Attorney General José Luis Santiago Vasconcelos acknowledged that Los Zetas' patron, Osiel, cut a deal to cooperate with Tijuana Cartel honcho, Benjamín Arellano Félix, to decimate the Sinaloa Cartel while both were "locked up" in La Palma.[5]

In January 2005, gangsters seized six employees of the Matamoros penitentiary and handcuffed, blindfolded, and shot them, leaving their cadavers in a white sport utility vehicle parked opposite the facility. This savagery may have been a response to the siege six days earlier of La Palma prison by 750 Federal Police and military. Clearly, drug dealers had corrupted the guards and were overseeing violent networks from inside. In early December 2008, enemies were believed to have executed two Zetas in the Mazatlán detention center.[6]

Thanks to widespread access to cell phones, prisoners find it easy to engage in extortion. A committee of the Chamber of Deputies estimated that convicts had extorted Mex$186,620 million in the 2001–07 period. The equipment installed in 2007 to block telephone signals in eleven prisons fell into disrepair and no longer functions.[7] This situation prompted Mexico State to invest Mex$10 million (roughly $770,000) to block telephone signals in its four largest penitentiaries— Neza-Bordo (Nezahualcóyotl), Barrientos (Tlalnepantla), Chiconautla (Ecatepec), and Almoloya de Juárez (Santiaguito).[8]

Just as in the United States, drugs flow freely inside Mexico's prison walls. Of the 37,000 inmates in Mexico City's penal institutions, an estimated 25,900 are addicts. Authorities admit that the availability of the substances, which may generate Mex$15.5 million a month, represents a convenient way to minimize melees and curb other violent outbursts. As an official told a city councilman, "Sir, if I cut off the flow of drugs, there will be a mutiny the next day."[9] In late 2008, authorities discovered fifty-one packets containing 119 kilograms of marijuana covered with sacks of toilet paper and boxes of soft drinks aboard a truck seeking to enter the capital's Reclusorio Sur.[10]

So ubiquitous were drugs in the Detention Center of Reynosa that it gained fame as a *narcopenal*, which was run by the convicts. "La Suburban," a gang linked to Los Zetas, not only ran the intramural drug trade but extorted money from their foes who lived in an adjoining structure known as "the Sinai" in the two-building compound.[11]

Overcrowding accentuates turmoil. Of Mexico's 439 federal, state, and local penal institutions, 228 are stuffed with an excessive number of inmates. In Mexico City's Reclusorio Oriente, seventy prisoners occupy one six-by-five-square-meter cell. They must sleep standing up, lie in hallways, and vie for green spaces to stretch out, or pay for access to a bunk.[12] Exacerbating the crisis is that 80 percent of federal prisoners (34,952) are in state prisons—with the remainder (9,494) in federal institutions. In 2010, Mexico had 222,771 men and women behind bars, according to the Ministry of Public Security (SSP).[13]

An especially brazen escape happened in Zacatecas on May 16, 2009, and all of it is available for public viewing on *YouTube*. Before dawn, thirty or more heavily armed thugs believed to be Zetas, riding in trucks adorned with Federal Agency of Investigation (AFI) logos, stormed into the Cieneguillas penitentiary as one of their helicopters whirred overhead. In the blitzkrieg assault, they extricated fifty-three prisoners, including Zetas, members of the Beltrán Leyva crime family, and other narco-felons. State and federal authorities immediately began apprehending escapees even as they investigated the director and his fifty subordinates to determine who fostered the escape.[14] One of several recaptured was Osvaldo "The Vampire" García Delgado, a kidnapping specialist whose Los Cotorros gang coordinates activities with Los Zetas in Hidalgo state.

In October 2009, actions of Los Zetas precipitated a riot in the Topo Chico prison in Nuevo León that the state police had to put down. Some hundred Zetas virtually controlled the four hundred other inmates in the facility through extortion and requiring them to hand over bribes for protection. Before the uprising, PRI Governor Natividad González Parás had brushed off turmoil in the penitentiary as "a squabble between one group of friends against another group of friends over personal problems."[15]

As in other facilities, Los Zetas practice virtual "self-rule" in the federal prison in Apodaca, Nuevo León (Cereso), where they attack members of the Gulf Cartel and other foes. The Mexican National Human Rights Commission (CNDH) found that this practice, called *auto-gobierno* in Spanish, existed in 37 percent of penal facilities in 2011—up from 30 percent in 2009.

Los Zetas also had the run of the state penitentiary in the industrial city of Saltillo. They sought to make their home away from home as habitable as possible. The criminals offered to repaint the prison chapel, but Chaplain Robert Coogan, a New York native and Catholic priest, turned down the offer because a leaking roof would ruin their handiwork. Not to be deterred, Los Zetas fixed the roof, and then painted the chapel in one day.

When Coogan asked the leader why he wasn't in politics, he answered, "I like things done quickly." The chaplain added that Los Zetas actively recruited inside prison walls, possessed cell phones, and air-conditioned their space. They even adopted a dog and hired their own cook. "The [Zeta] leader will talk proudly of how he's put order in the place . . . how no one gets robbed," Coogan told reporter David Agren, adding that "in a place where nothing works, they make things work."[16]

Job Creation

After federal, state, and local governments and perhaps WalMart and maquiladoras, Los Zetas represent the major source of employment in states like Tamaulipas. US authorities estimate that at least

1,500 people work for Los Zetas' number two leader, Treviño Morales, in Nuevo Laredo, Reynosa, and Matamoros alone. The vast majority of these individuals are not bona fide Zetas, but street vendors, policemen, truck drivers, convenience store operators, couriers, and other blue- or pink-collar workers who may earn only ten dollars a day working in maquiladoras. Although not combatants, these men, women, and children contribute to moving merchandise, laundering money, and keeping watch on the organization's enemies.

Cultural Activities

Just as city governments may sponsor book fairs, concerts, film fests, and other cultural activities, Los Zetas take a profound interest in entertainment events—generally in a negative rather than a positive way. They follow *narcocorridos*, the ballads sung by vocalists and played by bands that not only venerate drug lords but provide a form of popular "musical newspaper."[17]

Because many of the younger generations of sicarios relate more to hip-hop music than to corridos, a new genre of music has evolved, which is very similar to the gangsta rap from the 1990s. In Reynosa and Matamoros, musicians like Cano&Blunt, Lyric Dog, and Grupo Nektar, whose leader is believed to also be a CDG operative, sing about cartel lieutenants, the organizations' weapons, money, women, and power.

Artists who cater to one criminal group risk revenge by its enemies. A case in point is Valentín "The Golden Rooster"/"El Gallo de Oro" Elizalde, whom Los Zetas gunned down in an episode described in chapter 8. Elements of the Mexican Army and the PGR arrested Raúl "El Flander I" Hernández Barrón, one of the original Zetas, for the murder. His brother, Víctor Manuel "El Flander II," had been captured with Osiel on March 14, 2003, in Matamoros. Also suspected in the killing of Elizalde was another Zeta, Raúl Alberto "El Alvín" Trejo Benavides.[18]

The *Arizona Daily Star* reported the death of Sergio Gómez, thirty-four, founder of the popular group K-Paz de la Sierra, which features fast-paced drums and brass horns. A Chicago resident, Gómez disregarded warnings not to perform in his native state of Michoacán before being abducted and murdered. The same week, gangsters shot and killed Zayda Peña of Zayda y Los Culpables (Zayda and the Guilty) in a hospital in Matamoros. Samuel González Ruiz, former chief of a federal organized crime unit, said, "The cartels don't care about how they are seen by the public—they are worried about showing their absolute control of their territory, and they will impose their control at all costs . . . [killing a singer] is like planting the flag of their cartel in the ground."[19]

The military defectors even have their favorite *corrido*, "La Escolta Suicida" (The Suicide Escort), which emphasizes pride in defending their "patron":[20]

We are 20 the group of Los Zetas/	*Somos 20 el grupo de Los Zetas/*
United as a family/	*unidos como familia/*
We are 20 the force/	*los 20 somos la fuerza/*
With diplomas of suicide/	*con diplomas de suicida/*
Aware that in each action/	*conscientes de que en cada acción/*
We can lose our life . . .	*podemos perder la vida . . .*

Judiciary

Primacy of the rule of law is central to establishing a democracy in Mexico. In 2008, Congress and the states enacted a constitutional reform that will replace secretive proceedings and inquisitorial techniques with an Anglo-American-style adversarial approach. The changes include open trials, allowing recorded phone calls into evidence if one of the participants agrees, and permits prosecutors to hold organized-crime suspects without charges for up to eighty days.[21] The reform also introduced a presumption of innocence, the right of the defendant to face his accuser, and evidence-based procedures—with a greater emphasis on forensics and meticulous fact-gathering. "In what experts say is nothing short of a revolution, Mexico is gradually abandoning its centuries-old Napoleonic structure of closed-door, written inquisitions—largely a legacy of Spanish colonial rule—that had long been criticized as rife with corruption, opaque decisions, abuse of defendants and red tape that bogged down cases for years."[22]

In early 2009, legal specialists with the help of US attorneys were attempting to iron out the protocols of this legislation, which will not be implemented, if at all, in the thirty-one states and DF before 2016. Meanwhile, "we work with the same system that was used during the Spanish Inquisition," avers Alberto Barbaz, the then-Mexico State's attorney general. For example, information derived from electric shocks and other coercive interrogation techniques constitutes credible evidence. "In America, prosecutors investigate, but the judge and jury decide the facts," said human rights lawyer Santiago Aguirre Espinoza. "Here, statements made to prosecutors are facts. There is no cross-examination or right to confront accusers. If a person in Mexico confesses to a prosecutor that is considered sufficient evidence for a detention—so there is an inherent incentive to obtain confessions."[23] One survey found that 71 percent of convicted defendants said they never saw a judge before they were sentenced. About 47 percent of inmates in Mexico City's prisons are serving sentences for robbery involving sums of fewer than twenty dollars, law professor Ana Laura Magaloni said. Those who fall into the system are often subject to "arbitrary treatment," she added.[24]

The hermetic procedures of the current Kafkaesque regime have allowed Los Zetas and other DTOs to suborn and intimidate judges. In early April 2005, a lower-court judge freed a Zeta-linked gang known as Los Kelines, after a spectacular shoot-out in Matamoros. His reason? Insufficient evidence to proceed. Fortunately, a higher court reversed this decision and a trial took place,[25] but threats against members of the judiciary and their families often allow suspected felons to enjoy impunity.

Even more than Americans, Mexicans indulge in the illusion that if a statute is enacted, a pact signed, or a program announced, the problem at hand will be resolved.[26] For instance, Calderón promised an honest, effective police force by the time he left office in late 2012. The sad truth is that even if commanders vetted cadets, trained them in modern crime-fighting techniques, clothed them in attractive uniforms, provided them a decent salary, and offered low-interest mortgages and other fringe benefits, these men and women would become part of law-enforcement agencies bathed in corruption. If the newcomers refused to accept bribes or resisted intimidation from colleagues and hit men, they would risk their lives and the well-being of their loved ones: an ultimatum known as *plata o plomo*—silver or lead. The same applies to the pending judicial reform, which, though a good idea, suffers from opposition from those who have a vested interest in the status quo. In 2011, Congress cut funds for implementing this sea change in legal proceedings.

In addition, Los Zetas can hire the best lawyers money can buy. Attorney Pedro Israel Pena de León, known as an outstanding "narco-attorney," managed to convince a criminal court judge in Playa del Carmen, Quintana Roo, to free two of three imprisoned Zetas after they paid modest fines. Along with a fellow Zeta, they had been charged with extorting Mex$900,000 from a local business.[27]

Political Involvement

Similar to political parties, Los Zetas are heavily involved in campaigns. Like other cartels, they show the greatest interest in municipal and state elections because they want politicians who will protect—or turn a blind eye to—local growing areas, processing plants, commercial routes, and storage facilities. Favorite targets are mayors of municipalities that lie along their avenues from ports such as Salina Cruz, Lázaro Cárdenas, Veracruz, Coatzacoalcos, and Tampico to the US border.

If bribery does not work, Los Zetas intimidate public officials, many of whom—especially in Michoacán's Tierra Caliente where La Familia, the Sinaloa Cartel, and other criminal groups also operate—have begun wearing bulletproof vests. In the November 2007 municipal contests in the state, contenders for mayor of Múgica and Nuevo Italia stepped aside after receiving death threats. In Coalcomán, Aguililla, and Tumbiscatío, the paramilitaries barred opponents of their favored standard-bearers from voting. José Vázquez Piedra, the outgoing mayor of Turicato who won a seat in the state legislature, said that the imprimatur of the most powerful cartel in drug-infested areas was crucial to winning a public office.[28]

At least one attractive gubernatorial prospect in a north-central state decided not to enter the race in 2009, lest he place his family in harm's way. Should the criminals back a candidate for the Chamber of Deputies, it represents an investment in the future more than the hope of a proximate payoff; that is, the cartels are counting on the deputy's returning to his home state as a prosecutor, secretary of government, mayor, or governor—positions important to their industry.

Los Zetas show no preference for any one political party. In early 2009, the Federal Protective Police (PFP) captured Miguel Ángel Almaraz Maldonado, president of the leftist-nationalist Democratic Revolutionary Party (PRD) in Tamaulipas and contender for the mayoralty of Río Bravo. He was arrested for enjoying Los Zetas' protection as he sold gasoline stolen from PEMEX to US buyers. Almaraz Maldonado had been one of the state's most vociferous opponents of the military's combating Los Zetas in Tamaulipas.

Three days before the 2007 mayoral election in Río Bravo, Juan Antonio Guajardo Anzaldúa Almaraz claimed to have been threatened by forty Zetas carrying automatic weapons. The former state legislator, senator, federal deputy, and mayor was once again seeking the mayorship of this relatively tranquil Tamaulipas municipality, which lies across the border from Pharr, Texas. The besieged politician and his followers hid out in the local Casa de Cultura until an army unit managed to rescue them. During the heated campaign, he had accused Almaraz Maldonado of criminal behavior. In addition, he went on local television to warn of the involvement of organized crime in local elections. "I hold Governor Eugenio Hernández Flores responsible for anything that happens to me or my family, and . . . I wish to advise him that it will be an eye for an eye and a tooth for a tooth," he stated. Such charges precipitated death threats against Guajardo, who was gunned down along with four federal agents on November 29, 2007. The governor promised to "work with the federal authorities to find and punish those responsible for this act of violence" so that peace in Tamaulipas could continue. Several residents said they were certain Guajardo was targeted for saying the city should be cleared of corruption, and said the bloodbath showed the drug cartels were in power.[29]

In 2010, no one registered as a candidate for mayor of Ciudad Mier and the nearby municipalities of Camargo and Nueva Ciudad Guerrero. Citizens gradually returned to Ciudad Mier, whose population, 500 in December, rose to 2,200 inhabitants by mid-2011.[30]

The Zetas are believed to have executed the PAN's Valle Hermoso mayoral candidate José Mario Guajardo Varela, his son Luis, and an aide at their feed and seed store on May 13, 2010. In addition, the group allegedly murdered Reynosa's Public Works Director Roberto Arechandieta Ramos, who was gunned down on the city's north side on the same day.

The following month it appears that Los Zetas killed the PRI's gubernatorial nominee in Tamaulipas, Rodolfo Torre Cantú,[31] after reportedly forcing him to kneel and apologize for his "transgressions."[32] The assassins carried out the execution ten kilometers east of the Ciudad Victoria airport where they blocked his SUV in a stretch of the Ciudad Victoria–Soto La Marina highway that was not covered by surveillance cameras. The goal may not have been to murder Torres Cantú but to send a threatening message to Mexico's political class. PAN senator Santiago Creel called the tragedy "an attack on the nation's democracy."[33]

Los Zetas and other cartels directly or indirectly exert influence in hundreds of Mexico's 2,435 municipalities. A major difference is that elected office holders are subject to term limitations. Criminals do not have to worry about amassing ballots; their greatest concern is that foes will remove them from office with bullets.

Linkages between the "Shadow Governments"

Like the wooden ties that link rails on railroad tracks, the parallel governments are joined at multiple places. Local law-enforcement agents may enforce disorderly conduct, public drunkenness, and petty thefts in a municipality. At the same time, orders from the mayor and threats or bribes from organized crime may find them ignoring—or colluding in—drug-related activities.

In a similar vein, politicians and capos may discourage police from informing the press of criminal behavior. In mid-2009, only Monterrey-based *El Norte* carried a story of a shoot-out in Reynosa in which three soldiers perished.

Table 7 **Drug-Related Murders in Mexico from 2001 to 2012**

Year	Number of murders	% Increase
2011	12,366	6.8
2010	11,583	75.9
2009	6,587	28.4
2008	5,207	128.9
2007	2,275	7.3
2006	2,120	37.9
2005	1,537	17.9
2004	1,304	−4.4
2003	1,365	
2003	No consistent figures found	
2001	1,080	

Source: Office of the Attorney General; James C. McKinley Jr. "With Beheadings and Attacks, Drug Gangs Terrorize Mexico," *New York Times*, October 26, 2006; and the newspaper *Reforma*, which publishes a weekly tally of murders in its "National" section. *Reforma*, which reported 11,594 deaths through November 2011, estimated that the total for the year would be 12,674, based on 35 killings per day; see Rolando Herrera, "Repunta en 2011 narcoejecuciones," *Reforma*, December 2, 2011. The figure turned out to be 12,366.

Governors who benefit from the decentralization of power often cooperate with cartels or disregard their activities. Their excuse is that "drug crimes lie in the domain of the federal government." Of course, this fact should not prevent them from cleaning up local police agencies or seeking a change in the law to authorize them to fight criminal syndicates.

Notes

1. Crane Brinton, *The Anatomy of Revolution* (rev. ed; New York, NY: Random House, 1965),133.
2. Ibid.
3. Jorge Carrasco Araizaga, "Veracruz, bajo control de 'La Compañía,'" *Demócrata Norte de México*, February 8, 2010, http://democratanortedemexico. blogspot.com/2010/02/veracruz-bajo-control-de-la-compania.html.
4. William Sturgeon, "The Evolution of Security Threat Groups into the Twenty-First Century," *Corrections.com*, October 15, 2009.
5. "Mexican Army Urged to Take Over Prisons," *USA Today*, August 1, 2005.
6. "Executan a 'zetas' en cárcel in Mazatlán," *Reforma*, December 14, 2008.
7. Daniel Venegas, "Diputados exigen alto a la extorsión desde cárceles," *Milenio*, October 19, 2008.
8. "Inhiben señal de celular en 4 cárceles," *Reforma*, December 31, 2008.
9. Quoted in Henia Prado, "Toleran autoridades drogas en penales," *Reforma*, November 16, 2008.
10. Icela Lagunas, "Detectan 119 kilos de mariguana en aduana del Reclusorio Sur," *El Universal*, December 15, 2008.
11. Arturo Rodríguez García, "Tamaulipas: la massacre del narcopenal," *Proceso*, October 29, 2008.
12. "Llevan cárteles a penales guerra por territorios," *El Universal*, October 18, 2008; and Claudia Bolaños, "Cárceles, infierno de pobres," *El Universal*, May 16, 2009.
13. Rolando Herrera, "Saturan a estados con reos federales (I)," *Reforma*, October 25, 2010.
14. Luis Brito, "Amotina el narco penales," *Reforma*, May 24, 2009.
15. Arturo Rodríguez García, "Los Zetas, génesis de los conflictos en Topo Chico," *Proceso*, October 8, 2009.
16. Juan Cedillo, "Indgan 'atentado' en muerte de 14 internos," *El Universal. com.mx*, May 21, 2011; and David Agren, "Self-Rule on the Rise in Mexico's Prisons," *USA Today*, May 1, 2011.
17. See Elijah Wald, *Narcocorrido: A Journey into the Music of Drugs, Guns, and Guerrillas* (New York, NY: Rayo, 2001).
18. "Capturan a presunto asesino de Valentín Elizalde," *Terra*, March 26, 2008.
19. Quoted in Jeremy Schwartz, "Musician Killings Highlight Unrelenting Violence in Mexico," *Banderas News*, December 2007.
20. "Ex militares sirven de sicarios a cárteles mexicanos," *SeguRed.com*, July 25, 2006, www.segured.com/index.php?od=9&link=7765.

21. Olga R. Rodríguez, "Mexican Senate Approves Judicial Reform," *Associated Press*, March 7, 2008.

22. Quoted in Randal C. Archbold, "Mexican Prosecutors Train in U.S. for Changes in their Legal System," *New York Times*, April 24, 2009.

23. Lawson, "The Making of a Narco State"; and David Agren, "Self-Rule on the Rise in Mexico's Prisons," *USA Today*, May 1, 2011.

24. Héctor Tobar, "Mexico Gives Final OK to Judicial System Reform," *Tampa Bay Online*, March 7, 2008, www2.tbo.com/content/2008/mar/07/.

25. Jorge Fernández Menéndez and Víctor Ronquillo, *De los maras a los zetas* (Mexico City: Grijalbo, 2006): 285.

26. For an excellent examination of this characteristic, see Agustín Basave Benítez, *Mexicanidad y esquizofrenia: Los dos rostros del mexiJano* (Mexico City: Océano, 2010).

27. "Libran a presuntos 'zetas,'" *Noticaribe*, October 24, 2009.

28. Pablo César Carrillo, "Elección con tufo a narco," *EXonline*, November 17, 2007.

29. "Former Mayor of Rio Bravo, 2 AFI Agents Assassinated," *Mexico Trucker Online*, December 1, 2007.

30. Julio Manuel Guzmán, "Pese a violencia, regresan habitantes a Ciudad Mier," *El Universal*, July 20, 2011.

31. "Tamaulipas Elections Continue Despite Hurricane and Candidate's Assassination," *Brownsville Herald*, July 3, 2010.

32. Mauricio Suárez, "Justicia para todos," Código Topo, *Excélsior* suppl. ed. no. 24, July 2011.

33. Aurora Vega, "Zetas usaron 'monstruo' para matar a Torre Cantú; El Lazca lo ordenó: PGR," *Vanguardia*, June 29, 2011; and Olga Rosario Avendaño, "Senadores lamentan asesinato de Torre Cantú," *El Universal*, June 28, 2010.

5

Esprit de Corps

Introduction

Los Zetas go to great lengths to safeguard their members; it is a unifying gesture on and off the battlefield that lifts moral, as well as a spirit of belonging to something greater than oneself. This common attribute that is instilled within a nation's armed forces or even exists within some police units rarely, if ever, is practiced among rank and file members of criminal syndicates. With few exceptions, it's every man for himself. In contrast, Los Zetas attempt to invest a sense of pride and cohesion within their ranks. This characteristic, which springs from elite training, shared sacrifices, and pride in their service, abounds in such units as the US Marine Corps, the British Royal Marines, Napoleon's Imperial Guard, Hitler's elite Waffen-SS divisions, and many Special Forces or elite units like the Israeli Golani Brigade and the French Foreign Legion. Lest this point be overstated, Zeta cadres also fear the repercussions that will arise from failure to carry out orders and meet objectives. They also prize the cachet of belonging to a lethal organization, which provides opportunities to make money on the side or to intimidate and take advantage of women.

Los Zetas pay at least three times more than does the army, and provide much better food and housing. The armed forces boast a relatively high public-approval rating; yet they exist as a separate caste from civilians—a relationship evident in the number of children of military men who follow in the footsteps of family members who belonged to the army or navy, as well as marriages between the sons and daughters of military personnel. Few middle-class families would want a son or daughter to marry a member of the armed forces, much less a policeman. The one exception is the navy, which takes pride in greater social respectability. Increased pay, sophisticated weapons, and greater authority compensate for the lack of social standing among Los Zetas. Another form of "troop morale" lies in the significant wealth even lower-ranking Zetas can amass, and their ability to purchase expensive items.

The renegades are adept at taking advantage of ubiquitous, deeply rooted corruption in law-enforcement agencies and the armed forces. They exploit the venality among Mexico's local and state police agencies, offering sizable payouts to officers who provide inside information or help Los Zetas eliminate enemies. At the same time, they are on the hunt for military deserters. Their banners, hung on bridges and highway overpasses, promise "a good salary, food, and medical care for your families" to soldiers who switch sides, as well as "loans and life insurance." In addition, they pledge that recruits won't have to eat *sopa marucha*—an army staple made from packaged tasteless artificial noodles. There is a sizable audience for these appeals; low pay and difficult working conditions led to an astounding 100,000 desertions between 2000 and 2006, and nearly more than 30,000 more since Calderón's inauguration.[1] Those going AWOL since 2000 include 1,680 Special Forces members. The Ministry of Defense lacks a systematic way to pursue those who have disappeared from their posts. This situation has spurred more appeals for peasants to enlist in the army.[2]

Óscar Osvaldo García Montoya, a Mexican Marine whom Guatemalan Kaibiles taught to kill, confessed to carrying out three hundred murders and ordering six hundred more. Authorities arrested the deserter and suspected drug boss in early August 2011 at his home in Mexico City. Among other inhumane acts, Mexico State's attorney general accused him of engineering the September 2009 massacre of twenty-four people in La Marquesa forest outside of Mexico City. He had worked as a police officer in Baja California Sur and later in two towns in Sinaloa state. There he entered the BLO as a hit man and, subsequently, became a bodyguard for the group's chieftains.[3]

The benefits received contribute to the esprit de corps within Los Zetas' ranks. This rapport manifests itself in a striking effort to retrieve the bodies of fallen comrades-in-arms; no other DTO goes to such lengths to protect and give proper burial to cadavers. In what pundits labeled the "invasion of the body snatchers," four heavily armed men broke into "Los Jardines" private burial ground in Poza Rica, Veracruz, just before midnight on March 6, 2007. They quickly tied up a security guard, smashed Zeta Roberto Carlos Carmona's gravestone with hammers, disinterred his casket, and carried off the ornate coffin containing their collaborator's corpse. The deceased had perished three days earlier in a gun battle over a horse race in nearby Villarín.[4]

In the same vein, Los Zetas honor their dead. Three months after authorities killed Guzmán Decena—"Z-1"—in late 2002, a funeral wreath and four flower arrangements appeared at his gravesite with the following inscription: "We will always keep you in our heart: from your family, Los Zetas." Similarly, they placed a memorial to venerate deceased compatriots in Oaxaca. The inscription read, "Gulf Cartel [to which Los Zetas then belonged]. God keep in your memory Los Zetas who have died in Oaxaca," as well as "Arturo Guzmán [Decena] Z-1 and all of our fallen brothers in the Oaxaca plaza, that you will always remember them and their principles and ideals."[5] The organization has also laid wreaths or *narcocoronas* in public places to warn police and other foes of their presence.[6]

The frequency of Zeta-spearheaded penitentiary escapes has inspired black humor in Mexico's law-enforcement circles; that is, to save money, prison cooks survey inmates on Mondays, asking how many will be eating meals in the facility during the remainder of the week.

On December 23, 2010, 141 prisoners slipped out a side door of the CEDES prison in Nuevo Laredo, leading to the arrest of forty-one guards believed to have facilitated the escape. Orlando Monsivais Treviño, twenty-eight, a nephew of El 40 Treviño Morales, orchestrated the getaway. While behind bars, Los Zetas safeguard each other from other criminals and even kidnap and execute enemies. "There's been a bunch of retribution killings from inside the prison," observed Gary Hale of the intelligence firm Savant. "There's been kidnappings inside the prison. It's almost like a separate city inside itself. There's a lot of 'criminal justice,' in quotations, being administered . . .."

As described in Table 8, these paramilitaries make Herculean attempts to free imprisoned comrades. As mentioned, Jaime "El Hummer" González Durán earned both fame and a reputation for brutality among his comrades by rescuing Zeta narco-trafficker Daniel "El Cachetes" Pérez Rojas and three other inmates from the Santa Adelaida prison in Matamoros on December 28, 2002. They accomplished this impressive feat by donning AFI outfits. Los Zetas reprised this action when they freed twenty-five prisoners from a penal facility in Apatzingán, Michoacán, on January 6, 2004. The assailants penetrated the compound by wearing police and military uniforms.

Two months later (March 9, 2004), they took prisoner Tomás Aspland Aguilera, the warden at the Gómez Palacio prison in Durango state, and used the official as a bargaining chip to propel the escape of five Zetas. On May 16, 2008, the renegades again dressed as police officers entered the grounds of the Dupont-Ostión penal compound in Coatzacoalcos, Veracruz. Once inside the gates, they overpowered the guards and released five of their members and killed two other prisoners before escaping. The episode took place twenty-one days after the federal government had undertaken a major security initiative in the municipalities of Coatzacoalcos, Cosoleacaque, Minatitlán, and Nanchital. Such successful escapes aside, Los Zetas' plans sometimes misfire. Authorities frustrated their plot to free El Cachetes Pérez Rojas, arrested in April 2008, from a Guatemala City prison, which now has a tank guarding its entrance.

Still, authorities admitted that correctional officers lacked the weapons to thwart carefully planned and executed raids. "What can we do in the face of heavily armed groups?" asked Veracruz state director of corrections. "Neither this state nor any other in the Republic has the capacity to confront heavily armed, sophisticated bands, and [thus] we have asked the Federal government to take charge of federal prisoners." Los Zetas ran the Dupont-Ostión prison to the degree that they charged other inmates Mex$2,000 per week to avoid severe beatings or gain access to minor benefits known as *talachas* or both.

On December 4, 2009, Los Zetas stormed a prison in Escobedo, Nuevo León. Although the ensuing fire fight took the lives of twelve of the paramilitaries, including Monterrey regional leader Ricardo "El Gori" Almanza Morales, the assailants released twenty-three inmates. Among those set free were sixteen former municipal law-enforcement agents believed to be accomplices of the criminals. Members of the Federal Police charged with security at the facility were off-site eating. The commandos had sought to distract local authorities by engaging a military unit in a battle in nearby Juárez.

Despite rigorous military training, various Zetas have acted recklessly. For example, Efraín Teodoro "El Efra" or "El Z-14" Torres epitomized the cowboy mentality. An original Zeta, he—along with two comrades—controlled the Tamaulipas plazas of Ciudad Miguel Alemán and Ciudad Camargo. For recreation, he drank excessively, snorted cocaine, and bet heavily on horses, employing the pseudonym Roberto Carlos Carmona Gasperín. He died in a dispute over the winner of a clandestine race in rural Villarín, near Poza Rica, Veracruz, on March 3, 2007. El Lazca's escape from that bloody encounter inspired the theory that the Zeta leader had either masterminded the execution of his supposed ally or faked his own death.

Table 8   Zeta-Engineered Prison Escapes

Date and location	Prison	Outcome	Action
May 24, 2011, Reynosa, Tamaulipas	Detention Center of Reynosa	17 inmates dug a tunnel from the laundry area to the outside.	The director and eight guards are under investigation.
May 17, Reynosa, Tamaulipas	Center for Carrying out Sentences (Cedes)	17 inmates escaped	
December 17, 2010, Nuevo Laredo	Center for Carrying out Sentences (Cedes)	190 Zetas escaped, including Orland Monsiváis Treviño, the nephew of a Zeta leader "El 40," as well as several Zetas accused of murdering rivals behind bars.	Investigation still underway.
December 8, 2010	Malacatán Prison in Western Guatemala	Obtained the release of Elmer Zelada Galdámez, 20, who was suspected of abducting and butchering professional soccer player, Carlos Mercedes Vásquezal; a policeman and pedestrian were killed during the breakout.	Guatemalan police arrested 11 suspects.
September 10, 2010, Reynosa	Center for Carrying out Sentences (Cedes)	85 prisoners, including 66 federal convicts escaped.	
July 12, 2010, Tehuantepec, Oaxaca	Santo Domingo Regional Prison	3 inmates escaped.	
July 7, 2010, Reynosa, Tamaulipas	Center for Carrying out Sentences (Cedes)	12 prisoners escaped.	

(Continued)

Table 8 (*Continued*)

Date and location	Prison	Outcome	Action
June 22, 2010, Xochitepec, Morelos	Center for Social Readaptation (Cereso)	6 inmates escaped en route to trial.	
April 19, 2010, Tenancingo, Mexico State	Center for Prevention and Social Readaptation (CPRS)	8 inmates escaped.	
April 2, 2010, Reynosa, Tamaulipas	Center for Carrying out Sentences (Cedes)	12 federal convicts escaped.	
March 24, 2010, San Adelaida, Tamaulipas	Center for Social Readaptation (Cereso)	Between 4:00 and 5:00 a.m., 43 inmates—accompanied by two guards—walked out the front gate and stepped into waiting SUVs.	Authorities arrested and convicted 42 prison guards and employees.
September 8, 2008, Tuxpan, Veracruz	Center for Social Readaptation (Cereso)	40 prisoners escaped.	The PGR launched an investigation of the jailers.
May 16, 2009, Cieneguillas, Zacatecas	Center for Social Readaptation of Males (Cereso)	53 inmates escaped.	Cooperating guards and administrators were suspended for 30 days.
October 9, 2008, Reynosa, Tamaulipas	Center for Social Readaptation 2 (Cereso)	17 convicts, including 5 linked to Los Zetas, escaped.	
September 8, 2008, Tuxpan, Veracruz	Center for Social Readaptation (Cereso)	1 inmate escaped.	
May 16, 2008, Coatzacoalcos, Veracruz	Center for Social Readaptation (Cereso)	6 prisoners released.	

Table 8 (*Continued*)

Date and location	Prison	Outcome	Action
April 14, 2008, Cuautitlán, Mexico State	Center for Prevention and Social Readaptation (CPRS)	2 inmates escaped.	
February 25, 2008, Monterrey, Nuevo León	Center for Social Readaptation Monterrey "Topo Chico" (Cereso)	4 inmates tunneled out	
July 28, 2007, Zitacuaro, Michoacán	Center for Social Readaptation "Hermanos López Rayón" (Cereso)	6 inmates escaped.	
June 14, 2006, Nuevo Laredo, Tamaulipas	Center for Social Readaptation 2 (Cereso)	11 inmates escaped.	
October 2004, Nuevo Laredo, Tamaulipas	Center for Young Offenders in Tamaulipas	1 young convict released.	
January 5, 2004, Apatzingán, Michoacán	Preventive Center Apatzingán	Freed 6 members of the Gulf Cartel.	A four-month investigation proved inconclusive.
December 2002, Santa Adelaida, Tamaulipas	Center for Social Readaptation 2 (Cereso)	4 inmates freed.	No arrests made.

Sources: "Entérate fugas masivas de reos en México," *Vanguardia*, December 17, 2010; María Maeda, "'Los Zetas' Successfully Burst into Five Prisons," *Infosurhoy. com*, May 25, 2009; Guatemalan Police Arrest 11 in Prison Break," *Latin America Herald Tribune*, n.d., 2009; "Inmates escape Mexican prison," *Brownsville Herald*, March 25, 2010; "Guatemala: Los Zetas Free Suspected Killer from Prison," *InfoSurhoy.com*, December 9, 2010; "Analysis: More Carjackings Likely as Zetas Outfit Recruits," *The Monitor*, December 21, 2010; "191 reos se fugan de prisión en Nuevo Laredo," *ValleyCentral.com*, December 17, 2010; and "Escapan por túnel 17 reos en Reynosa," *Reforma.com*, May 25, 2011. For a directory of Mexican penal facilities, see "Directorio de Centros Penitenciarios," http://www.espora.org/vientodelibertad/ IMG/pdf/DIRECTORIO_CENTROS_PENITENCIARIOS.pdf.

While most narco-traffickers are Roman Catholics, some Zetas and other criminals carry images of mythical narco-saint Jesús Malverde. The alabaster-skinned mustachioed figure became a folk hero early in the twentieth century because he allegedly stole from the rich and gave to the poor. "Smugglers come to [his shrine outside Culiacán, Sinaloa] to ask Malverde for protection before sending a load [of drugs] north. If the trip goes well, they return to pay the shrine's house band to serenade the bandit, or place a plaque thanking Malverde for 'lighting the way.'"[7]

Some Zetas seek the good offices of Santísima Muerte, who takes the form of a clothed skeleton squeezing a scythe with her bony hand. From a distance, she resembles the Virgin of Guadalupe. "The narco-traffickers have always been very religious; they are not atheists. To the contrary, they are extremely superstitious," said University of Nuevo León psychologist José María Infante. "[*Santísima Muerte*] is a figure who accords with their activities where life and death are closely intertwined," he added.[8]

Zeta Luis Alberto "El Guerrero" Guerrero Reyes even wore as a charm a hand grenade dangling from a necklace. After he was massacred leaving the Wild West nightclub in Matamoros on May 2004, it took soldiers eight hours to defuse the device before removing it from his bullet-riddled cadaver.

Retaliation against Foes

Los Zetas retaliate with sadistic savagery against their enemies. Witnesses swear that the paramilitaries set fire to four Nuevo Laredo police officers crammed into barrels filled with diesel fuel. Their remains were buried there the next day.[9]

Like killers employed by the BLO, Los Zetas use various instruments to torture their victims. These include blow torches to burn the victims, carpenters' planes to peel away their skin, knives designed for mutilation, tourniquets, and appliances to administer electric shocks. In addition, the army has captured a variety of deadly chemicals, water-filled barrels in which to immerse captives, and special planks to rip away skin. More mundane instruments are razors, needles, sharp nails, staplers, candles, pliers, mallets, saws, hammers, ice picks, and salt to rub into wounds, and splinters to jam under fingernails.

Beyond torture, they break formerly well-established rules that govern whom to engage and whom to leave alone. A navy marine,

Melquisedet Ángulo Córdova, died in the successful December 16, 2009, attack on the bunker of Arturo Beltrán Leyva, leader of his eponymous cartel. Los Zetas, who have a working relationship with the BLO, immediately retaliated against the fallen hero's family by machine-gunning to death his mother, two brothers, and an aunt, while seriously wounding a sister. "The reprehensible acts show the lack of scruples of criminal organizations, attacking innocent people ... and we can only reinforce our determination to excise this cancer from society," affirmed Calderón. Not even the Sicilian Mafia attacks the families of military personnel.

Los Zetas showed their animus toward men in uniform when they decapitated a dozen members of the army in Chilpancingo, Guerrero, just before Christmas in 2008. The bodies, which lined a well-traveled thoroughfare, were accompanied by a sign. "For every one of mine that you kill, I will kill ten [of yours]." A sack of heads, some still gagged with tape, was uncovered nearby. This horrendous act obviated any chance to negotiate with the paramilitaries. Standing next to flag-draped coffins at the local army base, General Enrique Alonso Garrido, commander of the Ninth Military Region, said that this deplorable act constitutes "an offense against institutions in general and especially against those who wear military uniforms." Meanwhile, the president stated in a speech from Mexico City, "We will not take one step back in this fight, nor will there be any deal of mercy for the country's clear enemies."[10]

Socializing

As discussed earlier, El Lazca and El 40 traditionally threw an annual end-of-the-year party for their operatives across the country. This event, which usually takes place in Tamaulipas, features sumptuous food, an abundance of alcoholic beverages, the conferral of bonuses, rousing song fests, and a plethora of high-end prostitutes. These commandos don't have to wait for a special occasion to indulge their libidinous desires. A plaza chief may walk into an upscale restaurant, point to an attractive woman who is dining with her husband, and have one of his hoodlums spirit her into the Zeta's car where she must satisfy his sexual appetite or risk becoming yet one more victim.

Decorum sometimes surrounds Zeta activities. For instance, El 40 served as best man at the wedding of Salvador Alfonso "La Ardilla" Martínez Escobedo, held in Piedras Negras in late 2010. Authorities, who found out about that the event had taken place, believe that El Lazca and other high-level operatives in the organization also attended their ally's nuptials.

As described earlier, before carrying out an operation, plaza bosses offered their men Buchanan's whiskey, an expensive import from Scotland. When alcohol failed to stimulate sufficient Dutch courage, the hit men snorted cocaine. "Half a kilogram of cocaine for every five operatives that were used in the mission," said an ex-paramilitary.[11]

Notes

1. Hal Brands, "Los Zetas: Inside Mexico's Most Dangerous Cartel," *Air & Space Power Journal*, October 1, 2009; Manuel Roig-Franzia, "Mexican Drug Cartels Making Audacious Pitch for Recruits," *Washington Post*, September 20, 2007; and Alberto Najar, "Desertaron 100 *mil* militares con Fox," *Milenio*, July 20, 2007; "Mexico's Internal Drug War," *Power and Interest News Report*, August 14, 2006.

2. emorales, "Desertaron en 10 años 1,680 soldados de "elite," *Milenio.com*, March 7, 2011. According to the National Defense Ministry, desertions have fallen from a modern high of 20,224 (2005) to 16,641 (2007) to 9,112 (2008) to 4,398 (2010); see Benito Jiménez, "Recluta Ejército a campesinos, *Reforma*, July 3, 2011.

3. "Arrested Drug Cartel Hit Man Confesses to 900 Murders," *Sunday Mail* (Queensland, Australia), August 14, 2011.

4. "Invasion of the Body-Snatchers," *Reuters*, March 9, 2007.

5. "Aparecen 'Zetas' en panteón," *Reforma*, November 2, 2008.

6. Marcelo Beyliss, "Amenanzan con narcoflores a la policía de Sonora," *El Universal*, November 24, 2008.

7. Quiñones, "Jesús Malverde," *Front Line: Drug Wars*, PBS, www.pbs.org/wgbh, n.d.

8. "El culto de la Santísima Muerte, un boom en México," *Terra*, www.terra.com/arte/articulo/html/art9442.htm, n.d.

9. Alfredo Corchado, "Drug Cartels Operate Training Camps Near Texas Border Just Inside Mexico," *Dallas Morning News*, April 4, 2008.

10. Quoted in E. Eduardo Castillo, "Mexico Memorializes Soldiers Killed in Drug War," *Timesleader.com*, December 23, 2008.

11. "Zeta Recalls His Life, Warns Against It," *Brownsville Herald*, February 17, 2011.

6

Los Zetas and La Familia Michoacana

Introduction

Although begun several years earlier, La Familia Michoacana—or La Familia—held its coming out party on September 6, 2006, when ruffians crashed into the seedy Sol y Sombra nightclub in Uruapan, Michoacán, and fired shots into the air. They screamed at the revelers to lie down, ripped open a plastic bag, and lobbed five human heads onto the beer-stained black-and-white dance floor. The desperados left behind a note hailing their act as "divine justice," adding that "the Family doesn't kill for money; it doesn't kill women; it doesn't kill innocent people; only those who deserve to die, die. Everyone should know . . . this is divine justice."[1]

The day before these macabre pyrotechnics, the killers seized their victims from a mechanic's shop and hacked off their heads with bowie knives while the men writhed in pain. "You don't do something like that unless you want to send a big message," said a US law-enforcement official, speaking on condition of anonymity about an act of human depravity that would "cast a pall over the darkest nooks of hell."[2]

Origins

In 1985, Carlos Rosales Mendoza, a top lieutenant of Gulf Cartel chief Osiel Cárdenas, created the first iteration of La Familia, which was called La Empresa or "The Business." Other founders included Nazario "El Más Loco"/"The Most Crazy" and José de Jesús "El Chango"/"The Monkey" Méndez Vargas. La Empresa was struggling against the Milenio Cartel, operated by the Valencia brothers, for control of Michoacán. To help in this lethal tug-of-war, Rosales requested that Osiel dispatch Zetas to vanquish his foes. Shortly thereafter two of paramilitaries' deadliest elements—Efraín Teodoro "El Efra"/"Zeta 14"

Torres and Gustavo "The Erotic One" González Castro—led a cadre of gunmen to assist La Empresa.

They carried out their mission; however, once Rosales and Osiel were behind bars, Los Zetas began to pursue their own agenda. They had their eyes on lucrative plazas in Michoacán and Guerrero—with Lázaro Cárdenas constituting their highest priority. The importance of this coastal city derives from its strategic location: Half of Mexico's population lives within a 186-mile radius of the Pacific port through which cocaine and precursor chemicals for methamphetamines flowed into Mexico. This power grab angered La Familia's El Más Loco, El Chango, and their twelve top followers known as "The Apostles," who spearheaded a largely successful crusade against the newcomers.

Adopts Techniques of Los Zetas

Although La Familia became archenemies of Los Zetas in 2006, they adopted many of the ex-Special Forces' brutal techniques in seeking to oust Los Zetas from the state.[3] These included the following: castrating victims and placing their genitals in their mouths, mutilating, and even beheading them; accomplishing hit-and-run ambushes; employing psychological warfare (PSYOPS) by unfurling banners in public places, issuing taunting press releases, disseminating gruesome *YouTube* videos, and leaving menacing notes next to cadavers.[4] In late 2009, Los Zetas attempted to regroup in Uruapan under the leadership of the former commander of the municipal police, Gabriel "El Papí" Espinoza. Other reported leaders of the local cell were Arturo "El Ánfora" López Pérez and a man using the nom de guerre "El Jamaico."[5] Los Zetas retained a presence in the port, and the clash over Lázaro Cárdenas fueled the animus between the two criminal groups.

La Familia also battled for domination over marijuana- and poppy-growing areas, processing plants for synthetic drugs, and transit routes to the United States. At the same time, the messianic syndicate branched into extortion, kidnapping, human smuggling, contraband, loan-sharking, and small-scale sales of marijuana and cocaine.

Amid a rash of slayings in the summer of 2008, Federal Police apprehended Zeta activist Alfredo "El Chicles"/"L-46" Rangel Buendía, who was in the vanguard of the battle against La Familia for drug corridors in the Valle de Toluca and Mexico State municipalities adjacent to the DF. Rangel Buendía admitted that one of his missions was to assassinate El Más Loco and El Chango.[6] In a murderous tit-for-tat game, La Familia's Francisco Javier "The Camel" Torres Mora specialized in killing and kidnapping elements of Los Zetas and the Beltrán Leyva brothers in Guerrero.[7] "Narco-banners"—a symbolic declaration of war presumably installed by La Familia—blossomed on pedestrian bridges and along main thoroughfares in five Michoacán municipalities (Morelia, Pátzuaro, Acutzio, Lázaro Cárdenas, and Apatingán) and two towns in Guerrero (Coyuca de Catalán and Tlalchapa) on February 1 and 2, 2010. In effect, they warned Los Zetas to hit the road or die.

La Familia used the same technique to admonish Los Zetas to stay out of Guanajuato. In addition to Salvatierra, León, San Miguel de Allende, and Guanajuato city, these homemade pennants sprouted in eleven other municipalities in the state.

These messages emphasized that La Familia was battling "evil beasts" (*bestias del mal*) on behalf of the nation's law-abiding people and invited citizens to join in this struggle. Written in red and black crayon, the banners proclaimed that they were acting against Los Zetas, the Gulf Cartel, and the Milenio Cartel, indicating that La Familia would become the Guanajuato Family, the Guerrero Family, and, ultimately the "New Familia Michoacana will now become the Mexican [Family] against Los Zetas [and other criminal elements]. Sincerely. La FM."

La Familia was correct about the presence of their rivals in Guanajuato. In early February 2010, the armed forces captured five presumed Zetas in the Valle de Santiago, fifty miles south of the state capital. Their hideout contained grenades and assault weapons. Guanajuato's attorney general claimed that the men belonged to a well-organized cell.

Los Zetas responded with a vengeance to this challenge. On February 5, Michoacán ministerial police discovered five decapitated bodies in near Apatzingán, a La Familia stronghold. Los Zetas were the likely executioners inasmuch as the cadavers bore anti-Familia messages: "You're next Yupo [Dude] and all the La Familia dogs" and "Greetings to Frey, Sincerely Los Z." The killers had carved the letter "Z" in the backs of two of the dead men's torsos.

During the next two weeks, the clash between La Familia and Los Zetas produced twenty-one beheadings. On February 10, 2010, the killers had not only severed the heads of three victims, but they had cut up their cadavers, engraved them with the letter "Z," tossed them in black garbage bags, and dumped in downtown Morelia. The number of dismembered and/or beheaded corpses totaled seventy-seven during the first three months of 2009.

A Messianic Orientation

In contrast to Los Zetas and other Mexican capos, La Familia's leaders—especially the Bible-pounding El Más Loco—asserted that they were religiously motivated. They claimed to administer "divine justice" to rapists, robbers, corrupters of youth, and others whom the syndicate deems undesirable. The zealots even harshly disciplined teenagers caught spraying graffiti on colonial buildings in Morelia. They have pledged to "eradicate from the state of Michoacán kidnapping, extortion in person and by telephone, paid assassinations, express kidnapping, tractor-trailer and auto theft, home robberies done by people like those [undesirables] mentioned, who have made the state of Michoacán an unsafe place. Our sole motive is that we love our state and are no longer willing to see our people's dignity trampled on."[8]

In late January 2010, La Familia whipped with barbed wire and boards six presumed criminals in Zamora, Michoacán. After the sustained torture, it forced the men to walk in silence around a busy traffic circle for more than thirty minutes with signs reading, "Keep an eye out, you rats, we are coming for you, sincerely La Familia," "I am a rat and La Familia is punishing me," "This is for all the rats and 'recatos', sincerely La Familia Michoacana," and "This is for all delinquents. La Familia is here, citizens. Don't judge us. We are cleaning your city." After this episode, the young men refused to talk with police and the media, while spurning medical attention.[9]

The organization displayed a determination to safeguard women in its public debut in Uruapan in September 2006. This action, the first time in recent memory that lopped off heads had become propaganda artifices, was also designed to strike fear into the hearts of citizens. Local lore has it that the five decapitated men were involved in the murder of a waitress/prostitute who worked in the nightspot and had been impregnated by a member of La Familia. A few days before the ghastly incident, she allegedly refused to have sex with these men, who raped and killed her. La Familia began its own investigation and found guilty these individuals, who may have been Zetas. This story line may explain why the death note indicated that "La Familia doesn't kill for money, doesn't kill women, [and] doesn't kill innocent people. It only kills those who deserve to die."[10]

Proceso magazine's Richard Ravelo insists that the four thousand members of La Familia were born and raised in Michoacán, attend church regularly, carry Bibles, and distribute the Good Book in local government offices.[11] It's unclear whether these are King James versions of the Bible or ones that have been embellished by the teaching of La Familia's own leaders. They even justify executions as "orders from the Lord."

La Familia stalwarts focus their evangelical appeals on young people who are the poor and marginalized. They emphasize rehabilitation, empowerment, and self-renewal to drug addicts, alcoholics, juvenile delinquents, and others who feel alone and isolated. In fact, the organization operates a dozen or more rehabilitation centers, which gives immediate access to recruits. Of Michoacán's 4.7 million residents, 224,270 young people, aged twelve to twenty-five, are addicts, with cocaine being the substance of choice. There are at least 2,100 points of sale for drugs in the state.[12] The syndicate castigates the use of alcohol, tobacco, and drugs even as it preaches family harmony to raise members' motivation and spirits and respect for women. In addition, the cartel created "Youth: Art and Culture" ("Jóvenes: Arte y Cultura"), to lure teenagers into its ranks in the Tierra Caliente and Guerrero.[13]

Indoctrination

At the outset, recruits must clean up their lives by throwing off any drug- or alcohol addiction. Before his April 2009 arrest at a baptism, Rafael "El Cede" Cedeño Hernández, a self-described pastor and permanent observer of the state's human rights commission, took charge of indoctrination. He designed the six- to eight-week intensive educational programs, selected the texts and videos utilized in this brain-washing, and required periodic vows of silence by the class members as if they were religious brothers and sisters. Days without talking supposedly amplified spiritual concentration and facilitated the individuals' sense of solidarity, thankfulness, altruism, and complete loyalty to La Familia's leaders. Some of the events resemble Oral Roberts-type evangelical services, and El Cede claimed to have brought nine thousand people into the fold.[14]

El Milenio newspaper reported that La Familia took advantage of the works of American counselor John Eldredge to instruct and motivate their teetotaler recruits. Unlike La Familia, Eldredge does not espouse violence. Founder of the Ransomed Heart Ministries in Colorado Springs, Colorado, Eldredge has written that "every man wants a battle to fight, an adventure to live and beautiful rescue." The "big message" of his "small ministry" is "to set men and women free to live from the heart as God's intimate allies . . .. That's what we are devoted to—seeing men and women come fully alive as the image-bearers of a breathtaking God."[15]

The Christian author preaches a gospel that combines the rugged vigor of Teddy Roosevelt, the élan of Jesus expelling money changers from the Temple of David, and the bravery of Moses leading the Israelites out of bondage. In his *Wild at Heart: Field Manuel*, which, like many of his writings, has been translated into Spanish, he proclaims that "God created man to take risks."[16]

Nazario Moreno González, the most ostentatious religious advocate, even prepared a catechism that all present and potential cartel members had to read. It is called *Pensamientos de la Familia* (Thoughts of the Family) and signed by "El Más Loco." These "thoughts," which have gone through several editions, mirror the "Be-all-you-can-be" teachings of Eldredge, who has no connection to the criminal syndicate.[17]

Atrocities

Its enunciation of "civic" platitudes aside, authorities attributed seventeen decapitations to La Familia in 2006 alone. Between the murder of Rodríguez Valencia earlier that year and December 31, 2008, the syndicate killed scores, if not hundreds, of people. In 2010, there were 259 executions in Michoacán and 325 in 2011. In 2009, Michoacán ranked high in decapitations (18), which placed it behind only Guerrero (37), Chihuahua (33), and Baja California (24). In terms of tortured victims, Michoacán (97) came in second to Chihuahua (101), while the state led all others in messages attached to corpses (99). Most of the targets of brutality were police officers, armed forces personnel, or members of another narco-band.[18]

It remains to be seen whether this syndicate chopped up the corpse of a thirty-six-year-old man in Los Mochis, stuffed pieces of his body in different containers, and sewed a soccer ball onto the victim's skinned face. The location of the atrocity suggests another cartel may have sought to surpass La Familia and Los Zetas in insane machinations.[19] In mid-2010, Miguel "El Tyson" Ortiz Miranda, a captured La Familia activist, described the training of the organization's potential hit men. He said that a group of forty is taken to Jesús del Monte, a mountainous zone, and is directed to pursue, shoot, and cook fifteen victims. This exercise tests whether recruits can conquer their fear and overcome the sight of their quarries' blood.[20] He didn't say whether the initiates had to eat their prey, but there is a precedent for such cannibalism.

Before his mid-December 2009 demise, Arturo Beltrán Leyva would serve unsuspecting dinner guests meat, swimming in spicy sauces, sliced from the bodies of victims.

Amid rampant bloodshed that instills fear in the population, social scientists like Carlos Antonio Flores Pérez, an analyst formerly with the Mexican intelligence agency CISEN,[21] said that La Familia's public condemnations of certain ills helped it gain ground through what is effectively "psychological warfare" and win social legitimacy in a state plagued by violence. "[La Familia] is instituting its own actions to build social roots," said Flores Pérez. "It's a strategy to win over the goodwill of the people in areas in which it operates."

At least some *michoacanos* have bought into La Familia's message that the troublemakers, the killers, and the bad guys are outsiders—not locals or, heaven forbid, La Familia itself. "I applaud the emergence of La Familia Michoacana," wrote one Morelia blogger, adding that he thought the group's presence would result in a 70 percent drop in extortion, drug dealing, and kidnapping—another crime that La Familia publicly frowns upon but is said to engage in.[22]

No wonder that at a May 30, 2009, news conference, the then attorney general, Eduardo Mora Medina, labeled La Familia as Mexico's "most dangerous" cartel—a designation that he could have applied equally to Los Zetas. He based this assessment on the cruelty perpetrated by the shadowy, pious organization; its ability to suborn and terrorize politicians; its spectacular surge in constructing sophisticated laboratories to produce methamphetamines; and its access to high-powered weapons in a state where 10,311 arms were confiscated in 2008—tops in the nation. A "psychosis" of fear has invaded municipalities in this region, including Petatlán, Guerrero, known for its "miraculous saint" Jesús de Petatlán. The pervasiveness of violence and bloodshed in this small town prompted a former mayor to say "this municipality has been Colombianized."[23] In 2009, authorities killed or captured 174 members of the cartel. Meanwhile, various law-enforcement agencies sustained twenty-one deaths, the most at the hands of any criminal organization except Los Zetas since Calderón launched Mexico's version of the "war on drugs." [24]

Intimidation of Politicians

La Familia, which operates in seventy-seven of Michoacán's 113 municipalities,[25] also intimidates politicians, especially in the Tierra Caliente region. In the November 2007 municipal contests in the state, contenders for mayor of Múgica and Nueva Italia stepped aside after receiving death threats. In several other municipalities, La Familia dissuaded opponents of their favored standard-bearers from voting. José Vázquez Piedra, the outgoing mayor of Turicato, who won a seat in the state legislature, said that the imprimatur of the most powerful cartel in the drug-infested zone was crucial to winning public office. The same situation exists in Apatzingán.[26]

Like other cartels, La Familia shows the greatest interest in municipal elections because they want politicians who will protect—or close their eyes to—drug imports, processing facilities, storage compounds, and, above all, trafficking routes. Should they back a candidate for the Chamber of Deputies, it represents a medium- to long-term investment more than the hope of a proximate payoff; that is, the cartels are counting on the deputy's returning to his state as a prosecutor, secretary of government, mayor, or governor—positions important to their industry. Only in 2009 did La Familia begin paying attention to a few Chamber of Deputies aspirants. The PGR suspected that the cartel was backing nominees in Apatzingán, Lázaro Cárdenas, Morelia, Pátzcuaro, Uruapan, and Zitácuaro. Their alleged tactics included infiltrating nongovernmental organizations, providing funding, and mobilizing street vendors and other groups under their control on behalf of their candidates. By becoming involved in these contests, the syndicate sought to exert political control from the grassroots through the state capitals to the federal government.[27]

Even ex-mayors become targets if they are suspected of cooperating with La Familia's enemies. In early April 2009, authorities discovered the tortured, bullet-riddled body of Nicolás León Hernández, who had twice served as interim municipal president of Lázaro Cárdenas (1984 and 2001). A note left behind read, "This is for all who support los zetas. Sincerely FM [Familia Michoacana]."[28]

La Familia has extended its reach into Mexico State, where José Rubén "El Pony" Herrera Ramírez controlled or has conducted operations in more than a dozen major municipalities. The messianic merchants of death also have operated in Jalisco, Guanajuato, Nayarit, and Mexico City. They have brokered large loads of cocaine from Colombia or through Venezuela, Panama, and Guatemala. Its independent distribution cells have been identified in Houston, Dallas, Atlanta, and various locations in California and North Carolina.[29]

As indicated by the May 26, 2009, arrests, La Familia Michoacana homes in on Michoacán politicians, especially officials in municipalities along their trafficking routes. A protected witness avers that in the last election the criminal band contributed Mex$2 million ($155,000) to favored mayoral candidates who, if elected, would receive a stipend of Mex$200,000 ($15,000) per month. The same anonymous source swore that Leonel Godoy Rangel, who won the governorship in 2007, raked in $300,000 from each of La Familia's leaders—a charge he vehemently denies.[30]

Charges of a "narcoelección" filled the air after the PRI captured the governorship and a lion's share of mayors and state legislators on November 13, 2011. Luisa María Calderón Hinojosa, the PAN's standard-bearer and president's sister, recognized Fausto Vallejo Figueroa's triumph. In contrast, PRD President Jesús Zambrano attributed the "victory" of the PRI candidate, who ran strongly in Apatzingán and thirty-two localities with a notable La Familia presence, to support from this cartel. He alleged that the voice on an audio, possibly a taped telephone conversation, belonged to a La Familia member who urged voters to back the PRI candidate for mayor of Tuzantla. The governor-elect dismissed such assertions and pledged to intensify the battle against DTOs during his administration.

La Familia's expenditures on campaigns represent a drop in the bucket compared to the organization's earnings from methamphetamine alone. According to a laboratory operator, the organization invests approximately Mex$1 million ($77,000) in a plant to produce one hundred kilograms of ice weekly, which can generate earnings of Mex$3.5 million ($270,000).[31]

Federal forces demolished forty labs in 2010, many of which were in Apatzingán, nestled in the humpback hills of the remote Sierra Madre Mountains that hide marijuana and opium poppy farms, landing strips for light aircraft hauling cocaine from Colombia, and the increasingly sophisticated methamphetamine laboratories.[32]

At the beginning of his administration, the president dispatched large contingents of Federal Police and military personnel to fight La Familia and other cartels in Michoacán. Calderón even visited the Forty-third Military Zone in Apatzingán, a no-man's-land of narco-activities. There, he donned a floppy military tunic and sported an olive-green field hat bearing five stars and the national shield—all symbols of the commander in chief—to underscore his solidarity with the federal forces assigned to confront drug traffickers. In this "Operation

Michoacán," more than sixty soldiers and one hundred police officers lost their lives, even as they killed five hundred cartel gunmen. All told, the chief executive launched seven operations in Michoacán. In May 2009, though, he decided to zero in on politicians.

Focus on Politicians

After the first five military incursions into the state, Calderón changed his strategy to focus on politicians who were enabling La Familia and other cartels to act with impunity. Pressure from Mexico City forced the February 2009 resignation of Citallí Fernández González, a former state legislator who was Michoacán's secretary of public security. She was required to step down because of her lack of success against DTOs and possible ties to La Familia. On May 27, 2009, federal authorities arrested Fernández González as part of a stunning thrust against thirty-two public officials, including twelve mayors.

In addition to Fernández González and the mayors, the federal forces took into custody various municipal security directors (Arteaga and Tumbiscatío), ranking law-enforcement personnel (Lázaro Cárdenas, Morelia, and Zitácuaro), as well as state public servants (chief of advisers to the attorney general, the economic development director, police agents, and the head of police training). A spokesman for the PGR, who eschewed the idea of political motivation, stressed that the strike was nonpartisan and derived from intelligence amassed by SIEDO. In provincial areas, there are few secrets about the conduct of public figures. The focus was on Lázaro Cárdenas and trafficking routes from the port. Even though several cartels absorbed hits, La Familia's allies took the brunt of the assault.[33]

In 2007, Uriel "El Paisa"/"The Confidant" Farías Álvarez, brother of "The Grandfather" and a PRI stalwart, won a landslide victory for the mayoralty of Tepalcatepec, which—along with Aguililla, Apatzingán, and Buenavista Tomatlán—graces a drug-smuggling corridor that connects the Tierra Caliente with Jalisco. He dismissed the idea that he or his relatives had ties to the underworld: "My brother only kept a lookout on orders of the army. And as a result they said he was a narco." Federal forces took El Paisa into custody, along with nine other mayors, on May 27, 2009.[34]

The arrests sparked a thunderous outcry from Mexico's political nomenklatura. It was one thing for the government to pursue criminals; a quite different thing was rounding up public officials who cooperated with narco-traffickers. For politicians, it was the policy version of penalizing jaywalkers. After all, the syndicates had much more firepower and money than officeholders, who—if they resisted the pressure exerted by the cartels—endangered themselves and their families. The shrillest condemnation of this "occupation" by federal forces came from the leftist-nationalist PRD, the party of Michoacán's state executive Leonel Godoy. He decried the failure of Calderón to consult with him before sending forces into his state. His colleagues in the nation's Senate chimed in, "We oppose the weakening of the Michoacán government that the people elected at the polls," thundered Silvano Aureoles Conejo, vice-coordinator of the PRD's senators, and an unsuccessful candidate to succeed Godoy in the November 13, 2011, election. The head of Mexico's CNDH also took the government to task for not notifying Michoacán's chief executive in advance "as a political courtesy."[35]

Of course, one reason for not keeping the move under wraps was that Godoy's half brother Julio César Godoy Toscano won a federal congressional seat from Lázaro Cárdenas as a PRD candidate. After the election, Monte Alejandro Rubido, the then technical secretary of the National Security Council, claimed that the legislator-elect had ties to money laundering and organized crime. He evaded a 2009 arrest warrant by sneaking into his own swearing-in ceremony in order to obtain parliamentary immunity. In March 2010, a judge issued an *amparo* (injunction) against his arrest, but Godoy Toscano ultimately gave up his legislative seat.[36]

Godoy was later disavowed by the party and stripped of his office when an audio recording was released of his apparently speaking with La Familia big shot La Tuta Servando Gómez. He remains a fugitive.[37]

The PRI, which scored a thumping victory in the July 5, 2009, congressional contests, even questioned the effectiveness of troop movements under Calderón. State party president Mauricio Montaya Manzo lambasted the detentions, seizures, and arrests carried out by elements of the federal government over the previous two-and-a-half years.[38]

La Familia sought to drum up support by organizing a convoy of buses to drive hours to Mexico City to protest the arrest of Uruapan's mayor. "I'm just here because they [La Familia] told me to come," said a migrant deported from the United States, who is hoping the organization will find him a job in the local police force. "I know they

[La Familia] are really crazy. In fact, I think they are sick sometimes, but they are the only people in my town who can help you out if you get in trouble, so that's why I joined the group," he added.[39]

Interior Secretary Fernando Gómez Mont brushed aside the bellyaching and encomiums, emphasizing that the gravity of the situation required "an immediate, frontal, and determined response."[40]

Moreover, he made a direct challenge to La Familia: "We are ready for you; deal with authority and not with citizens; we are waiting; this is an invitation to you." Deputies and senators across the spectrum decried this bravado as provocative, which signaled Gómez Mont's frustration over the government's inability to quell drug-incited ruthlessness with large military detachments (he subsequently apologized for his statement). The units may tamp down violence in one area only to face an upsurge elsewhere in what one scholar called a "whack-a-mole" dynamic. Yet reliance on the army and navy was essential in light of the venality and unprofessionalism that infused police departments.[41]

The officials ultimately gained their freedom, largely because the government could not produce sufficient evidence or enough witnesses to convict them. Still, authorities affirmed that it would continue investigating the freed suspects. Despite a tirade from Governor Godoy about the misuse of power, both Interior Secretary Gómez Mont and SSP Secretary García Luna adamantly refused to ask the liberated mayor for forgiveness because a probe of their links to narco-traffickers was still underway.[42] Six months before late May 2009 foray into the state, federal agents had captured Wenceslao "El Wencho" Álvarez Álvarez, an ally of La Familia who ran an international operation out the Michoacán municipality Nueva Italia. Like many growers in the Tierra Caliente, El Wencho claimed that he produced agricultural crops. He vows to have turned to narco-trafficking to avenge the 1999 kidnapping and murder of his father by a vicious gang.

The PGR has connected "El Wencho" to La Familia. His cocaine network allegedly extended from Colombia through Guatemala, Honduras, El Salvador, Venezuela, and the Dominican Republic, as well as to Atlanta and other US cities. The US law-enforcement experts have linked him to Rosales Mendoza and to El 40, the number two operatives in Los Zetas. Álvarez Álvarez called the charges against him "false," insisting that he was only a grower of tomatoes, peppers, mangos, and other crops on land rented by his entire family. Credible official sources insist that El Wencho's worked with Los Zetas, as well as La Familia. For the latter, he moved millions of dollars to Monterrey and Nuevo Laredo before laundering them in Atlanta.[43]

Project Coronado

On October 22, 2009, US federal authorities announced the results of a four-year investigation into the operations of La Familia Michoacana in the United States. "Project Coronado" was the largest US raid ever against Mexican drug cartels operating in the United States. A coordinated effort by local, state, and federal law enforcement that took forty-four months of planning resulted in the apprehension of 1,186 suspects in nineteen different states. These agents seized more than 1,999 kilograms of cocaine, 2,710 pounds of methamphetamine, 29 pounds of heroin, 16,390 pounds of marijuana, 389 weapons, 269 vehicles, two sea vessels, and $32.8 million in US currency.[44]

Since the start of "Project Coronado," the investigation has led to the arrest of more than 1,186 people and the seizure of approximately $33 million. Overall, almost two metric tons (2.2 short tons) of cocaine, 1,240 kilograms of methamphetamine, 13 kilograms of heroin, 7,430 kilograms of marijuana, 389 weapons, 269 vehicles, and the two drug labs were seized.

"Multiagency investigations such as Project Coronado are the key to disrupting the operations of complex criminal organizations like La Familia. Together—with the strong collaboration of our international, federal, state, and local partners—we have dealt a substantial blow to a group that has polluted our neighborhoods with illicit drugs and has terrorized Mexico with unimaginable violence," said FBI Director Robert S. Mueller III. Attorney General Eric Holder added that the raids, conducted in thirty-eight cities from Boston to Seattle, "dealt a significant blow to La Familia's supply chain."[45]

"Project Delirium," another investigation spearheaded by the Department of Justice, culminated in the mid-2011 arrest of 221 people linked to La Familia in the United States. This twenty-month, multiagency operation also yielded $770,499 in cash, 635 pounds of methamphetamines, 118 kilograms of cocaine, and twenty-four pounds of heroin. "The arrests and seizures we are announcing today have stripped La Familia of its manpower, its deadly product, and its profit, and helped make communities large and small safer," Deputy Attorney General James Cole said in a statement released to the press.[46]

La Familia Splits

A love–hate relationship has characterized Los Zetas and La Familia Michoacana. The two factions of La Familia—El Más Loco's and El Chango's—agree to send troops to join the Sinaloa and Gulf Cartels in the North in 2010 after receiving a direct appeal from the imprisoned Osiel Cárdenas, who used a cell phone provided by US authorities, an action revised in chapter 11. This loose accord, the so-called Fusion of Anti-Zeta Cartels (*Fusión de Cárteles Antizetas*— FCAZ), sought to eradicate Los Zetas, who have links to the weakened Beltrán Leyvas, the badly crippled Juárez Cartel, and remnants AFO based in Tijuana.

Nonetheless, a schism in La Familia emerged in the aftermath of the reported death of co-leader Más Loco Moreno González on December 8, 2010. Calling themselves the Knights Templars (*Los Caballeros Templarios*),[47] El Más Loco's acolytes—notably Servando "La Tuta" Gómez Martínez and Enrique "El Kike" Plancarte Solís—challenged Juan de Jesús "El Chango"/"The Monkey" Méndez Vargas for the leadership of the organization.

The Knights Templars got the upper hand when authorities captured El Chango in Aguascalientes on June 21, 2011. This same year his cultlike adversaries "expelled" El Chango from La Familia for allying with Los Zetas. A communiqué in the form of a banner explained the action: To the *michoacana* society in general: We are informing you that the Familia Michoacana separates itself from all acts by Chango Méndez and his allies who formed part of La Familia Michoacana, because el Chango's degrading actions . . . [which have caused us] to expel him because of his links to the social cancer of Los Zetas. We wish to make clear that La Familia [represents] all *michoacanos* not Chango Méndez.[48]

Before his arrest, El Chango called for outside help. The Beltrán Leyvas were too weak to pull his chestnuts out of the fire, and he got a thumbs-down from two warring minicartels in Jalisco—"La Resistencia" ("The Resistance") and the "Cártel de Jalisco Nueva Generación" ("The Jalisco New Generation Cartel"). He used his contact with El Wencho to seek assistance from El 40, but the aid was too little, too late. Authorities captured eleven Zetas at the Jalisco Michoacán border before they could lend a helping hand to El Chango.

Even as a growing number of their paladins suffered arrest, the Knights Templars were passing out twenty-two-page booklets claiming that they were determined to battle poverty, tyranny, and injustice. This publication, *The Code of the Knights Templars of Michoacán*, claims that the group "will begin a challenging ideological battle to defend the values of a society based in ethics." Another passage reads, "God is the truth and there is no truth without God." Illustrations include medieval knights in tunics bearing red crosses like the ones worn by the original crusading order.[49] In addition, a shield is embellished with pictures of El Más Loco and Jesus, leading some credible law-enforcement agents to believe that El Chayo will reappear in his own version of the "Second Coming."[50]

For reasons unknown to close observers, there are white crosses that carry Muslim names like "Muhammad," "Abdul Azim," "Sulaiman," and "Abu Sufian" near El Chayo's alleged burial site.[51] El Chango's arrest spurred an exodus of his supposed loyalists to the Knights Templars, including Ignacio Rentaria Andrade, Alfonso "La Moraleja" Morales, Javier Suárez, and Javier "El Borrado" Barragán. The Federal Police arrested two other defectors in late July: Bulmaro "El Men" Salinas Muñoz, the reported plaza chief in Morelia, and Neri "El Yupo" Salgado Harrison, who is believed to have become the Knights Templars' chief in Apatzingán.[52]

Jesús "El Changito" Méndez, one of El Chango's fourteen children, heads what is left of his branch of La Familia. His handful of allies includes El Changito's younger brother, Fernando, "El Pony" Herrera Ramírez, and Martín Rosales Magaña.

As long as they cooperate with the Sinaloa Cartel, El Chapo is likely to provide protection to La Tuta's motley organization, which lost several important cadres in 2011. For example, in mid-November, the army took into custody Juan Gabriel "El Gasca" Orozco Favela, the plaza boss in Morelia who allegedly killed twenty-one people in the periphery of the state capital on June 8. He was also in charge of extorting merchants, trafficking in marijuana, providing weapons to comrades in the south of the state, and unfurling narco-banners that condemned La Familia.

Two weeks after Orozco Favela's arrest, a banner appeared in Morelia, Apatzingán, Buenavista Tomatlán, and elsewhere in support of a Christmas-time truce between the government and organized crime. Poet-novelist Javier Sicilia, whose son was kidnapped, tortured, and executed on March 28, 2011, had advocated this cease-fire as part of his crusade to reduce bloodshed in the country.

Table 9 Compares Los Zetas and La Familia/Knights Templars.

Table 9 Comparison of La Familia and Los Zetas

Characteristics	Los Zetas	La Familia
Origins	Gulf Cartel boss Osiel Cárdenas Guillén, now in prison in the US, enticed Lt. Arturo Gúzman Decena to recruit GAFES and other military to become his Praetorian Guard and enforcers in 1997.	Emerged from "La Empresa," formed in 2000 by Carlos Rosales Mendoza—with important roles played by José Jesús "El Chango" Méndez Vargas and Nazario "El Chayo"/"El Más Loco" Moreno González.
Leadership	Heriberto "The Executioner" Lazcano and Miguel Ángel "El 40" (Treviño Morales); secondary leaders include 1. Omar "El 42" Treviño Morales, 2. Alberto José "El Paisa" González, 3. Iván "Z-50"/"El Talibán" Velázquez Caballero, 4. Jorge "La Chuta" López, 5. Victor Nazario Castrejón Peña, 6. Francisco "El Quemado" Medina Mejía, and 7. Gustavo "El Erótico" González Xalate, and others mentioned in Figure 2.1.	Other key figures in the Knights Templars include 1. Servando "La Tuta" Gómez Martínez—a mercurial ideologue and key public relations man, 2. Enrique "Kike" Plancarte Solís—main coordinator of narcotics sales to US, and 3. Ignacio "Cenizo" Rentería Andrade—Uruapan plaza boss who is under indictment by a US federal court.

Organization	Regional lieutenants oversee plaza bosses under which subunits called *estacas* conduct operations through segregated cells. Each *estaca* has 5 to 7 operatives; although all *estaca* members kill, various *estacas* in a state or large city will have different specialties—that is, kidnapping, extortion, prostitution, contraband, carjacking, human smuggling; lookouts report to the security detachment of each plaza boss, who enjoys considerable leeway as long as he meets financial goals; Los Zetas maintain a separate financial structure with financial operators, who collect the receipts of illegal activities each day and report not to the plaza boss but to El 40 or his brother Omar; floating auditors keep tabs on plaza financial operators.	25 to 50 plaza chiefs, many of whom control several municipalities; weaker control over plaza bosses from the center.
Areas of operation	Most of 20 coastal and interior states—with less penetration of the northwest, where the Sinaloa Cartel remains dominant; US—mainly, Houston, Los Angeles, Dallas, and Atlanta; and Central America.	Michoacán, Colima, Guerrero, Jalisco, El Bajío, Aguascalientes, Mexico State, the DF, and Tamaulipas; present in scores of US cities, Central America, and Europe via "El Wencho."

(Continued)

Table 9 (*Continued*)

Characteristics	Los Zetas	La Familia
Ideology	Strict discipline arising from military background of founders.	La Tuta and other followers of El Más Loco extol a perverted fundamentalist Protestantism used as an artifice to attract alienated, unemployed, uprooted young men, who may also suffer drug and alcohol addiction, into a community—namely, "La Familia." Requires recruits to clean up their lives before they are accepted into the fold; in March 2011, they began calling themselves the Knights Templars and issued a code of conduct for their members.
Drugs sold	Cocaine, heroin, marijuana, and some meth.	Major meth processor and seller; also small amounts of cocaine, heroin, and marijuana.
Number of members	Possibly 1,000 or so ex-military, police, and drug/alcohol addicts from across the country (although principally in the north); illegal aliens, as well as Kaibiles.	A few thousand—with emphasis on recruiting *michoacanos*, including young men who receive treatment at La Familia's rehabilitation centers.
Alliances	Situational alliances with the badly weakened Beltrán Leyvas, the even-more debilitated Juárez Cartel, and La Resitencia in Jalisco.	An arrangement with Juan José "El Azul" Esparragosa, who allowed them to move into Guanajuato without a fight. As a result of the Gulf Cartel's attempting to reassert dominance over Tamaulipas, from the Zetas, a working alliance has been formed among

		1. La Familia,
		2. the Sinaloa Cartel,
		3. the Gulf Cartel,
		4. the Guadalajara Cartel,
		5. the weak Milenio Cartel, and
		6. shards of the Baja California band once operated by the imprisoned Eduardo Teodoro "El Teo" García Simental. This grouping, which calls itself the "Fusión de cárteles 'antizetas,'" is battling (1) Los Zetas, who are linked to the (2) reeling BLO, (3) the weak Juárez Cartel, and (4) remnants of the decimated Arellano Félix Organization.
Non-narcotics activities	Kidnapping, murder-for-hire, extortion, contraband, human smuggling, loan-sharking, stealing and selling petroleum products to US, hijacking trucks, organizing prostitution rings, selling protection, operating casinos, and investing in "legal" businesses.	Kidnapping, murder-for-hire, extortion, contraband, human smuggling, loan-sharking; La Familia spurns prostitution, but shakes down pimps.
Level of violence	Extremely high as evidenced in their executing family members of the fallen Marine who was involved in the attack on Arturo Beltrán Leyva.	Extremely high; yet unlike Los Zetas, they claim to respect the president and the armed forces.
Training	Green Beret-type instruction, carried out in the organization's camps in Mexico, Guatemala, and, possibly, Texas.	Less rigorous military training; intense indoctrination that may involve 6 to 8 weeks of lectures, videos, and other teaching devices.

(Continued)

Table 9 (*Continued*)

Characteristics	Los Zetas	La Familia
Propaganda	*YouTube*, narco-banners, *corridos*, decapitations, newspaper ads, young people and senior citizens paid to mobilize antimilitary/Federal Police operations, and threatening notes left alongside corpses.	La Familia uses the same propaganda techniques; in addition, it kills, tortures, and humiliates alleged criminals to show that it "protects" the people of Michoacán from bad actors.
Involvement of women	Los Zetas use *Las Panteras* to cut deals with authorities, whom they may kill if discussions do not crystallize; also, employed to handle the funds in some plazas; in these cases, they report to "El 40" rather than to plaza boss.	Few female members; one exception is Leticia Martínez Guzmán, who assists her husband Armando Quintero Guerra in the syndicate's financial transactions.
Social work	Except for El Lazca's yielding to his mother's request to build a chapel in Apan, Hidalgo, there is little civic activity; in fact, Los Zetas want to inspire fear through sadistic cruelty rather than cultivate the image of benevolent godfathers.	Cosmetic road, church, and lighting improvements to attempt to curry local favor; small loans to farmers in return for their growing drugs.

Sources: Manuel Olmos, "Caen seis integrantes de 'La Familia Michoacana," *La Prensa*, July 30, 2009; and "Cártel del Golf pierde un brazo," *EXonline*, February 4, 2010; "Narcoguerra' en Michoacán llega a 21 decapitados este año," *El Universal*, February 20, 2010; Manuel M. Cascante, "Los 12 'narco-apóstoles' que dirgen La Familia Michoacana," *ABC International*, December 16, 2010; "Ligan a 'Templarios' con laboratory," *Reforma*, July 14, 2011; and Benito Jiménez, "Delatan al 'Changó' sicarios de Familia," *Reforma*, June 23, 2011.

Notes

1. This may explain why the death note indicated that they "do not kill women."

2. James C. McKinley Jr., "Mexican Drug War Turns Barbaric, Grisly," *New York Times*, October 26, 2006.

3. Alejandro Suverza, "El evangelio según La Familia," *Nexosenlinea*, January 1, 2009.

4. "Quitan puerto a 'Los Zetas,'" *Reforma*, October 4, 2009.

5. "Luis Brito, Detectan egreso de 'Los Zetas,'" *Reforma*, December 16, 2009.

6. "Multiplica 'Familia' violencia en Edomex," *Reforma*, September 14, 2008.

7. "Cae presunto jefe de La Familia Michoacana," *Noroeste.com*, April 22, 2009.

8. This paragraph, taken from an enunciation of La Familia's principles, was prepared by Juan Carlos García Cornejo and translated by Mark Stevenson of the Associated Press; the entire document appears as Appendix 1 in this monograph; see George W. Grayson, *Mexico: Narco-Violence and a Failed State?* (New Brunswick, NJ: Transaction Publishers, 2010): 212–13.

9. Rafael Rivera, "'La Familia' castiga y exhibe a ladrones," *El Universal*, January 30, 2010.

10. Quoted in "Van 28 degollados en agosto 7 estados," *El Universal*, August 30, 2008.

11. Malcolm Beith, "La Familia: Society's Saviours or Sociopaths," *Mexidata. Info*, October 20, 2008.

12. See George W. Grayson, "The PRI Makes a Comeback in Mexico," *E-Note*, Foreign Policy Research Institute, July 9, 2009.

13. See Centro Independente de Art y Cultura de Michoacán/Facebook, http://www.facebook.com/pages/Centro-Independiente-de-Arte-y-Cultura-De-Michoac%C3%A1n/121613971230313?v=wall.

14. "La nueva fe de los narcos," *Milenio Semanal*, May 30, 2009; "La Familia da cursos de liderazgo y altruismo a sus integrantes," *La Crónica*, August 28, 2009; and "'El Cede' adiestró a más de 9 mil integrantes de 'La Familia Michoacana,'" *Cambio de Michoacán*, April 19, 2009.

15. Ransomed Heart Ministries, "Ransomed Heart Is a Small Ministry Devoted to a Big Message," www.ransomedheart.com/ministry/who-we-are.aspx.

16. Published by Thomas Nelson Publishers, Nashville, 2002.

17. John Eldredge, "Re: Mexican Press—John Eldredge," electronic mail to author, August 9, 2010.

18. Rolando Herrera, "Acelera narco ejecuciones," *Reforma*, January 1, 2010.

19. Olga R. Rodriguez, "Mexico Cartel Stitches Rival's Face on Soccer Ball," *Associated Press*, January 8, 2010.

20. Rolando Herrera and Karla Portugal, "Detallan ataques contra Bautista," *Reforma*, July 1, 2010.

21. Centro de Investigación y Seguridad Nacional (National Security and Investigation Center).

22. Quotations in the two preceding paragraphs came from "La Familia: Society's Saviours or Sociopaths," September 25, 2008, http://cyanide257.wordpress.com/2008/09/25//.

113

23. Antonio Armenta Miralrío quoted in Adriana Covarrubias, "Pobladores prefieran callar ante inseguridad," *El Universal*, November 30, 2008.
24. "Arrecian ataques en Michoacán," *Reforma*, December 11, 2008.
25. Drug Enforcement Agency, Office of Public Affairs, "La Familia Michoacana Fact Sheet," October 2009.
26. Pablo César Carrillo, "Elección con tufo a narco," *EXonline*, November 17, 2007; and Abel Miranda, "Intimidan a los penales de Guerrero," *Excélsior*, January 8, 2009.
27. Francisco Gómez and Alberto Torres, "'La Familia' quería colocar políticos federales propios," *El Universal*, May 29, 2009.
28. "Executan a ex Alcalde michoacano," *Reforma*, April 3, 2009.
29. DEA, "La Familia Michoacana Fact Sheet."
30. "Dicen que 'La Familia' apoyó campañas," *Reforma*, June 20, 2009.
31. Francisco Gómez, "'La Familia' extiende sus redes hasta Europa y Asia," *El Universal*, July 26, 2009.
32. "Descubren 'megaloaboratorio' en Michoacán," *Reforma*, March 10, 2010.
33. "Ligan a Alcaldes con 'La Familia,'" *Reforma.com*, May 27, 2009.
34. "Capturan a seis presuntos integrantes de La familia michoacana," *Milenio.com*, June 12, 2009.
35. Jorge Ramos Pérez, "Gobierno debió avisar a Godoy 'por cortesía': CNDH," *El Universal*, May 28, 2009.
36. "Alaude la bancada del PRD el amparo ortogado a Julio Godoy," *El Universal*, March 26, 2010.
37. Armando Estrop, "Gastan diputados . . . y pagan en 2012," *Reforma.com*, August 30, 2011.
38. Quoted in Azucena Silva, "PRI critica aumento de fuerzas federales," *El Universal*, July 21, 2009.
39. Jo Tuckman and Ed Vulliamy, "Drugs 'Taliban' Declares War on Mexican State," *The Observer*, July 19, 2009.
40. Quoted in Jorge Ramos, "'Legítima defensa' despliege en Michoacán Gobernación," *El Universal*, July 19, 2009.
41. Quoted in Hal Brands, *Mexico's Narco-Insurgency and U.S. Counterdrug Policy* (Carlisle, PA: Strategic Studies Institute, 2009): 34.
42. "García Luna niega disculpas a alcaldes," *El Mañana*, February 4, 2010.
43. "Entra 'Wencho' al narco en busca de revancha," *Reforma*, November 12, 2008; and María de la Luz González, "Mapaches 'lavaron' en siete países," *El Universal*, October 15, 2008.
44. Tracy Russo, "Project Coronado—By the Numbers," *The Justice Blog*, US Department of Justice, October 22, 2009.
45. Warren Richey, "US Strikes at Mexican Cartel's Drug-and-Gun Trade," *Christian Science Monitor*, October 22, 2009; Ed Pilkington, "Crackdown on La Familia Cartel Leads to More Than 300 Arrests across US," *The Guardian*, October 23, 2009; and Spencer S. Hsu, "La Familiar Drug Cartel Target of Sweep in U.S.," *SignOnSanDiego.com*, October 23, 2009.
46. Wendell Marsh, "Justice's 'Project Delirium' Targets Major Mexican Drug Cartel," *Reuters*, July 21, 2011.
47. In approximately 1119, Hugues de Payens, a nobleman from France's Champagne region, began the order with eight loyalists. Their goals

were to protect pilgrims on journeys to the Holy Land. They made their headquarters in a mosque, which had been the site of King Solomon's Temple. At first they called themselves the "The Knights of the Temple of King Solomon," abbreviated to "Knights Templars." The Roman Catholic Church condemned them in 1129. They sought donations to defend Jerusalem, and to ensure the charitable giver of a place in Heaven; see "The Knights Templars," *The Catholic Dictionary*, www.newadvent. org/cathen/14493a.htm.

48. Quoted in "Rompe La Familia nexus con 'El Chango,'" *Reforma.com*, June 28, 2011.

49. E. Eduardo Castillo, "Mexico Cartel Issues Booklets for Proper Conduct," *Associated Press*, July 20, 2011.

50. It should be noted that his demise has yet to be substantiated with pictures, fingerprints, or a body.

51. Policía Federal, "Cruces de los Integrantes de la Organización 'La Familia Michoacana', Presuntamente Abatidos en el Enfrentamiento, del Día 09 de Diciembre de 2010," Secretaría de Seguridad Pública, Mexico City, n.d.

52. "Cae jefe de 'Temparios' en Morelia," *Reforma*, July 25, 2011; and Rolando Herrera, "Detienen a jefe de plaza de Templarios," *Reforma*, August 1, 2011.

7

"Zetanization" of Mexico

In early August 2011, Amnesty International expressed concern that Mexico might become a dictatorship like those in the Southern Cone in the 1970s and 1980s. A spokesman for the organization downplayed the possibility of a coup d'état but warned that the quest for order might lead citizens to become more tolerant of repression and, he added, "paradoxically the army had intensified the insecurity." A month later, students commemorated the forty-third anniversary of the "Tlatelolco Massacre," in which government forces gunned down hundreds of protesters and innocent bystanders in downtown Mexico City. Raúl Álvarez Garín, a leftist survivor of the blood bath, warned against growing militarism. He said that Calderón is "dragging the people into a war and the people have become the victims. The logic is absolutely incomprehensible that there are narcos fighting other narcos or narcos battling the police or Navy ... [and] the army fighting another gang." Is he correct about the nation's becoming militarized? After all, "Zetanization" has influenced Mexico's landscape in various ways: in the tactics of rival DTOs, in the reconfiguration of state and municipal security forces, and in media self-censorship (discussed in the next chapter).[1]

To begin with, cartels that once focused on earning money from drug smuggling now engage in the kind of butchery associated with the paramilitaries. No longer are torture, dismemberment, and decapitation measures monopolized by La Familia, which appropriated these techniques from Los Zetas.

For instance, the Sinaloa Cartel's El Chapo has sought to depict himself as a Godfather whose good works in the community, donations to the church, and job creation complement elicit business transactions. Now, even he has begun to sanction gratuitous and grotesque violence. Local lore has it that peasants in the municipality of Badiraguato,

Guzmán Loera's bailiwick, wear no clothing other than caps, which they doff when the famed capo passes by. On October 29, 2009, heavily armed gunmen fired at a high-ranking police intelligence agent dining in a Ciudad Juárez restaurant. They killed another policeman and wounded the official and two bodyguards. Authorities later found a sign indicating that responsibility for the attack lay with El Chapo.[2]

The horrific scene in San Fernando was eclipsed in early May 2011 when authorities discovered 226 corpses buried in the Vicente Suárez and Valle de Guardia neighborhoods of Durango—another state where the Sinaloans ride roughshod over their opponents.

At 2:00 p.m. on March 25, 2011, authorities in Guerrero received calls reporting carnage at the Sam's Club in Acapulco. Upon reaching the store, they found an abandoned van next to which lay a farrago of human remains. The butchers had placed duct tape over the victims' eyes and proceeded to sever heads, arms, hands, legs, and other body parts. Four of the subjects were policemen who had gone missing the night before. Guzmán Loera's name appeared on the narco-message deposited at the scene.[3]

Just over a month later, police discovered five decapitated corpses in Los Almendros, a community along the Acapulco–Zihuatenejo highway in Guerrero's Costa Grande. A note at the site read, "For all of you who are casting your lot with the enemy and those who are backing you, take care. Attentively, El Chapo Guzmán."[4]

Los Zetas also pioneered the use of low-level lawbreakers to sell drugs on the street and commit small-scale robberies. Other cartels are copying this tactic, according to Secretary García Luna.[5]

Military Appointments to Civilian Posts

In an attempt to cope with the horrors meted out by Los Zetas, various states and large cities have recruited ex-members of the armed forces to fill traditional civilian posts in law enforcement. Table 10 illustrates this phenomenon. The number of military men in these roles has risen from six in February 2009 to fourteen in April 2011—with six officers in charge of state police forces. Of the twelve governors elected in 2010, seven opted for a general in charge of the State Security Ministry: Carlos Lozano de la Torre (Aguascalientes), Roberto Borge Angulo (Quintana Roo), Mario López Valdéz (Sinaloa), Egidio Torre Cantú (Tamaulipas), Mariano González Zarur (Tlaxcala), Javier Duarte de Ochoa (Veracruz), and Miguel Alonso Reyes (Zacatecas).

Meanwhile, in 2011 men with military backgrounds occupied the position of the secretaries of public security in 36 percent of the municipalities with the most homicides in the country, according to the National System of Public Security. Retired generals head the ministry in the five cities that have registered the most killings: Acapulco, Chihuahua, Ciudad, Juarez, Culiacán, and Tijuana.

On January 13, 2011, nine retired officers were named chiefs of the nine municipalities in war-torn Tamaulipas: Altamira, Ciudad Victoria, Madero, Mante, Matamoros, Nuevo Laredo, Reynosa, Río Bravo, and Tampico.

While by no means new to Mexico, this approach appeared to offer several advantages.

First, many of the officers selected have served as regional or zone commanders and have years of experience combating drug Mafias.

Second, they are likely to have ties to—and the confidence of— current regional and zonal military chiefs with whom they often coordinate assaults on cartels.

Third, whether retired or on leave, military officers may be familiar with the tactics of Los Zetas, the original contingent of which served in the GAFES. Gen. Rolando Eugenio Hidalgo Heddy, the former public security secretary in Aguascalientes, once headed these commandos.

Fourth, generals, admirals, and colonels have the background to bring a culture of discipline to civilian police forces that have often acted in a venal, freewheeling manner—to the point that thousands of serious kidnappings and other felonies go unreported because many citizens believe that the cops are in league with the miscreants. Even if military leaders cannot change behavior patterns, they can oust incompetents and malefactors. For instance, General Salinas Altés removed two hundred elements of Acapulco's Municipal Preventive Police when he took over as Guerrero's security boss.

Fifth, officers are in a good position to recruit active-duty or retired members of the armed forces as policemen in the jurisdictions that they serve.

Sixth, in light of the relatively low pensions received by retired officers, assuming a civilian post supplements their income and reduces pressure to increase retirement income. Overall security expenditures have skyrocketed. The Calderón government sought an 11 percent increase to $11.785 billion in 2012 for the army, navy, PGR, SSP, and states and municipalities to combat organized crime and improve police forces.

Finally, every public-opinion survey shows that the armed forces enjoy a much better reputation than do the police. Such praise centers on their efforts in disaster relief, as well as their anticrime missions. Although 58 percent of respondents to a late November 2011 survey conducted by *Reforma* perceived human rights violations on the part of the army, 81 percent backed its deployment against DTOs. As one anonymous source indicated, "Even if military security chiefs are as corrupt as their civic counterparts, they give a psychological lift to the public."

Preliminary Results

How have the officers in mufti fared?

Upon taking office, retired generals, colonels, or captains often encounter law-enforcement personnel who are afraid to challenge the narcos. Retired General Juan Heriberto Salinas Altés, the public safety minister in Guerrero until June 1, 2011, and a seasoned officer, found that eight members of the police force in the Zirándaro, near Acapulco, never returned to work after either the Sinaloa Cartel or Los Zetas killed a thirty-two-year-old man in a May 2008 shoot-out.[6]

Military men have clashed with local police, especially when they attempted to cleanse their ranks. After all, Los Zetas and other cartels often demanded the appointment of a "reliable" security chief in municipalities that lay along trafficking routes. Soon after reaching Tijuana to head the municipal police on March 10, 2009, Lt. Col. Julián Leyzaola Pérez oversaw the dismissal or resignation of six hundred law-enforcement agents, including eighty-four who were arrested for allegedly cooperating with organized crime. Meanwhile, 2,325 people, among them forty-three policemen, had died during the previous three years. A confluence of factors produced a drop in the crime rate on Leyzaola's watch: the city's population is relatively compact; Governor José Guadalupe Osuna Millán (2007–13) cooperated in the fight against organized crime; he got along well with the military commander in the region. In addition, the increasing hegemony of the Sinaloa Cartel, which supplanted the AFO, meant that one DTO ruled the roost, minimizing intercartel warfare. The fall in violence aside, the state human rights commission and the CNDH charged the police chief with torture before the Inter-American Human Rights

Commission. Meanwhile, the NGO Human Rights Watch criticized Leyzaola for 390 disappearances, including four young *tiajuaneses*.[7]

"The case of Julián Leyzaola is a rare mirage in which tough action in response to a security crisis has other costs: human rights' abuses. He has transgressed the fundamental principle of democracy whereby civil authority must control the military," stated Erubiel Tirado, a security analyst at Mexico City's Ibero-American University.[8]

These accusations did not prevent the convulsed city of Ciudad Juárez from hiring Leyzaola as its public security secretary in a latter-day example of a sheriff facing bad men at high noon. In this office, he leads a force of 2,400 police, working in six crime-ridden districts where 456 murders had been recorded by June 1, 2011.

Brig. Gen. Carlos Bibiano Villa Castillo also believes in an ultra hard-line toward criminals. As director of public security in Torreón, Coahuila, this descendent of Pancho Villa and one of thirty-six children, told a reporter that he preferred to kill members of organized crime rather than interrogate them. "I like to feel the flow of adrenaline. On patrol, when I capture a Zeta or Chapo, I kill him. Why interrogate him? Here we beat the hell out of a bad actor. I have no confidence in the Federal Police because they do not kill [suspects], only arrest them. The Army and Navy execute them," he said six days after the March 2, 2011, confrontation with cartel gunmen.[9] Either because of or despite the retired brigadier general's bravado, Quintana Roo's new governor Roberto Borge Ángulo appointed him secretary of public security.

Upon leaving Torreón, Villa Castillo emphasized his loyalty: "My father is the Army, my mother is the Patria," he affirmed. He also claimed to have been "sleeping with the enemy . . . Of the 1,100 elements under his command, 1,000 were corrupt; they sold uniforms; they sold gasoline; even when on patrol they carried out their dirty business everywhere."[10] Soon after arriving in Cancún, a "narco-message" threatened death to the general. It was signed by "Los Zetas Special Forces."

Although conditions vary from state to state, the presence of military men in top security roles has not diminished the violence afflicting their areas of responsibility (see Table 11). In view of venal police forces, the governors and mayors may have had no choice other than to reach into the barracks for public safety czars. The next move may be to place military officers in charge of the worst prisons, a takeover that has already occurred in Quintana Roo.[11] Three weeks after the

Table 10 Military Personnel in Public Safety Posts

State/municipality	Position	Incumbent	Date appointed
Acapulco (Guerrero)	Secretary of Public Security	Col. (Ret.) Manuel Paz Espinosa	Late July 2011
		Gen. (Ret.) Héctor Paulino Vargas López (took over after Brig. Gen. (Ret.) Serafín Valdéz Martínez resigned on Feb. 16, 2010)	Feb. 16, 2010
Baja California	Director of State Ministerial Police	Brig. Gen. Florencio Raúl Cuevas Salgado, former commander of II Military Zone headquartered in Tijuana	March 27, 2008
	Director of State Preventative Police	Lt. Col. (Ret.) Eusebio Alecio Villatoro Córtez	Feb. 20, 2009
Chiapas	Secretary of Public Security	Maj. Rogelio Hernández de la Mata	Dec. 30, 2010
Chihuahua	Director General of Unified State Police	Div. Gen. (Ret.) Julián David Rivera Bretón	Oct. 3, 2010
Ciudad Juárez	Director of Public Security	Lt. Col. Julián Leyzaola Pérez[a]	March 10, 2011
	Police Chief	Div. Gen. Julián David Rivera Bretón	March 16, 2009
	Director of Security Operations	Col. (Ret.) Alfonso Cristóbal García Melgar	March 16, 2009
Coahuila	Director General of State Investigative Police	Brig. Gen. (Ret.) Jesús Ernesto Estrada Bustamante	Aug. 12, 2008
	Undersecretary of Prevention and Social Readaptation	Gen. José Luis García Dorantes	Feb. 24, 2009

Location	Position	Name	Date
Colima	Chief of the State Preventative Police; equivalent to Secretary of Public Security	Brig. Gen. (Ret.) Raúl Pinedo Dávila	Dec. 6, 2010
Ensenada, Baja California	Commissioner (in charge of security and director of Municipal Police	Div. Gen.(Ret.) Florencio Raúl Cuevas Salgado	Sept. 21, 2011
Federal District	Secretary of Public Security	Rear Adm. Manuel Mondragón Y Kalb (Physician)	
Gómez Palacio (Durango)	Director of Municipal Public Security	Lt. Col. (Ret.) Antonio Horacio Ramírez Morales	Feb. 14, 2008
Guanajuato	Secretary of Public Security	Gen. Miguel Pizarro Arzate	March 2, 2010
Guerrero	Secretary of Public Security and Civil Protection	Div. Gen. Juan Heriberto Salinas Altés (Ret.), former army chief of staff	April 1, 2005 to April 1, 2011
		Salinas Altés was replaced by a civilian, Ramón Almonte Borja, who promised to promote tourism by hiring 18- to 35-year-old female cops and dressing them in sexy uniforms for beach patrol duty in Acapulco	April 1, 2011
Matamoros (Tamaulipas)	Secretary of Public Security	Lt. Col. Gabriel López Ordaz	Jan. 18, 2011
	Operations Director of Secretary of Public Security	Lt. Rafael Antonio Huerta Méndez	Jan. 18, 2011
	Director of Transit	Lt. Roberto Guerrero Roldán	Jan. 18, 2011
Michoacán	Secretary of Public Security	Div. Gen. (Ret.) Manuel García Ruiz	Aug. 8, 2010
	Coordinator of State Preventative Police	Capt. (2nd) Manuel García Ruiz	Oct. 26, 2010

(Continued)

Table 10 (*Continued*)

State/municipality	Position	Incumbent	Date appointed
Monterrey	Secretary of Preventive Police	Gen. (Ret.) José Pablo Leonel Vargas Martínez	Jan. 4, 2012.
Morelos	Secretary of Public Security	Div. Gen. Gilberto Toledano Sánchez[b]	April 10, 2011
Nuevo Laredo	Secretary of Public Security	Brig. Gen. (active) Manuel Farfán Carreola	Jan. 1, 2011
Nuevo León	Secretary of Public Security	Div. Gen. Jaime Castañeda Bravo	Feb. 3, 2011
Oaxaca	Secretary of Citizen Protection	Lt. Col. (Ret.) Javier Rueda Velásquez	March 31, 2008
Puebla	Secretary of Public Security	Div. Gen. Mario Ayón Rodríguez (Ret.), former director general of personnel for National Defense Ministry	March 1, 2005
Querétaro	Secretary of Public Security	Capt. Adolfo Vega Montoto	Oct. 4, 2009
Quintana Roo	Secretary of Public Security	Brig. Gen. (Ret.) Carlos Bibiano Villa Castillo[c]	April 5, 2011
Saltillo (Coahuila)	Director General of the Municipal Preventative Police	Brig. Gen. (Ret.) Marco Antonio Delgado Talavera	Jan 29, 2009
San Luis Potosí	Secretary of Public Security	Brig. Gen. (Ret.) Heliodoro Guerrero Guerrero	Jan. 15, 2011
Tabasco	Acting Secretary of Public Security	Maj. (Ret.) Sergio López Uribe	Feb. 1, 2009
Tamaulipas	Secretary of Public Security	Brig. Gen. (Ret.) Ubaldo Ayala Tinoco	Dec. 30, 2010
Tijuana (Baja Calif.)	Municipal Secretary of Public Security	First Capt. (Ret.) Gustavo Huerta Martínez[d]	Nov. 26, 2010
Tlaxcala	Secretary of Public Security	Brig. Gen. (Ret.) Valentín Romano López[e]	Jan. 15, 2011
Veracruz	Secretary of Public Security	Lt. Arturo Bermúdez Zurita[f]	July 3. 2011

| Zacatecas | Secretary of Public Security | Gen. (Ret.) Jesús Pinto Ortiz | Sept. 11, 2010 |
| | Director of State Preventative Police | Gen. (Ret.) Víctor Manuel Bosque Rodríguez | Nov. 3, 2010 |

Source: Jésica Zermeño, "Toman generales mandos policiacos," *Reforma*, February 15, 2009; Jésica Zermeño et al., "Optan estados por mando militar," *Reforma*, February 15, 2009; "Encabezan los hermanos Ayón Rodríguez mandos policiacos en el país," *E-consulta*, February 15, 2009; Roberto Aguilar, "Torre Cantú nombra a general titular de la SSP," El *Universal.com.mx*, December 31, 2010; Mauro de la Fuente, "Asume militares policía de Matamoros," *Reforma.com*, January 19, 2011; Juan Cedillo, "NL: general asume cargo de titular de Seguridad," *El Universal.com.mx*, February 5, 2011; Óscar Guadarrama, "El gobernador de Morelos cesa al secretario de Seguridad pública," *CNN México*, April 10, 2011; Andro Aguilar, "Militarización sin resultados," *Reforma* ("Enfoque"), April 10, 2011 (the authors relied heavily on this source); and Édgar Ávila Pérez, "Arturo Bermúdez Zurita fue designado a la dependencia luego de la renuncia del general Sergio López Esquer," *El Universal*, July 3, 2011.

[a] Leyzaola replaced Col. Laurencio Rodríguez.

[b] Replaced Div. Gen. Gastón Menchaca Arias (fourteen days after seven people were killed in the state, including the son of writer and social activist Javier Sicilia).

[c] Bibiano replaced Vice Adm. Miguel Ángel Ramos Real.

[d] Replaced Lt. Col. (Ret.) Julián Leyzaola Pérez, who became secretary of public security in Ciudad Juárez.

[e] Replaced Div. Gen. José Leopoldo Martínez González (Ret).

[f] Replaced Div. Gen. Sergio López Esquer, former zone commander for the states of Coahuila, Baja California, Baja California Sur, and Veracruz.

Table 11   Crimes Committed in States with Military Law-Enforcement Chiefs

State	Robberies (%)	Kidnappings (%)	Homicides (%)	Executions
Aguascalientes	13	−54	1	85
Chiapas	20	92	−6	NA
Chihuahua	4	−39	−3	1,008
Coahuila	NA	NA	NA	NA
Colima	18	518	73	NA
Guanajuato	−7	−55	9	128
Michoacán	7	18	46	216
Morelos	7	160	15	433
Nuevo León	12	NA	27	NA
Querétaro	32	60	28	21
Quintana Roo	NA	NA	NA	NA
San Luis Potosí	NA	NA	NA	NA
Sinaloa	−3	278	1	NA
Tamaulipas	−3	123	−9	NA
Tlaxcala	NA	NA	NA	NA
Veracruz	−37	−100	−37	357
Zacatecas	3	27	17	18

Source: Monthly reports of the Executive Secretariat of the National System of Public Security (SESNSP) as compiled by Andro Aguilar, "Militarización sin resultados," *Reforma* ("Enfoque"), April 10, 2011.

August 25, 2011, burning of the Casino Royale in Monterrey, which took fifty-three lives, the Defense Ministry announced formation of a brigade of fire fighters.[12] Are customs and immigration assignments in the offing? In the United States, politicians often place the burden of solving social ills on the public schools. Similarly, civilian leaders in Mexico are quick to rely on the armed forces to tackle ever-more intractable problems. In confronting Sisyphean challenges, the military men frequently assume security roles without the benefit of having their staffs accompany them.

Alexandro Poiré Romero, technical secretary of the National Security Council, denied any trend toward militarizing the country.

He insisted that most of their operations do not involve fighting organized crime. "Neither the Army nor the Navy . . . is supplanting police agencies. At present the elements deployed, together with the Federal Police, are temporarily . . . assisting civilian authorities, not acting alone," he affirmed. "The use of the Armed forces to combat organized crime will be less necessary when local police forces improve their professionalization and [achieve] certification," Poiré added.[13] Improving the quality of local police is a slow process at best, a chimera at worst. The political class, often for self-serving reasons, has fiercely opposed a national police force similar to those in Chile, France, and Spain, and the lion's share of governors adamantly resists dissolving their own forces into a national agency.

Middle-class young people recoil from a career in law enforcement. On May 6, 2011, the federal government launched a campaign to attract candidates for 422 positions in a new Accredited State Police (Policía Estatal Acredible). "We believe that with your talent, your ethical integrity, you, young people . . . can contribute to this force that is so important to the Mexican State," averred Education Secretary Alonso Lujambio Irazábal. The students explained their lack of interest in terms of "corruption," "bad image," "fat," "drug addicts," "danger," and other pejoratives.[14]

Just as Los Zetas recruited Kaibiles for training and support, the Mexican government has backed "Project Sparta," which reportedly involves the L-3 MPRI paramilitary consortium based in Alexandria, Virginia. *Reforma* reported that the organization's cadres are ex-US military personnel, who will establish twelve "virtual military training centers" where they will teach counterinsurgency, urban warfare, infantry tactics, and defense against improvised explosive devices. When contacted by telephone, Rick Kiernan, the company's senior vice president of strategic communication, denied that his firm had a contact in Mexico and that "there has been no contract awarded that I know of."[15]

Meanwhile, the protracted anticartel conflict has taken its toll on trust of federal forces. According to a national survey, between 2010 and 2011, the percentage of respondents who expressed "much confidence" declined for the army (52.5–46 percent), the navy (55–51 percent), and the Federal Police (24.6–17.2 percent).[16]

Few analysts take seriously Public Safety Secretary Genaro García Luna's claim that Tamaulipas will have an effective, qualified police force by 2012. In the meantime, the more contact the ex-army and navy officers have with cartels nationwide, the more likely they are to succumb to the lure of illegal enrichment. Corruption frequently escalates during the last year of a sexenio, known colloquially as "The Year of Hidalgo" after independence champion Father Miguel Hidalgo whose pinched face once graced the peso coin. During the "Año de Hidalgo," public officials traditionally lay aside nest eggs in case they don't secure a suitable post in the next presidential administration.

Notes

1. "Teme Amnistía dictadura military en México," *Reforma*, August 2, 2011; and Luz González and Penélope Aldaz, "Exigen detener Militarización," *El Universal.com.mx*, October 3, 2011.
2. Bernd Debussman Jr., "Latin America: Mexico Drug War Update," *StoptheDrugWar.org*, November 6, 2009.
3. "El Chapo Guzman Claims Credit for Butchering of 5 in Acapulco," *El Blog del Narco*, March 26, 2011.
4. "Hallan cuatro decapitados en Zihuatanejo," *Reforma.com*, April 27, 2011.
5. E. Eduardo Castillo, "Official: Mexican Cartels Hiring Common Criminals," *Associated Press*, April 6, 2011.
6. "Mexico Town's Entire Police Force Quits in Fear of Assassination," *Associated Press*, May 23, 2008.
7. "Leyzaola Takes Post in Ciudad Juárez," *SanDiegoRed*, June 6, 2011.
8. Quoted in Andro Aguilar, "Militarización sin resultados," *Reforma* ("Enfoque"), April 10, 2011.
9. Quoted in Sanjuana Martínez, "Si agarro a un *zeta* lo mato; para qué interrogarlo?: jefe policiaco," *La Jornada*, March 13, 2010.
10. Quoted in "Por ordenes militares, Villa Castillo dejará Torreón," *La Jornada*, March 15, 2011.
11. Sergio Caballero, "Nombran a militares en penales de QR," *Reforma.com*, April 26, 2011.
12. Silvia Otero, "Sedena capacita a brigada de rescate," *El Universal*, September 18, 2011.
13. Quoted in Antonio Baranda, "Niega Poiré militarización," *Reforma*, June 7, 2011.
14. Henia Prado, "Rehúsen jóvenes empleo de policía," *Reforma.com*, May 23, 2011.
15. "Entrenan mercenarios a soldados en País," *Reforma.com*, April 6, 2011; and Bill Convoy, "U.S. Private Sector Providing Drug-War Mercenaries to Mexico," *The Narcosphere*, April 3, 2011.
16. The government's National Institute of Statistics and Geography conducted the "Encuesta Nacional de Victimización y Percepción of Seguridad Pública"; see Henia Prado, "Cae confianza en Marina, PF y el Ejército," *Reforma*, September 21, 2011.

8

Psychological Operations

A scratchy, homemade video began on December 1, 2005, with the shaky image of four beaten and bloodied men sitting in a row atop black plastic bags. Their bruises indicated torture. As the video advanced, each of the four men was interrogated when, suddenly, a gloved hand entered from the left side of the screen to aim a pistol at the head of the last individual to speak. He looked at the camera with zero emotion, zero fear, blinked, and died instantly after a gloved finger squeezed the trigger.

A separate video pictured a tortured man, wearing only underwear, tied to a chair, gazing at the camera as the lens panned his battered body; it was March 2007. Messages were engraved on his upper thighs, chest, and head, and on his forehead was emblazoned the letter "Z." Once prompted, the captive began explaining what he did and for whom he worked. He recited his short story in a solid voice, demonstrating no fear as he eyeballed the camera. Once he finished his tale, two figures materialized on the scene. Viewers could see the standing men only from the chest down as one shadowy figure looped a wire around the victim's head before the second man slid two foot-long skinny plastic tubes at both ends of a wire. Then the second man began twisting, slowly choking his prey whose stare never wavered. The scene ended just before the decapitation took place.[1]

Beginning in 2005, various Mexican social media and some traditional outlets regularly depicted the most such gruesome acts that one human can inflict on another, from photos of the—now common—quartered remains of victims to the macabre photograph of two young men who were found skinned with their hearts removed.[2]

Soon after the Gulf Cartel and the Zetas began their war in 2010, pictures surfaced of a small shrine, presumably in Valle Hermoso, where the heads of various *sicarios* had been mounted on top of the structure. Human limbs adorned three nearby tree branches in an arrangement reminiscent of a Christmas tree.

Mexico's various killers expertly manipulate the new options to inflict observers with a level of hideous visual stimulation beyond what even the early theorists of the "CNN effect" considered possible.[3] Beyond the impact that real-time information-sharing may have on the population, photos, videos, and other new media such as *Twitter* accelerated the pace by which Mexico's rival DTOs dramatized the cruelty visited on one another. Mexican outlets, the criminals' own blogs, and *YouTube* channels displayed this barbarism for the viewing public at large, but the violent content was intended to intimidate their foes. Most observers remained on the edge, sickened, disheartened, and scared, while analysts, academics, and other observers debated what new transmitters lay ahead.

Martín Barrón Cruz, a researcher with Mexico's National Institute of Penal Science, observed that criminals and DTOs seek reputations by engaging in ever-greater savagery through their nicknames and the reputations of the groups to which they belong. "Before, we didn't observe mutilations and decapitations . . . but there were violent crimes . . . Now atrocities come to the public's attention . . . through videos on the web that did not exist previously."

It's anyone's guess about the future of this new barbarism. The number of criminals-in-training ready to wield a razor-sharp machete and a handheld camera will grow as the youth bulge in such cities as Reynosa, Matamoros, Ciudad Juárez, Chihuahua, and Hermosillo converges with the syndicates' constant need for street gangs and other hirelings. The tendency for large cartels to fragment and kingpins to fall under pressure from law enforcement portends a new level of ruthlessness in the Americas.[4] Violence in Mexico is approaching a viciousness not seen since the Central American civil wars of the 1980s when Guatemalan Kaibiles and other commandos massacred insurgents and civilians in jungles and villages.[5]

It is difficult to trace Mexico's sadism to a single individual or group. The initial ranks of Los Zetas carried out violence unprecedented in modern Mexico. Los Zetas' original commander, Guzmán Decena, and the current leader, The Executioner, and, above all, Treviño Morales infused the Gulf Cartel with exceptional brutality, even as they safeguarded Osiel Cárdenas.

To augment their cadres, Los Zetas hired Kaibiles. The antiguerrilla warriors earned a reputation for excruciating torture that left survivors with the impression that they had been tormented by demons, not mere mortals.[6] The Guatemalans emphasized the importance of castrations, beheadings, and other inhumane acts.[7] Reviled as "killing machines," these tough fighters and counterinsurgency specialists had trained in an isolated camp known as "The Hell," 260 miles north of Guatemala City. Softer aspects of their instruction involved biting off heads of live chickens and drinking river water out a fired artillery shell with the burnt residue still inside.[8]

One reporter compared the Kaibiles to a combination of "US Rangers, British Gurkhas, and Peruvian Commandos." They adhered to the maxim, "If I advance, follow me. If I stop, urge me on. If I retreat, kill me."[9] The Kaibiles helped Los Zetas master intimidation techniques that cowed adversaries and militated against defections from the organization. In addition, the Guatemalans introduced the airing of hideous torture on *YouTube*. It was said that "you had to kill to become a Zeta; and die to leave their ranks."[10]

Israel Nava Cortes a.k.a. "El Ostión"/"The Oyster" was believed to be an ex-Kaibil, who joined Los Zetas, served as a bodyguard for El 40, ruthlessly oversaw activities in Oaxaca city, and received shipments of the cocaine and marijuana from Colombia. He died in April 2009 when federal agents shot him through the eye near his house located in Fresnillo, Zacatecas, where two of his bodyguards also perished and eight police officers suffered wounds.[11] "They took delight in torturing victims before finally killing them. They would decapitate, dismember, burn and dissolve victims, all with a military precision and detachment hitherto not seen in Mexico."[12] As Los Zetas grew in strength and presence across Mexico, they relied on former Kaibiles to provide security and terrorize enemies.[13]

As noted in chapter 6, La Familia Michoacana learned inhumane punishments from Los Zetas, as well as the basic premise of PSYOPS: "[I]f you frighten your enemy enough, you may defeat him without having to fight."[14]

Los Zetas' adversaries displayed their own penchant for *YouTube* horrors when, in 2005 and 2007, they posted videos of the interrogation and death of presumed Los Zetas operators. These men functioned as pawns in a parallel world of psychological combat that DTOs had used against each other for more than a decade. Dating back to the late 1990s, Los Zetas have employed a spectrum of tactics to misinform and frighten their antagonists. In contrast to others, Los Zetas learned to disguise their own angst on film, rendering themselves less vulnerable to psychological manipulation. Their stoic acceptance of a miserable demise earned them the local underworld's version of martyrdom. They did not show dread; their criminal brand was one of hunters—not the hunted.

Los Zetas made their first significant PSYOPS foray into popular music world on November 25, 2006. As alluded to in chapter 2, Valentín Elizalde had just given a loud and raucous concert in Reynosa. Widely known as the Golden Rooster, he was a young man blessed with roguish good looks and a swagger earned by years of top-ten hits, vast wealth, and a multitude of adoring fans at home and abroad. Following a bravura performance, the talented singer-songwriter boarded his 2007 black Chevrolet Suburban en route to his next tour stop. He would never arrive.

Not twenty minutes after the entertainer climbed off the stage, Los Zetas had identified Elizalde's Suburban, which they began to follow. Once the small convoy sped out of the city, the two trucks tailing Elizalde's van accelerated. The pursuers rolled down their windows and began to shoot. Hot lead shredded the Suburban. All told the gunmen fired some seventy rounds, eight of which perforated the star's body.

Los Zetas had apparently targeted the singing sensation for having recorded and played a *narcocorrido*, a song about the exploits of Mexico's drug-trafficking elite. Only this ballad, titled "A Mis Enemigos" or "To My Enemies," was produced on behalf of Los Zetas' rival El Chapo Guzmán. It was bad enough for the Golden Rooster to record the song on his popular 2006 album titled *Vencedor*, but he showed up at a Zeta hotbed, and opened and closed his show with the piece that excited cheers from his fans and outrage among the *matazetas*, or "Zeta Killers," known to be linked to the Sinaloa Cartel.

In what may have been an omen of Elizalde's assassination, these Zeta foes had posted on *YouTube* pictures of dead Gulf Cartel and Zeta members as "To My Enemies" played in the background. Two days before the show, a presumed Gulf Cartel follower wrote that "videos like these cause the death of Chapitos," referring to men who work for the Sinaloa capo.[15]

The Golden Rooster's last *corrido* included the lyrics, "Why talk behind my back? That's what you are good for. Why don't you talk of me in my presence? Is it that you are afraid of the fellow? You know who you are messing with, come risk your luck."

An unknown cameraman filmed Elizalde's autopsy in gory detail, zooming in as an attendant plucked the shards of lead embedded in the singer's disfigured corpse. The film immediately aired on *YouTube* and other hosting sites in what aficionados believed was a provocative violation of their idol's human rights. This video flashed a signal to other audacious musicians: "Death awaits those who appear on our turf and pay tribute to our enemies."

As in other countries, power brokers have long manipulated journalists in Mexico. For instance, governors continue to attain favorable coverage by advertising heavily in print and electronic media. A few years ago, one of the authors attended an Oil Workers' Union convention that did not adjourn until late Saturday night. "Too bad the concluding session's exceptional length will prevent coverage in Sunday's newspapers," the naïve American remarked. "Not to worry," replied a labor official, "the papers already have the story." True to form, top-of-the-fold front-page headlines adorned the next day's editions and featured the conclave in glowing terms.

Before the appearance of *Proceso* magazine (1976) and newspapers like Mexico City's *Reforma* (1993) and Guadalajara's *Mural* (1998)— both spin-offs of Monterrey's *El Norte* (1938)—reporters covering the travels of prominent officials could expect the government to pay for their airfare, meals, and hotels, as well as $1,000 a day in "walking around money." There were—and still are—*gacetillas*, articles prepared by government figures or private citizens and published as news items for a fee. Mexico's intellectuals long benefited from *embutes*, columns subsidized by an ambitious cabinet minister or other mucky-mucks. PRI administrations went so far as to bestow "journalistic prizes" of $450 per month on two thousand intellectuals.[16]

While cash is still dished out, the cartels use violence to discourage the media's exposing the brazenness of chieftains and the reluctance of law-enforcement agencies to give chase to the culprits. In 2005, if not sooner, Los Zetas began targeting journalists in a stratagem that caught on among other syndicates even though El Chapo and similar warhorses had long cultivated benevolent images through the media. The mercenaries heaped riches on pliable reporters and persecuted detractors.

Watchdog groups such as the Committee to Protect Journalists regard the 1984 daytime slaying of Manuel Buendía, a muckraking columnist for *Excélsior*, the beginning of serious attention to hazards facing the country's Fourth Estate. Cries for justice aside, five years passed before José Antonio Zorrilla Pérez, the ex-DFS chief and protector of drug barons, was convicted with four accomplices for masterminding the cold-blooded murder that they called "Operation News."[17]

Pablo Pinesa Gaucín, a *La Opinion* reporter who lived and worked in Matamoros, became the first journalist whom Los Zetas are believed to have murdered. In April 2000, US Border Patrol agents found the man's body ten miles west of the Los Indios Bridge near Brownsville. Alleged Gulf Cartel hit men, probably Los Zetas, had abducted the newspaperman from outside his office. They administered torture before shooting him in the back of the head, swaddling him in a white sheet, and dumping him north of the Rio Grande in an attempt to deceive detectives. One report indicated that before his execution, Pinesa had received threats, some from specific state policemen.[18]

Four years later, the Gulf Cartel/Los Zetas alliance struck again. On the morning of March 19, 2004, hit men stabbed Roberto Javier Mora García in front of his middle-class home. He was editorial director of the Nuevo Laredo daily *El Mañana*, the oldest newspaper in the embattled border city. That he had not been robbed prompted observers to conclude he had been killed for his work. "Drug battles have become bloodier, and gangs have no code of ethics. They don't respect human life; why should they respect reporters?" warned Daniel Rosas, *El Mañana*'s managing editor. "It's the new trend of drug gangs: Journalists are warned, paid off or killed," Rosas added.[19]

Several months after Mora García's demise, Los Zetas, sometimes called *la maña*, struck again.[20] Francisco Arratia Saldierna was known in Matamoros and across Tamaulipas as *El Profe*, the professor. He was a high school counselor who moonlighted as a columnist. His hard-hitting commentary *El Portavoz* or "The Spokesman," considered a "gossip column about drug trafficking," appeared six days a week in several daily and online publications covering Tamaulipas. These essays established Arratia as an unrelenting critic of politicians and their ties to the underworld. He even capitalized the names of his subjects. "He went for the jugular. He had guts. He pursued the police, the narcos, and the government," remembered a longtime friend and fellow journalist. Arratia was working toward full-time reporting before his abductors ruined his hands and, eventually, took his life.[21]

"La maña" kidnapped and tortured Arratia on August 31, 2004. Authorities surmised that his assailants had used an iron bar and acid to smash and mutilate his hands and fingers even as they burned him with cigarettes and knocked out his teeth.[22] The week before his disappearance, El Profe had published an eye-catching series on especially reprehensible mobsters, including Osiel Cárdenas, who was conducting the Gulf Cartel's business from posh prison confines, and Carlos Rosales Mendoza, a founder of La Familia Michoacana and a ranking Osiel lieutenant. A thirty-second phone call from either man could have sealed the muckraker's fate. The valiant Arratia survived three hours in the torture chamber, only to suffer a fatal heart attack after being unloaded at the local Red Cross office.[23] He was the fifth journalist killed in Matamoros since 1986.[24] An investigation netted Raúl "El Escorpión"/"The Scorpion" Castelán Cruz, a member of Los Zetas. Two months later, the brigands attacked the head of the Tamaulipas state antikidnapping unit, pouring twenty-eight rounds into his vehicle before he miraculously escaped. Reportedly, the assault constituted revenge for the arrest of Castelán, who claimed to have beaten Arratia to scare him, not take his life.[25]

Although a victory for law enforcement, Castelán's capture failed to abate Los Zetas' coercion of newswriters. On October 11, TV, radio, magazine, and newspaper professionals staged a national day of protest at the Monument to the Revolution in downtown Mexico City. This demonstration didn't faze the paramilitaries and other DTOs determined to muzzle the press. "All the journalists are upset and outraged by our impotence," said the president of the Matamoros journalists association.[26]

At 7:40 p.m. on February 6, 2006, editor René Martínez was staring at a stack of articles that he had to edit when he heard the thud of military boots outside the *El Mañana*'s Nuevo Laredo newsroom. The intruders opened fire in the messy room, cursed the journalists, and tossed fragmentation grenades before speeding away in latest model SUVs. Martínez crawled from under a desk to find Jaime Orozco Tey, a forty-year-old rewrite man and father of three, bleeding profusely. He had taken several rounds in the abdomen and back during the early evening onslaught.[27] Days after the horror, the daily's editor Ramón Cantú said the newspaper would scale back even more its coverage of *narco* crimes, which had already been pared in the aftermath of Mora García's 2004 murder.

Nearly a year later, Los Zetas employed thinly veiled threats, blackmail, express abductions, and beatings to highlight the fate that awaited zealous reporters. Sinister men hovered outside the newspaper's front door to remind the staff that they were under surveillance. "They spy on everyone inside the newspaper, and almost everyone knows they get money from Los Zetas to do it," an anonymous reporter told a visiting journalist.[28] By the end of 2006, after at least two assaults and relentless intimidation, the management of one of the most prestigious newspapers in Tamaulipas, and indeed northeastern Mexico, had knuckled under.

Despite concerted efforts by Mexican authorities and NGOs, media professionals remained soft targets in 2011 and early 2012.[29] More damaging than the actual attacks was divisiveness in the press community and even within the same newsroom. A 2006 special report filed from Nuevo Laredo stated simply that "reporter suspects reporter."[30] Long before the rifle and grenade storming of *El Mañana*, a veteran editor of *El Bravo*, another Matamoros paper, ceased to work directly with or even talk to reporters on the crime beat, lest he suffer retribution from the police or *la maña*.[31] Los Zetas and their proxies kicked off their PSYOPS campaign against Nuevo Laredo and Matamoros journalists and reprised their tactics in other parts of the country.

Rodolfo Rincón Taracena was a middle-aged, chain-smoking reporter who worked for the *Tabasco Hoy* daily in Villahermosa, Tabasco's capital. He was a hard-working veteran and a street-smart newshound. Such experience didn't prevent his disappearance on January 20, 2007.[32] After working a crime scene story, Rincón called his office to say that he had to rendezvous with a contact. That was the last anyone heard from him alive.

Rincón appeared prominently on Los Zetas' radar in 2007 after he exposed drug trafficking in Tabasco, including one piece that revealed the location of a Villahermosa safe house. There, the renegades had stored cocaine imported through Guatemala before shipping it north for transport into the United States. This trenchant reporting infuriated the mercenaries. Soon after his last article appeared, local drug dealer Miguel Ángel Payró Morales approached Rincón outside the *Tabasco Hoy* offices. The mafioso said he had to "make arrangements" to prevent his working on "these types of publications." He then forced the journalist into his car, where two goons were waiting.[33]

The three men drove the writer to La Quinta El Bambú, in the suburbs, where they lined him up with four other men and shot them all in the head. One of the hitmen chopped Rincón's body into pieces and "cooked" them in a vat of gasoline and acid—to the point that his corpse was unrecognizable.[34] For telling the truth, the journalist had been "disappeared" on the command of a local boss determined to stress the oft-repeated message: "You write about us, you die." Other cartels also participate in such intimidation.

Mexico was already an extremely dangerous place for journalists, and Rincón was the first of many reporters to suffer at the hands of Los Zetas during Calderón's administration. The cutthroats continued to attack journalists in Tabasco, Tamaulipas, Veracruz, Campeche, Nuevo León, and elsewhere. A drug gang reportedly added at least one American journalist to its hit list.[35]

In early October 2008, Michoacán-based newspaper editor Miguel Ángel Villagómez Valle was abducted on his way home from work. The editor and publisher of the tabloid *Noticias de Michoacán* suffered multiple gunshot wounds before his body was thrown on a garbage pile in Guerrero State, about thirty miles from Lázaro Cárdenas. He was one of twelve journalists killed in Mexico during the year.

The motive for the murder of Villagómez is not yet known; however, he had received a threatening phone call from a member of Los Zetas about a month before his death and had warned his family to be alert. *Noticias de Michoacán* often reports on organized crime, corruption, and drug trafficking. Neither the state police nor the PGR's Special Prosecutor for Crimes of Violence against Journalists, created in February 2006, turned up suspects.

Eight Ciudad Juárez journalists received intimidating calls from self-described cartel members in January 2008. The messages were identical: "Don't get mixed up with the wrong people," or face the consequences. José Armando Rodríguez Carreón of *El Diario* was one of those contacted. When he reported the threat to the Chihuahua state prosecutor's office, he was told he should get out of the city, for there was no way to guarantee his safety. After two months, "El Choco," as he was called, returned to work, while other journalists preferred self-exile. Triggermen gunned him down on November 13 when he was driving his three children to school. There were menacing calls to reporters during his funeral the next day. As a result, an increasing number of journalists left the region or went abroad.[36]

Michoacán State has one of the highest rates of violence in Mexico, with regular confrontations between and among the Los Zetas, La Familia, and the Sinaloa Cartel. Abductions, disappearances, and murders of journalists are common. For example, Mauricio Estrada Zamora of *La Opinión de Apatzingán* and *La Opinión de Michoacán* had been missing since February 14, 2008, and José Antonio García Apac of *Ecos de la Cuenca* since November 20, 2006. Gerardo Israel García Pimentel of *La Opinión de Michoacán* was shot dead on December 8, 2007.[37] Rodríguez Carreón was the eleventh writer killed in Mexico in 2008.

Gangsters are not the only ones who direct violence toward reporters. In mid-March 2009, cops in Puebla stopped a vehicle carrying journalists for *Intolerancia*, *El Columnista*, and *Cambio*. When the police learned their profession, they bellowed that the press humiliated law-enforcement officers. The policemen then hurled the three men to the ground, handcuffed them, and continuously beat and threatened them during a twenty-five-hour detainment. Each year newspapers, TV networks, radio stations, and press associations report scores of incidents of similar brutal treatment.[38]

Such was their dread that some news writers decided to do the unthinkable and switch sides, going to work for the very organizations that had killed many of their colleagues. More pragmatic reporters allegedly accepted payoffs from Los Zetas, including Lázaro Tejero Juárez and Roberto Carlos Abreu Suárez, journalists for *Presente* in Tabasco's Balancán and Emiliano Zapata municipalities.

The cartels paid $500 or more per month to journalists who paid no heed to their crimes.[39] Some reporters chose not to curtail their treatment of the news but to spin it in favor of one or another criminal organization. Others elected to work as police informants or accept communication roles with Los Zetas or others DTOs. Guadalupe Garcia Escamilla's decision to represent the wrong cartel may explain her April 2005 death. Although many thought she had become an El Chapo's mouthpiece in Nuevo Laredo, no conclusive evidence supported this conjecture.[40] Personal safety may dictate whether a journalist performs PR duties for a syndicate as evinced by Los Zetas' PSYOPS campaign in Nuevo Laredo that eroded the accurate, objective presentation of news. Where survival trumped ethics, it wasn't a hard decision to make. Still, pro-criminal reporters often found themselves as exposed as their reputable counterparts inasmuch as they became bull's-eyes of their employer's competitors.

Newspapermen in Matamoros, Reynosa, and other narco-controlled cities indicate that a veteran journalist frequently becomes the *enlace* or "link"—specifically, the DTO's spokesman, who informs reporters what they can write, broadcast, or must keep under their hats. The link typically informs the press corps to lay off hard crime stories and focus on public drunkenness, auto accidents, soirees, and other relatively innocuous topics. The reporters may receive a *plata-o-plomo* offer, with silver filling the pockets of those who excoriate the government without mentioning criminal groups. Such journalists, who—like municipal cops—earn miserable salaries, often endure public contempt "as literary harlots."

Table 12 indicates journalists killed from 2008 through the first half of 2011.

Table 12   Mexican Journalists Murdered from 2008 through 2011

Year	Event
2011	José Luis "La Gata" Cerda Meléndez, 33, host of a program for Televisa in Monterrey, kidnapped outside the TV station and killed (March 25). Cerda was also identified as one of the *enlaces* that worked for the Zetas in Monterrey. He was also allegedly a small-time pusher of drugs in the show business elite of the Metropolis.
	Luis Emanuel Ruíz Carrillo, 20, reporter for *La Prensa* (Coahuila), suffered the same fate as Cerda Meléndez; next to their bodies lay a note: "Now you won't collaborate with Los Zetas. Sincerely, DCG. Saludos arquitecto El número uno" (Greetings architect number one); March 25.
	Noel López Olguín, journalist for *La Verdad de Jalipan* (Chinameca, Veracruz) and, formerly, stringer for the weeklies, *Noticias de Acayucan* and *Horizonte*; kidnapped March 8; body found nearly three months later (May 31); recent and former colleagues distanced themselves from the deceased lest they excite the fury of Los Zetas.
	Miguel Ángel López Velasco, author of the *Milo Vela*, a well-known column in *Notiver* (Veracruz); killed while sleeping in his home, along with his wife and 21-year-old son, in the Boca del Río neighborhood of Veracruz (June 20).
	Yolanda Ordaz de la Cruz, police reporter for *Notiver* (Veracruz); she was found with her throat slit behind the offices of another newspaper and near a radio station in the neighboring city of Boca del Rio. A note beside her corpse read, "Friends also Betray. Sincerely, Carranza"—a possible reference to a former traffic police officer, Juan Carlos Carranza Saavedra (July 25).
	Ana María Yarce Viveros, 45, reporter and founder of the weekly *Contralínea*; discovered bound, naked, asphyxiated, and shot in a park in the Iztapalapa borough of Mexico City, apparently a victim of theft (August 31).
	Humberto Millán Salazar, 43, radio host of "Sin Ambages" ("Plain Language") on *Radio Fórmula* and founder, editor, and columnist for the only newspaper *A-Discusióin* Culiacán, Sinaloa; frequently criticized politicians and drug traffickers; abducted on August 24 and found dead from a gunshot wound the next day (August 25).

(Continued)

Table 12 (*Continued*)

Year	Event
	Rocío González Trápaga, 48, ex-reporter for Televisa and an independent journalist, who owned a casa de cambio in the Mexico City airport; like her companion, Yarce Viveros, she was discovered bound, naked, asphyxiated, and shot in a park in the Iztapalapa borough of Mexico City, apparently a victim of theft; she and her companion were carrying $71,800 (August 31)
	Maria Elizabeth Macías Castro, 39, a freelance journalist who lived and worked from her residence in Nuevo Laredo, published her views on Twitter (*@nuevolaredovivo*) and wrote for *Nuevo Laredo en Vivo*. Her decapitated body was found along with headphones, a keyboard, and a note that stated she had been killed for writing on social media websites (September 24). Her murder was the first homicide recorded by the Committee to Protect Journalists where the aggression was directly related to work on a social media website.
2010	Valentín Valdés Espinosa, reporter for *Zócalo* of Saltillo, Coahuila, killed (January 8).
	José Luis Romero, crime reporter for the radio program *Líneas Directa*, Mochis, Sinaloa; kidnapped in Ahome and killed (January 12).
	Jorge Ochoa Martínez, director and editor of the weeklies *El Oportuno* and *El Despertar de la Costa*, killed in Ayutla de los Libres, Guerrero; authorities claimed that two Mixtec Indians participated in the murder, which may have stemmed from an automobile accident (January 29).
	Jorge Rábago Valdéz, 49, reporter for Radio Rey group; kidnapped in Reynosa, along with seven journalists of various media; tortured and after 14 days was freed; a diabetic, he died of torture wounds in a local hospital (February 19).
	Evaristo Pacheco Solís, reporter for the weekly *Visión Informativa*; found shot to death alongside the Chichihualco–Chilpancingo highway, near the municipality Eduardo Neri, Guerrero (March 12).
	Enrique Villicaña Palomares, columnist for La Voz de Michoacán and political analyst for CBT Television and other media; kidnapped April 5 and killed even though the family paid the ransom; body found in Morelia, Michoacán (April 11).
	María Isabella Cordero, former host on Televisa (Chihuahua) and subsequent employee of CANACO (National Chamber of Commerce) in Chihuahua; machine-gunned to death (April 10).

Table 12   (*Continued*)

Year	Event
	Miguel Ángel Bueno Méndez, collaborator with the newspaper *Nuestro Distrito*; kidnapped and massacred in Huisquitecan, Mexico State (June 26).
	Francisco Rodríguez Ríos, correspondent for *El Sol de Acapulco* and *Objectivo de Chipancingo*; killed in Cayuca de Benítez, Guerrero (June 28).
	María Elvira Hernández, journalist for *El Sol de Acapulco* and *Objectivo de Chilpancingo*; killed along with spouse in Cayuca de Benítez, Guerrero (June 28).
	Marco Aurelio Martínez Tijerina, 45, director of the *Contrapunto* news program on Radio Station XERN and TV Azteca correspondent; shot to death in Montemorelos, Nuevo León (July 10).
	Guillermo Alcaráz Trejo, 24, worked for the online newspaper *Omnia*, and was a cameraman for the Human Rights Commission; machine-gunned to death in Chihuahua city (July 10).
	Hugo Olivera Cartas, active in the Tierra Caliente, director of the *ADN* news agency, collaborated with the *Agencia Quadratín*, edited *El Día of Michoacán*, and was correspondent for *La Voz de Michoacan*; bound and shot inside his car (July 6).
	Marcelo de Jesús Tenorio Ocampo, 64, radio announcer focusing on religious subjects; worked for PEMEX and served on city council; killed in his home on the Centro neighborhood of Campeche (September 7).
	Luis Carlos Santiago, 22, cameraman for *El Diario* of Ciudad Juárez; machine-gunned while in commercial center of the city in an attack that injured other reporters (September 16).
	Carlos Alberto Guajardo Romero, 37, had worked for the dailies *El Bravo*, *El Mañana* (Matamoros), and *Contacto*; covered the police beat for *Expreso* when he died in cross fire between federal forces and cartel gunmen in the Victoria neighborhood of Matamoros, Tamaulipas (November 5). Several journalists in both Matamoros and Reynosa identified Guajardo as the *enlace* with the Gulf Cartel in Matamoros and actually held a rank in the organization. He was killed in one of the many firefights that took place on the day Tony Tormenta was killed. According to the journalists, Guajardo was off duty but arrived at a firefight to act as a lookout for the criminal organization. The white SUV driven by the alleged *enlace* had more than 16 bullet holes.

(Continued)

Table 12   (*Continued*)

Year	Event
2009	Jean Paul Ibarra Ramírez, photographer for *El Correo de Iguala*, Iguala, Guerrero; shot on his motorcycle after covering a story (February 13).
	Luís Daniel Méndez Hernández, reporter for *La Poderosa* of the *Radiorama* chain; shot four times in the back in la Huasteca region of Veracruz (February 22).
	Juan Carlos Hernández Mundo, director of the local newspaper *El Quijote*; assassinated in Taxco de Alarcón, Guerrero (February 27).
	Carlos Ortega Melo Samper, lawyer and correspondent for *Tiempo de Durango*; shot to death in Santa María de Oro, Durango (May 3).
	Elisio Barrón Hernandez, 36, crime reporter for *Milenio-Torreón*; kidnapped from his home on May 25, shot eleven times, and found dead in an irrigation canal in Torreón (May 26).
	Juan Daniel Martínez Gil, news broadcaster for *Radiorama Acapulco*; savagely beaten and killed in La Máquina, Guerrero (July 28).
	Norberto "El Gallito" Miranda Madrid, 44, radio journalist who covered criminal activities in his program "Cotorreando con El Gallito," broadcast on *Radio Visión* in Ciudad Juárez; shot in Casas Grandes in northeast Chihuahua (September 24).
	Gerardo Esparza Mata, worked in social communications for the municipality of Durango, specializing in reporting on crime and taking pictures of suspects who had been arrested; shot in the head in Durango (October 12).
	Fabián Ramírez López, 42, announcer for a *La Magia 97.1* radio station in Mazatlán, Sinaloa; throat slashed and markings carved on his back in Mazatlán (October 13).
2008	Claudia Rodríguez Llera, founder of the publication *CineMagazine* and host of the news program *En Pantalla Grande* on *Radio Mix* of Ecatepec, Mexico State; shot in the temple (January 7).
	Francisco Ortiz Monroy, correspondent for the daily newspaper *El Diario de México*; shot dead in Camargo, Tamaulipas (February 5).
	Bonifacio Cruz Santiago and his son Alfonso Cruz Pacheco, director and editor, respectively, of the weekly *El Real de Ciudad Nezahualcóyotl*; killed in Chimalhuacán, Mexico State (February 7).

Table 12   (*Continued*)

Year	Event
	Felicitas Martínez Sánchez and Teresa Bautista, radio journalists for an indigenous station "La Voz que Rompe el Silencio," in San Juan Copala, Oaxaca; shot to death (April 7).
	Candelario Pérez Pérez, independent journalist and editor for crime magazine *Sucesos*; shot dead in Ciudad Juárez (June 24).
	Miguel Ángel Gutiérrez Ávila, anthropologist, linguist, author, and indigenous rights activist; beaten to death in Guerrero state (July 25 or 26).
	Alejandro Zenón Fonseca Estrada, host of the news program "El Padrino" on radio station "Exa FM" in Villahermosa; assassinated by commandos (September 23).
	David García Monroy, columnist for *El Diario* and contributor to various publications in Chihuahua; killed along with ten other people in a shoot-out in a bar (October 9). The incident was apparently unrelated to the murder of Villagómez.
	Miguel Angel Villagómez Valle, publisher and editor of *Noticias de Michoacán*; executed near Lázaro Cárdenas (October 8 or 9).
	Francisco Javier Salas, spokesman for *El Mexicano* of Tijuana; killed for having reported threats to authorities (October 17).
	José Armando Rodríguez Carreón, reporter for *El Diario* (Juárez); killed while taking his children to school (November 13).

Sources: "Mexico: Incontenible el ritmo de asesinatos de periodistas; caen tres en un més," Federación Latinoamericana de Periodistas, Mexico City, April 5, 2009; "Amenaza narco a periodistas y soldados," http://kikka-roja.blogspot.com/2009/05/amenaza-narco-periodistas-y-soldados.html; "UNESCO Director-General Condemns Murder of Mexican Journalist Carlos Ortega Melo Samper," May 18, 2009; "Ejecutan a periodista en Ciudad Juárez, Chihuahua," *Terra*, September 24, 2009; "Periodista asesinado de modo horripilante en Guerrero," *IFEX*, August 12, 2009; "Suman 10 periodistas asesinados este año en México, según una organización civil," *EFE*, October 13, 2009; "Director-General Condemns Murder of Mexican Reporter Fabián Ramírez López," UNESCO, October 21, 2009; "Relación de periodistas asesinados en México," *El Figaro*, February 2, 2011; and "México: Dos periodistas asesinados en Nuevo León," *Reporteros sin fronteras*, March 28, 2011; "Drug trafficker confesses to killing missing Mexican reporter," *Committee to Protect Journalists*, June 1, 2011; "Matan a periodista y familia en Veracruz," *Reforma.com*, June 20, 2011; Miguel Ángel Hernández, *Associated Press*, July 27, 2011; "Sospechosos de asesinar a periodistas en la Ciudad de México son Detenidos," *CNNMéxico*, October 3, 2011; and "Fiscalía: Robo es móvil de asesinato de Dos periodistas mexicanas," *Associated Press*, September 1, 2011.

The Paris-based Reporters without Frontiers cited ninety-five attacks on journalists during the first half of 2008, while a World Journalists' Report on Press Freedom castigated Mexico as "one of the most dangerous countries for journalists in the world"—with twenty-four reporters killed, eight missing, and dozens threatened, intimidated, or harassed for practicing their profession during the last eight years.[41] Alejandro Junco de la Vega, owner and publisher of major dailies—- *Reforma* (Mexico City), *El Norte*, (Monterrey), *Mural* (Guadalajara*)*, and *Palabra* (Saltillo)—has moved to Texas in response to threats. In a letter to Nuevo León's governor, the newspaper tycoon said he considers himself a "refugee" and faced the dilemma of either "compromising the editorial line of the paper[s] or protecting my family," adding that "we lost faith."[42] In contrast, Jesús Blancornelas, who was severely wounded in 1997, continues to edit the weekly *Zeta*, which has no relationship to the cartel except to expose their activities. Blancornelas believes that Los Zetas—possibly its leader The Executioner—were responsible for the 2004 slaying of one of the newspaper's co-editor, Francisco Ortiz Franco.[43]

In late May 2009, banners dotted the landscape in Torreón, warning soldiers and journalists to "watch out." The names of El Chapo and the unknown Cartel of the West (Cártel del Poniente) graced the placards, which appeared one day after the discovery in an irrigation canal of the bullet-ridden body of Elisio Barrón Hernández, a thirty-six-year-old crime reporter for *Milenio-Torreón*.[44] In mid-June 2009, five suspects were arrested for Barrón's execution. One of the men, Israel Sánchez Jaime, confessed membership in Los Zetas and admitted to killing the kidnapped reporter.[45]

"Journalism is dead in Reynosa," wrote *Milenio* news director Ciro Gómez Leyva on April 3, 2010.[46] If that were true, Los Zetas had done their work well, but the murder of singers and journalists was only one of several PSYOPS ventures. Others were not as direct or dramatic and employed the use of several thousand followers on the periphery, who lived normal lives, but jumped at the chance to support Los Zetas. Various journalists in Reynosa and Matamoros claimed that a number of the reporters attacked or executed in Reynosa since 2010 were in fact working for the Zetas and were killed by the Gulf Cartel after being warned to cut their ties with the paramilitaries.

From periphery to core, Los Zetas operators communicated in many forms: hand signals and Nextel cell phones, messengers, hacked police radio frequencies, and notes left on or carved into dismembered body parts. Publicly placed banners, known as *narcomantas*, became a mainstay of Los Zetas' PSYOPS efforts.

Hung on overpasses with messages for the government, rivals, and potential recruits, the banners were frequently reprinted in local media and aired on television, even as authorities scrambled to rip them down. Photographers snapped pictures of the displays, often scrawled on bedsheets. Newspapers translated the hastily scribbled propaganda into clear readable prose. Wire services circulated the declarations across the country, even across the world. The *narcos* not only allowed the journalists to cover these examples of agitprop but exalted in the free publicity. *Narcomantas* fed into this warped news cycle in a way that satisfied the public's appetite for information, while enabling Los Zetas and other groups to manage the news without heaving a bomb into a printing plant or a television studio. All DTOs have taken advantage of this artifice, but none more effectively than Los Zetas. They raised the bar on how, when, and where to disseminate messages to maximize their psychological effects, eliciting fear or cooperation from specific audiences.

By early October 2008, Mexico had endured years of escalating violence, which was only surpassed by the terrorism that the Colombian don Pablo Escobar rained on his nation's cities. Would Mexican cartels pursue the same course? It appeared they might on September 15, 2008, when masked gunmen detonated two grenades in downtown Morelia where men, women, and children celebrated the traditional Independence Day ceremony known as "El Grito." The blasts killed eight and wounded eighty-five revelers.[47] Had Mexico's Mafias shifted from criminal violence to terrorism?

The PGR narrowed the list of likely perpetrators to members of either La Familia or Los Zetas.[48] The latter sought to shape rather than respond to public opinion. On October 5, 2008, they unfurled *narcomantas* that blamed La Familia for the bloodshed. Los Zetas pledged to eliminate La Familia's bosses, not because they had acted against them but because they threatened the Mexican people. The Executioner's organization offered a $5 million reward—"paid in dollars, in pesos, or in whatever currency desired"—for information leading to the arrest of La Familia's leaders. Other banners read, "You already know where to find us. We are people of our word" and "To all those in charge of the Michoacán plaza [territory] we request that you come together, and you will have our support."[49]

By early 2009, Los Zetas had mastered the weapon of fear. At the same time, they realized how well-placed "donations" could advance their cause. In Nuevo León, the renegades, who collaborated with local police, sought to take advantage of human rights violations. They gave poor people—often children—cell phones, school supplies, and toys. In return, the recipients hoisted placards, bellowed slogans, and mobilized opposition to the presence of the military and Federal Police in their state. "Soldiers Go Home!," "We Want Peace; Out with the Army," "The Soldiers Scare Us!"—these were among the chants intoned by thousands of so-called Hidden Ones, or *Los Tapados*, in metropolitan Monterrey.[50]

About the *tapados*, one observer noted, "What's happening is that the kids get together in the streets; if someone comes with a ball and says 'We're going to play soccer,' they go; if someone comes with a forty (beer) and says 'We're going to go get drunk,' they go to get drunk; if someone shows up with rocks and says 'We're going to throw stones,' they go." It's no secret here that the people who went out to protest against the military in March 2009 are the same clientele that politicians round up for elections and other big events. There is a long tradition of parties dispensing tortillas, soft drinks, beer, and even sewing machines and bicycles to a throng of people at gatherings.

The mother of a *tapado* from Monterrey's Sierra Ventana neighborhood says, "One day we woke up and there were backpacks with Mex$200 bills on our doorsteps with a message, 'This is yours if you participate in today's protest; if you're not interested, leave everything where you found it.'"[51]

Similarly, Father Juan Pedro Alanis, the parish priest in the Independencia neighborhood, said, "They go to the demonstrations; they don't even know what it's about or why, they just go. They go," the clergyman continued, "because of the pay. It's a time-honored tradition in Mexico, where political parties, unions, and other organizations reward people for showing up at rallies. There's even a word for it here, *acarrear*, which in Spanish means to transport but in Mexican slang adds the elements of payoffs and gifts."

In February 2009, Monterrey withstood four consecutive days of protests that left tires burning, windows smashed, roads blocked, and a confused, scared populace. By mid-month, a deep sense of foreboding hung over citizens accustomed to residing in an affluent, bilingual, pulsating modern city—a virtual island where tranquility had prevailed.

Residents of this northern business hub did not realize that they were viewing a preview of coming attractions.

On the second consecutive day of protests against the Mexican military, authorities arrested Juan Antonio "El Keko" Beltrán Cruz, whom they concluded had orchestrated the convulsion.[52] As the suspect was being carted off, his supporters, masked with bandannas and dark sunglasses, unleashed another torrent of violence. Wielding sticks, stones, and bottles, they blatantly challenged rank and file municipal and state law-enforcement officers who lacked shields and helmets. Buses rumbled in with more aggressive young protestors who blockaded main thoroughfares and assaulted the offices of the state transport authority, located not two hundred meters from a military base. Another fist of ruffians killed a state ministerial police commander.[53]

Days after his capture, El Keko admitted that he and a handful of young toughs belonged to a small cell or *estaca*, which protected Zeta operators while they worked in Monterrey. They had given the malcontents money and gifts to ignite the protests. Beltrán Cruz headed just one of scores, if not hundreds, of *estacas* that function under plaza bosses in Monterrey and other Zeta bastions.

El Keko's detention confirmed what many observers considered a cynosure of Los Zetas' psychological warfare, namely, the ability to assemble groups of poor, marginalized children and adults, who for a few hundred pesos would go to war against a corrupt, elitist regime. These street vendors, convenience store operators, unemployed youngsters, jobless adults, and pensioners served as the cartel's eyes and ears, as well as part-time PSYOPS activists. Some were on call to pick up a pistol or a rifle and, when necessary, foment civil unrest against a government indifferent to their plight. They allowed the paramilitaries to muster armed protesters with a single phone call. The existence of this part-time reserve army partially explained how some observers erroneously concluded that perhaps five hundred men and some women composed a force that is actually larger.[54] This so-called puffer-fish effect, or exaggeration of size, was another victory in Los Zetas PSYOPS.

On the chilly morning of February 12, 2010, citizens of Monterrey began their day with yet another salvo from Los Zetas. This time the syndicate's publicists had suspended their banners from the metropolitan cathedral in the city's center, just a stone's throw away from the mayor's office. This communication lacerated the Sinaloa Cartel for the massacre of eight students in Ciudad Juárez on February 10, 2011. They also took to task El Chapo's men for the February 11, 2010, kidnapping in Gómez Palacio of two adolescents, who turned up dead in neighboring Torreón, Coahuila.[55]

This transparent "hearts and minds" gambit exemplified Los Zetas' expertise in crafting public messages, similar to those circulated in political campaigns. When this approach came a cropper, the desperados resorted to the tried and true game plan of kidnappings and executions.

The effectiveness of Los Zetas' long-term PSYOPS became evident in the so-called War in the North, in Tamaulipas, where Los Zetas fought with their former employers, the Gulf Cartel, for control of the plazas in Matamoros and Reynosa. Even though the Northeast was aflame with fighting, the mainstream media largely avoided the intermural clash. "The big philosophical question in this gritty border town does not concern trees falling in the forest but bodies falling on concrete," opened a March 2010 report that detailed the media's silence about the warfare besetting Reynosa.[56] A journalist who worked for the *El Mañana* disappeared on March 1, 2010, increasing to six the number of journalists who vanished during February. The March affronts included the death of a local radio reporter from a vicious beating, the severe thrashing administered to a *TV Milenio* crew in Reynosa, and threats against *Dallas Morning News* staff members who were run out of town because "they lacked permission to report there."[57]

Los Zetas' cowing of the media in Tamaulipas was so complete that a Reynosa-based communications professor encouraged his journalism students to focus on covering politics, culture, or sports—"anything but crime."[58] Even as these young men and women graduated, the Mexican government unconvincingly sought to link Los Zetas to Lebanese brothers Kamal and Salim Boughader Mucharrafille: the former accused of attacks on the Scotia bank in Mexico; the latter, proprietor of the La Libanesa restaurant in Tijuana, sentenced to fourteen years in prison for smuggling Middle Easterners to San Diego. The only tie to terrorists was Salim's admission that one of his clients had worked for a TV network owned by the Hezbollah.[59]

In one of his first publicized statements, US Ambassador E. Antony Wayne expressed support for the CNDH and reported that the Department of State-sponsored "Secure Coverage" program, based in the Digital Journalism Center of the University of Guadalajara, had trained

120 reporters from throughout Mexico in professional techniques for carefully covering high-risk events.[60]

Notes

1. Colleen Cook, "CRS Report for Congress: Mexico's Drug Cartels," *Congressional Research Service*, October 2007.
2. Rigoberto Ventura, "Les arranaron la piel cuando aún estaban vivos," *Nayaritpuntocom*, April 6, 2011, http://www.nayaritpuntocom.com/portada/52228.html.
3. A cursory review of "the CNN effect" may be found via its Wikipedia entry: http://en.wikipedia.org/wiki/CNN_effect.
4. "The Four Corner Stones of Mexico's Criminal System," *Southern Pulse*, March 24, 2011.
5. Coauthor (Logan) has conducted interviews in El Salvador (most recently in January and February 2011) specific to the civil war, insurgencies, torture, extreme violence, and how these cultural scares have translated into the country's current struggle to manage public security.
6. Coauthor (Logan) interview with a former Guatemalan military officer (name withheld), November 2010.
7. Ricardo Ravelo, *Los Capos* (Mexico City: Debolsillo, 2007): 251, 257, and 258.
8. Albert De Amicis, "Los Zetas and La Familia Michoacana Drug Trafficking Organizations (DTOs)," capstone paper, Masters of Public and International Affairs, Graduate School for Public and International Affairs, University of Pittsburgh, March 12, 2011 (updated).
9. "Los Kaibiles: Las 'maquinas de matar,'" *Terra*, October 2, 2005.
10. Ricardo Ravelo, *Los Capos* (Mexico City: Debolsillo, 2007): 251, 257, and 258.
11. María de la Luz González, "'Los Zetas' llegaron a Zacatecas desde 2007," *El Universal*, May 20, 2009.
12. Quoted in Beith, *The Last Narco: Inside the Hunt for El Chapo* (London: Penguin Books, 2009).
13. Francisco Gómez, "'Los Zetas' por dentro," *El Universal*, December 31, 2008.
14. Ibid.
15. Buggs, "The Strange and Tragic Story of Valentín Elizalde," *Borderland Beat*, June 20, 2009.
16. Patrick Oster, "The Periodista," in *The Mexicans: A Personal Portrait of a People* (New York, NY: HarperCollins, 2002).
17. John MacCormack, "Journalism is a Dying Profession in Mexico: At Least Five Matamoros Reporters and Editors Have Been Killed for Their Drug-Trade Coverage," *San Antonio Express News*, October 10, 2004.
18. César Peralta González, "Investigan en Tamaulipas crimen de reportero gráfico," *El Universal*, April 11, 2000.
19. Susana Hayward, "Mexican Reporters Fear Gang," *Knight Ridder Newpapers*, August 14, 2005.
20. Coauthor (Logan) interview with a reporter for *El Bravo* (name withheld), August 2010.

21. Quoted in MacCormack, "Journalism is a Dying Profession in Mexico."
22. Ibid.
23. Olga R. Rodriguez, "Mexican Journalists Fear Killing May Have Chilling Effect," *San Diego Union Tribune*, September 2, 2004.
24. Quoted in MacCormack, "Journalism is a Dying Profession in Mexico," *San Antonio Express News*, October 10, 2004.
25. "Balean al jefe del Grupo Antisecuestros en Tamaulipas," *El Siglo de Torreón*, October 2, 2004.
26. MacCormack, "Journalism is a Dying Profession in Mexico," *San Antonio Express News*, October 10, 2004.
27. James C. McKinley Jr. "A War in Mexico: Drug Runners Gun Down Journalists," *New York Times*, February 10, 2006.
28. Sara A. Carter, "Mexican Journalists Caught in the Crossfire of City's Drug-Cartel Wars," *San Antonio News Express*, December 28, 2006.
29. See Carlos Lauría, Sauro González Rodríguez, "Mexico: Dread on the Border," Committee to Protect Journalists, February 2006; and "Getting Away with Murder: The Committee to Protect Journalists' 2011 Impunity Index," June 1, 2011.
30. Ibid.
31. Coauthor (Logan) interview with editor of *El Bravo* newspaper (name withheld), August 2011.
32. "Atribuyen a Los Zetas el asesinato de periodista en Tabasco," *IFEX*, March 2, 2010.
33. Samuel Logan and John P. Sullivan, "The Gulf–Zeta Split and the Praetorian Revolt," *ISN/ETH*, Zurich, April 7, 2010.
34. "Zetas quemaron cuerpo de periodista," *El Universal*, March 1, 2010.
35. In the wake of the threat, the San Antonio Express News temporarily reassigned its Laredo correspondent; see Jose Simon and Carlos Lauría, "Mexican President Must Protect Freedom of Expression," *San Francisco Chronicle*, July 23, 2007.
36. "The Dilemma Mexican Journalists Face: Self-Censorship, Exile or Certain Death," *Mexidata.info*, January 26, 2009.
37. International Pen, "Mexico: Editor Abducted and Shot Dead," October 15, 2008, www.internationalpen.org.uk.
38. "Mexico-Media Safety: Police Assault and Threaten Three Journalists," *IFEX*, March 19, 2009, www.newssafety.org.
39. Logan and Sullivan, "The Gulf–Zeta Split."
40. Committee to Protect Journalists, "Dolores Guadalupe García Escamilla," April 16, 2005.
41. "Shocking Culture of Impunity and Violence," www.freemedia.at/cms/ipi/statements_detail.html?ctxid=CH0055&. . .&year=2008.
42. "Por qué se fue Alejandro Junco," *Reporte Indigo*, September 12, 2008, www.reporteindigo.com.
43. Kevin Sullivan, "Tijuana Gang Figure Held After Slaying of Journalist," *Washington Post*, June 26, 2004.
44. "Amenaza narco a periodistas y soldados," *Reforma.com*, May 28, 2009.
45. Elisabeth Malkin, "Mexico: Arrests in Reporter's Death," *New York Times*, June 13, 2009.

46. Ciro Gómez Leyva, "Dos reporteros de Milenio: el día que el periodismo murio," *Milenio*, April 3, 2010.
47. "Atentados en Morelia: Suman ocho muertos," *El Universal*, September 16, 2008.
48. Ibid.
49. Miguel Ángel, "Aparecen narco-mantas!," *Notiver*, October 5, 2008.
50. Juan Alberto Cedillo, "Pandillas al servicios del narco," *El Universal*, March 3, 2009.
51. Quoted in Diego E. Osorno, "In Two Years the Number of Gang Members Doubles in Monterrey"; the article, which originally appeared in *Milenio*, was reproduced by Kristin Bricker, *The Narcosphere*, March 23, 2009.
52. "Confirman apoyo del narco en protestas de Monterrey," February 14, 2009.
53. "Exige narco retirar militares de NL," *Reforma*, February 13, 2009.
54. "Datos—Los Zetas, un cártel narco que secuestra inmigrantes," April 11, 2011.
55. "Los Zetas' acusan a gobierno en narcomantas," *El Universal*, February 12, 2010.
56. Marc Lacey, "Fearing Drug Cartels, Reporters in Mexico Retreat," *New York Times*, March 13, 2010.
57. Ibid.
58. Ibid.
59. Sandra Dibble, "Judge in Mexico City Sentences Smuggling-Ring Leader to 14 Years," *Signon San Diego*, May 23, 2006.
60. "Manifiesta Wayne apoyo a CNDH," *Reforma*, October 4, 2011.

9

Zetas in Central America

Two decades ago, the Coast Guard, the DEA, and allied US agencies cracked down on cocaine shipments into Florida and other Southeast states. The exporters quickly chose Central America as the new avenue for sending drugs to Mexico en route to America—with Guatemala suffering the worst ravages of criminality.

Its wide open frontier with Mexico—more of a surveyor's line than a border—made Guatemala an ideal venue for Mexican syndicates. There, they found a sanctuary to stockpile drugs and weapons before moving their assets north, in the case of narcotics, across the Rio Grande. Mexican DTOs—notably, Los Zetas and their nemesis, the Sinaloa Cartel—deployed superior force against local criminal bands. Until late 2007, the Lorenzana, Mendoza, and León clans dominated organized crime in Guatemala. For these local entrepreneurs, drugs represented just one of several illicit ventures, which included fraud, embezzlement, money laundering, weapons trafficking, and cardamom spice smuggling. Ever the opportunists, Los Zetas took advantage of the sales channels, relationships, and local know-how accumulated by local Mafias. In addition, Los Zetas also penetrated Belize, Honduras, El Salvador, and Nicaragua.

Guatemalan President Álvaro Colom, who swore the presidential oath on January 14, 2008, is a thin, tall man with long bony fingers. Throughout his tenure, he wore a gaunt face and his yellowed teeth betrayed effects of chain-smoking. The nervous man never set foot outside the colonial presidential palace without a platoon of body-guards. Violence, venality, and an assortment of pressing social needs in a country characterized by poverty, hunger, and murder besieged the seemingly well-intentioned politician.

Guatemala teetered on the brink of a failed state when Colom took office. A wave of criminality slammed his regime before the new leader completed one hundred days in office. To make matters worse, he already struggled with a crooked law-enforcement apparatus, which had neither the resources nor the incentives to stand up to foreign and domestic DTOs. Interior Minister Vinicio Gómez lamented that it was "humanly impossible" to protect the nation's 13 million inhabitants with only 18,744 national policemen—the equivalent of one officer for every 2,400 civilians.[1] By comparison, there were 2.4 sworn officers for every 1,000 people in the United States or 5.8 policemen for every 2,400 inhabitants.[2] In terms of homicides per 100,000 inhabitants, Guatemala (42) came in third after Honduras (78) and El Salvador (65), which was followed by Panama (22), Mexico (18), Nicaragua (13), and Belize (7).[3] In 2010, the US Department of State observed that "the influence of non-state criminal actors rivals or exceeds that of the [Guatemalan] government in up to 40 percent of the country."[4]

Before Colom came to power, analysts considered that less than 1 percent of the six hundred to seven hundred tons of cocaine trafficked north from Colombia to Mexico passed through Central America.[5] Over the course of Colom's four-year rule, cocaine trafficking by truck, air, or ship gave the impulse to the violence that spiraled out of control on his watch. In 2010, US authorities estimated that 70 percent of the narcotics entering Mexico came through, over, or around Guatemala[6]—a figure that has shot up in light of Calderón's pursuit of criminal organizations.

For a decade, one of the more active Guatemalan traffickers was Otto "El Profe" Roberto Herrera García, who linked the Lorenzana syndicate with Colombian and Mexican drug traffickers until his mid-2007 arrest.[7] Once in custody, he famously offered each arresting officer $700,000 if they would let him go. The same generous bribe had vaulted him from a Mexican prison in 2005, but it didn't work in Colombia, where the criminal justice system was more professional.

A constant tug-of-war for power and wealth characterized Guatemala's three largest clans, as well as between and among these organizations and smaller families entrenched at the city level. Based in Zacapa and controlled by Juan José "El Juancho" León Ardón, Los Leones won distinction as the most aggressive underworld family. Los Leones and the Lorenzanas had configured a pact through marriage and, before 2007, had expanded their operations beyond Zacapa into the important, jungle-infested northern departments of the Petén and Alta Verapaz. There, they purchased land, acquired businesses, and practiced intimidation.[8] Their expansion offended his rivals, particularly Hearst Walter Overdick, who would become a notable Zeta ally. Drug boss Otoniel Turcios Marroquín may also have welcomed the Mexican paramilitaries into his country.[9]

Los Zetas Move into Guatemala

In 2007, the Gulf Cartel ordered Los Zetas to Guatemala to "adjust accounts" and assassinate selected local criminals. "Peter," the first Zeta to operate in the country, kept a low profile.[10] The men who followed him did not. The next year the Mexican paramilitaries used sophisticated tactics and horrendous might to subdue Los Leones.

By March 2008, Colom had decided to confront the nation's flagrant insecurity, but he was neither prepared nor equipped to respond to the rapid collapse of Guatemalan barons at the hands of the invaders. As Colom committed his administration to the Herculean goal of public security, Walter Overdick, who operated out of the coffee-producing Alta Verapaz capital of Cobán, was slowly becoming acquainted with Los Zetas, who readily paid for cocaine with thick wads of hundred dollar bills and transported their purchases to Mexico.

As the relationship strengthened, Overdick and his Guatemalan cohorts, who also suffered under the strong-arm treatment administered by the Leones family, began to work closely with the free-spending Mexicans. An unprecedented influx of drugs proved what bureaucrats call a "game changer": the stakes were raised, lives threatened, and, ultimately, men with Los Leones ripped off a cargo of cocaine that Los Zetas had protected for the Gulf Cartel.[11] Until that moment, the Mexican renegades seemed content to remain above the fray in the conflict between and among local kingpins. However, Los Zetas had labored assiduously to establish a criminal brand, highlighted by fear driven by unspeakable cruelty. No one stole from Los Zetas and got away with it in Mexico! Guatemala would be no different. In keeping with their credo, Los Zetas hatched a plan with Overdick to eliminate "El Juancho" León Ardón, also known to Colombia's National Civil Police (PNC) as "Juancho León" or "Mister J." They took advantage of a requested audience to coax their adversary into a death trap.

El Juancho arrived on March 25, 2008, in the village of Rio Hondo, Zacapa—a picturesque region known for its crystal clear river, hardened cheese, hand-rolled cigars, and European ancestors. The "department," the name of the country's state-level jurisdictions, lies roughly halfway between the Caribbean port of Puerto Barrios and Guatemala City. It goes without saying that El Juancho had traveled in a convoy of bulletproof SUVs to meet with Los Zetas' and Overdick's men.

Bodyguards ringed the mustachioed, beady-eyed crook as he alighted from his truck in the parking lot of the Laguna spa. It was nearing 2:30 p.m. on a weekday, and El Juancho nonchalantly waited for his contacts to show up.[12] He seemed oblivious to the fact that he was standing dead center in a kill zone, part of an ambush that had been planned for months. El Juancho's Zeta contacts had enticed him to get together to smoke the peace pipe so everyone could make even more money. Minutes before his arrival, two groups of thirty and fifty thugs formed a loose circle around the parking area. Out of sight, they immediately assumed firing positions and awaited the command to attack.

Juancho began chitchatting with his reception committee. After fifteen minutes, the stilted bonhomie evaporated when the lead Zeta gunman squeezed off his first round.[13] A cacophony of automatic rifle fire erupted. Juancho's men fought back. They managed to keep their boss alive for more than forty minutes as storeowners and other citizens belly flopped to the ground and scrambled under parked vehicles. Not even local police or security units dared approach the battleground.[14] Armed with AK-47 and AR-15 rifles, fragmentation grenades, and grenade launchers, the attackers demolished two trucks and littered the pavement with corpses before speeding off. Two of El Juancho's men were found charred to a husk, still gripping their M-16 rifles. Once the smoke cleared, local police showed up to inspect the site and figure out what had happened. El Juancho, one of his brothers, and six of his henchmen had perished. Two others, including El Juancho's cousin, later succumbed to wounds at a nearby hospital.

The PNC were not certain of the Zetas' involvement until the investigation led them to a house in Mixco, just outside of Guatemala City, where on April 9, 2008, they captured several Mexicans who claimed to be Guatemalans.[15] One of the men, Juan González Díaz, told the arresting officers that he sold cars for a living, but investigators discovered that he was actually Daniel "El Cachetes"/"Puffy Cheeks" Pérez Rojas, a high-ranking Zeta and the second-in-command of the paramilitaries in Guatemala.[16] They recovered from El Cachetes' belongings a map that pinpointed Los Zetas' beachheads: the department of Zacapa, the region around Sayaxché in the Petén, and Cobán, in Alta Verapaz.

By late April 2008, Colom had learned that a Zeta-supported pirate radio station was blasting recruitment advertisements every five hours to listeners in Sayaxché and La Libertad. They offered employment to ex-members of the Guatemalan armed forces, with a preference for the deadly Kaibiles. The recruits would help guard vehicles used to move cocaine from various points in the Petén west into Mexico.[17]

In late 2007, residents of Cobán, less than one hundred miles south of Sayaxché, smelled a rat when heavily armed men rolled through their streets in spanking new pickups. The strangers openly brandished automatic rifles, and the PNC didn't seem to notice or even care. Los Zetas finally displayed their local muscle five months after El Cachetes'

Map 3 Map of Guatemala

Source: GraphicMaps.com.

arrest. On August 16, 2008, they trumpeted their presence in the Cobán area by killing two street dealers.

Overdick and his Mexican allies profited from murdering El Juancho, but at a steep price. As Los Zetas settled into Cobán, they began to take advantage of the lax police presence and submissive populace. Although Overdick functioned as the local criminal boss, he could not rein in the newcomers. Still, he felt safe. After all, Los Zetas required his network—it extended from the Guatemalan Congress to weapons' smugglers to local police commanders—to manage their nascent enterprise in Guatemala. As Los Zetas settled into Cobán, Raymundo "Comandante Gori" Almanza Morales replaced the jailed El Cachetes as the paramilitary's *número uno* in the country.[18]

A week after Los Zetas' high-profile murders in Cobán, law-enforcement personnel in northern Huehuetenango department discovered seven Zeta safe houses near the village of La Democracia, close to the Mexican border. That the outlaws had acquired real estate furnished ironclad evidence that they had expanded operations from the Petén and Alta Verapaz to Huehuetenango. In 2008, however, they remained focused on Alta Verapaz, a department nestled in a strategic enclave surrounded by Izabal on the east coast, Zacapa to the south, and the Petén to the north.

On September 3, 2008, only a few weeks after executing the Cobán street sellers, Los Zetas kidnapped and killed a third vendor. Police found Carlos Humberto Alvarado's body punctured by more than three hundred single cocaine doses, locally referred to as *colmillos*. If they were powerful enough to kill El Juancho with impunity, the Mexicans could wield the whip hand throughout the country.

Crews were still cleaning up the debris around Alvarado's body when Cobán traffickers foolishly provoked a midday firefight with Los Zetas. At the end of the shoot-out, police found eleven grenades, two M-16 rifles fixed with grenade launchers, one AK-47, and a car apparently stolen in Mexico. "It used to be relaxed around here," a local cop told reporters after the shoot-out.[19]

Los Zetas were only getting started. El Cachetes' March 2008 arrest momentarily disrupted their projecting their brand over a broad swath of Guatemalan territory, stretching from the Caribbean coast to the Mexican border. Looking back from 2011, it is clear that Los Zetas had identified Cobán as its center of activities for Central America, not just Guatemala. Consequently, before lunging southward, they had to stabilize their Guatemalan field operations and intelligence networks.

In September 2008, Colom authorized the issuance of warrants for the arrest of ex-Security and Administrative Affairs Minister Carlos Quintanilla and former director of the Secretariat for Strategic Analysis, Gustavo Solano. The men stood accused of bugging the president and first lady's home and offices and attempting to destabilize the government. Were they guilty? And if the charges were true, were they freelancing or might Los Zetas have been their clients? Rumors swirled that Los Zetas has penetrated the Colom administration and, by extension, the police and military.[20]

While on helicopter patrol in early October 2008, elite Guatemalan soldiers detailed to fight local drug syndicates received orders to intercept a single-prop aircraft that was about to land in Fray Bartolomé de las Casas, Alta Verapaz. As the helicopters neared the parked plane, automatic rifle fire sounded. The soldiers dove to cover. They quickly learned, though, that they were outmatched when five pickup trucks filled with gunmen arrived to support Los Zetas, who had already engaged the troops. Two more trucks roared onto the scene. Even with the help of the local PNC, the military men had to cede the terrain to the Mexican aggressors.[21] And so Los Zetas expanded their might and presence across Guatemala. As in Mexico, the paramilitaries demonstrated their readiness to face off successfully with police and military squads.

From their base in Cobán, the Mexicans secured routes to move cocaine into Guatemala from the Caribbean, Honduras, and El Salvador. The Petén department played a significant role in this strategy and helped illustrate why Los Zetas aligned with Kaibiles. Traditionally, Guatemala's Mendozas, working for the Sinaloa Cartel, had held sway over drug corridors. As Los Zetas' presence in the remote, inhospitable department evolved, the Mendozas' grip on this region loosened—to the point that key members of the clan fled to Spain rather than face the deadly insurgents.[22]

A horse race in which the prize was a new car purchased in Chiapas and smuggled into Guatemala detonated a clash between Los Zetas and the Sinaloans in Huehuetenango. According to local reports, Los Zetas and their Guatemalan counterparts had organized the competition. It was a day of celebration and relaxation until El Chapo's men ruined the party by inciting a shoot-out. Police arrived in Agua Zarca, a village in Huehuetenango, soon after the fusillade had stopped. Sinaloa loyalists supposedly dominated the pueblo, which would explain the fracas with Los Zetas. Police arrested the wounded and surveyed the blood-drenched landscape, finding seventeen bodies, as well as a red truck smashed against a tree. The Tamaulipas-registered vehicle contained a small arsenal in its cab. Among the firearms and grenades, the officers discovered a shaving kit, cologne, and other personal effects. They learned that the truck had never been recorded as passing through an official border crossing. The driver had apparently left Tamaulipas to make the two-day drive for the horse race. Investigators suspected that he was in town only to deliver cash and supplies and had only planned to hang around for the festivities.[23]

Authorities found a second pickup with Guatemalan plates on the Mexican side of the border. More than ninety-four bullet holes had perforated the side paneling and rear of the vehicle.[24] One eyewitness remembered that a helicopter had arrived from Mexico to rescue the injured and ferry them north. Los Zetas likely lost that battle, waged over control of a specific slice of turf, but had managed to gain a foothold in the important Huehuetenango department and eventually acquire a remote ranch for storage and, possibly, training, near La Democracia.

Amid a year of impressive Zeta expansion into Guatemala, in December 2008 the PNC apprehended Abel Díaz Alzate. He allegedly ran the organization's business in the east: from Los Amates, Izabal, a department with access to the strategic Caribbean port of Puerto Barrios. This arrest brought to sixteen the number of Los Zetas whom Guatemalans had thrust behind bars during the year.[25] Though important, the seizures did little to impede the ex-Special Forces' inexorable march into Central America. Guatemalan officials proclaimed that Los Zetas traveled across the country in caravans of thirty, forty, and fifty armored vans, crammed with men hefting AK-47s and brandishing grenades.[26]

Before New Year's Day that welcomed in 2009, a Guatemalan interior ministry official claimed that approximately 80 percent of the population lived in abject poverty. Thus, performing a simple job as a lookout or messenger for Los Zetas could earn in a few days more than the individual could hope to pocket in a year.[27] Echoing the official statement, US Ambassador Steven G. McFarland declared in late 2008 that approximately four hundred metric tons of cocaine, worth some $7 billion, passed through Central America annually, and most of it through Guatemala.[28] It was a significant departure from just three years before, when a local report suggested that 150 tons transited the country annually.[29] The government took some satisfaction from making sixteen arrests, yet it had done little to stanch the cocaine entering at a volume that had tripled in three years.

Early in 2009, Colom's office reported that more than four hundred Zetas operated inside Guatemala, indicating that the group had zeroed in on Alta Verapaz, San Marcos, the Petén, and the capital, Guatemala City. In light of the map confiscated after El Cachetes' April 2008 arrest, Los Zetas maintained a presence in eight of Guatemala's twenty-two departments, a block of real estate equal to the size of Virginia, including the entire top half of the country from the Caribbean to the Pacific and the length of the six-hundred-mile-long Guatemala–Mexico border.[30]

By early 2009, Los Zetas had transcended simply laying siege to geography. The lethal group had established a connection with a guard who opened the Mariscal Zavala military depot to the Mexicans, allowing them to pick and choose among the available weapons, ammunition, and explosives. At the same time, Colom received an intelligence report that between July 2007 and January 2008, Los Zetas had stolen more than five hundred military-style weapons, including automatic rifles, pistols, machine guns, and grenade launchers from the presumably well-protected base. Los Zetas operators had also filched thousands of fragmentation grenades and rounds of ammunition.[31]

A year after taking office, Colom appeared to grasp the scope of criminality afflicting his country. On the basis of a limited police capability and need to ramp up security, the chief executive commanded the military to concentrate on drug trafficking in the Petén, many areas of which were a no-man's-land. The presence of the Mexicans had a peculiar result when the national emergency hotline—number 110—registered three phone calls, none of which sought to help capture wrongdoers. When one caller vowed to kill the president on March 1, 2009, officials concluded that Los Zetas or their sympathizers had made the threats.[32] Undeterred by the death message, Colom dispatched one thousand soldiers to the Petén to shore up Guatemala's border with Mexico's Tabasco state. Armored vehicles, helicopters, and surveillance aircraft supported the boots on the ground.

Days after the chief executive issued this command, a scandal burst into the headlines, precipitating demonstrations in Guatemala's Central Plaza and attracting worldwide attention. Lawyer Rodrigo Rosenberg claimed to have "direct knowledge" of a conspiracy that involved embezzlement and murder orchestrated by Colom and his ambitious wife, Sandra, a formidable figure in her own right who invited comparisons with Eva Perón. The episode had more twists and turns than a John Grisham novel. The highly respected corporate attorney, who had earned advanced law degrees from Cambridge and Harvard, prepared an eighteen-minute video. He looked into the camera and said, "My name is Rodrigo Rosenberg Marzano, and alas, if you are hearing or seeing this message, it means that I've been murdered by President Álvaro Colom, with help of [the chief executive's private secretary] Gustavo Alejos."[33]

In fact Rosenberg was killed on May 19, 2009, while riding his bicycle and listening to his iPod on a side street in the capital. An assassin suddenly materialized and began pumping 9 mm bullets into the forty-eight-year-old lawyer's head. The unfolding of this bewildering story line, which haunted Colom's hapless administration for more than two years, lies beyond the purview of this study. As it turned out, the UN-backed International Commission against Impunity in Guatemala conducted a lengthy, painstaking investigation only to conclude that Rosenberg, depressed over the death of his girlfriend and her father, had contrived his own death to discredit the Colom government and its military-intelligence apparatus.[34]

Weeks after Rosenberg's damning accusation, Colom benefited from a modest accomplishment when, in late March 2009, soldiers in the Petén seized five hundred fragmentation grenades and an armful of AK-47s. This action took place a year after the Los Zetas had eliminated El Juancho, and the situation proved to be just as volatile. While Guatemalan soldiers scoured the Petén for signs of Los Zetas, the PNC picked up an unidentified aircraft on radar and pinpointed its landing on a clandestine airstrip on the San Jorge ranch in Río Dulce, Izabal. The police acted to intercept the plane. Once they entered the compound, Los Zetas laid down a blanket of gunfire, pinning the officers and enabling the criminals to unload the aircraft and fly away.[35] Police quickly secured the scene and found a twin-engine aircraft, five luxury SUVs, a motorcycle, an ATV, three AK-47 rifles, eleven fragmentation grenades, a laptop, and a satellite phone.[36] Such an outburst prompted a Brookings Institute analyst to suggest that policymakers should regard Guatemala, rather than Mexico, as a failed state.[37]

Less than a week after Los Zetas had again bested local forces, elite Guatemalan antinarcotic soldiers discovered a ranch near Playas Grande in Quiché department, situated between Alta Verapaz and Huehuetenango. The new soldiers, who encountered no resistance upon entering the area, seized five hundred fragmentation grenades, five AK-47 rifles, and an assortment of military equipment. Investigators later determined that 157 of the 500 grenades had been stolen from the Mariscal Zavala military base and that the ranch was a Zeta training camp, the first detected in Guatemala. They surmised that at least two Zetas could have run the facility, which trained as many as thirty-five enlistees in each recruiting class. Neither the military nor the police managed to track down Álvaro "El Sapo"/"The Toad" Gómez, reportedly an Overdick confidant who oversaw the compound.[38]

Colom's anticartel offensive achieved results on October 28, 2009, when police stumbled upon a Zeta-operated ranch near Nuevo Progreso, a tourism center in the Huehuetenango area near the Mexican frontier. Since arriving in Huehuetenango more than a year earlier, the invaders had invested in infrastructure that betokened plans for protracted initiatives. There were a dozen safe houses on the property. Each had been recently constructed, and according to one investigator, the buildings contained neither furniture nor other trappings of family life. After a meticulous search, police discovered 934 kilograms of cocaine buried in an empty water tank next to one of the residences. Even though the PNC seized twenty-four luxury SUVs, they had to ward off an attack on the highway while transporting the vehicles to Guatemala City.[39]

Days after finding the ranch, Colom admitted that Mexican syndicates dominated Huehuetenango. After nearly eighteen months of butting heads with Los Zetas, the president was forced to confess that his efforts had not met his ballyhooed expectations for improving the nation's security.

Los Zetas Drive into El Salvador

Guatemala served well as a training ground. Los Zetas exuded such belief in their safety in the country that they reached south along the isthmus. El Salvador, an over-populated, impoverished nation, furnished eager cadres among the Mara Salvatrucha (MS-13), who attended training seminars in the Petén, reportedly near the Laguna del Tigre national park.[40] From July to August 2009, Los Zetas instructors hosted as many as forty MS-13 gangsters from various municipalities in El Salvador, Honduras, and Guatemala. Investigations later revealed that one of the three men, "El Burro," who ran El Salvador's "Cartel de Texis," had organized the field trip.[41] In all likelihood, the street thugs received weapons training, instruction on a rifle range, and guidance in military tactics.[42]

When news of the camp surfaced in the Salvadorian media, then director of the Anti-Gang Center in San Salvador, Douglas García Funes, claimed that MS-13 members in El Salvador had no direct connections with the intruders. He made this assertion even though the Mexicans clearly planned to reach beyond their well-fortified Guatemalan bastion, deep into El Salvador and Honduras.

Indeed, Los Zetas were quietly projecting their influence in El Salvador, where gang members were ready, willing, and eager to perform contract work.[43] In El Salvador, the Mara Salvatrucha provided access to the underworld. The country's other major street hoodlums, the Eighteenth Street gang, initially shied from cooperating with the Mexicans. Finally, they decided that collaboration advanced their best interests.[44] Los Zetas hired these goons to perform such low-level jobs as trafficking small amounts of cocaine or shipping pistols and gun parts. In this case, Los Zetas' interests were logistical and business oriented—not violent. Their presence in the small country appeared to be limited, though their actions accentuated unrest.

Map 4 Map of Caribbean Basin

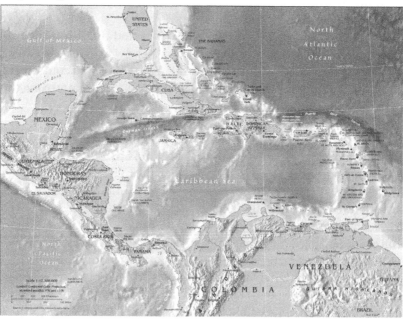

Source: Courtesy of the University of Texas Libraries, The University of Texas at Austin.

In mid-2009, Defense Minister David Munguía Payés admitted that the ruffians and drug traffickers committed 85 percent of the crimes in his nation.[45] The closer the relationship between Los Zetas and the MS-13, the more the latter absorbed skills and deviousness from their considerably more organized, sophisticated, and potent Mexican patrons. To make matters worse, the Mexicans often paid with drugs, which the local hooligans then cut and sold on the retail market. These *narcomenudeo* sales heightened the recipients' earning power as well as their control over specific slices of turf. Gangbangers suddenly had more to win or lose over battles, and violence took off like Roman candles. Not interested in the public security fallout in El Salvador, Los Zetas continued to recruit and operate in the postage stamp-sized Central American republic, engaging ever more fiercely the national security apparatus that even in 2012 lacked the money, troops, and will to challenge superior Mexican DTOs.[46]

Los Zetas also penetrated the Salvadorian armed forces, though for different reasons. The Mara Salvatrucha and other street gangs were ultimately contractors; Zeta military contacts in El Salvador opened an arms smuggling pipeline from the Salvadorian army's stockpile into the hands of gunmen in Mexico. Los Zetas' operators in El Salvador convinced several men to work on their behalf inside the Salvadorian military, but one stands out—Major Élmer Espinoza Hércules. His decision to switch allegiances constituted a coup for the Mexicans.

Espinoza was widely respected within the armed forces, had obtained a relatively high rank, was on the fast track for promotion, and, above all, was considered one of the military's top explosives experts. He met the second man in Los Zetas' arms smuggling ring while traveling from San Salvador to Santa Ana, where he stopped to purchase watermelons. The vendor turned out to be a former policeman, who was a confidant of the number three in their growing network. He was an armorer, who for most of 2008 and 2009 had gained the respect and confidence of many National Civil Police members by adroitly repairing and modifying their weapons. The fourth figure rounded out Major Espinoza's smuggling ring. The outfit worked with the Engineering Command of the Armed Forces, charged with destroying weapons in poor condition. Together, the men boasted the skills and linkages to spirit weapons out of Salvadorian armories. They often buried their illegal cargo under mounds of watermelons.[47]

In September 2009, Major Espinoza arrived at a friend's residence in northwest Santa Ana province, contiguous to Guatemala, to deliver a crate of weapons and other supplies, claiming that it would be a while before he could return for the material. Five months later police arrived at the house, seized the armaments they believed destined for Los Zetas, and captured the former policeman—the only one of the four conspirators to have been apprehended to date. Thanks to suspected informants within the police and PGR, the other three caught wind of the arrest and left the country. One source consulted by local reporters was convinced that Espinoza fled to Guatemala, where he took up residence in Cobán.[48] The major continued his arms smuggling operation with impunity, allegedly dispatching orders to his younger brother, a sergeant who was privy to information about weapons to be destroyed.

Salvadorian authorities believe that Espinoza continued to traffic arms, to the point that a unit of his network attempted to steal a box of 1,800 M-67 fragmentation grenades by feigning their shipment to an unknown foreign destination. Military investigators recovered the explosives in April 2011, arrested six military officers, and cashiered four high-ranking officials.[49] Later, other members of the Salvadorian brass were found to be in league with Mexican criminals.

Apart from the United States, where dealers ensured a steady stream of long-barrel rifles, shotguns, and pistols, Central America was the second largest source of armaments. Los Zetas needed to sustain their position in Mexico. Guatemala and El Salvador proved to be wellsprings of weapons, which were increasingly more difficult to procure above the Rio Grande. Bullets and grenades obtained in El Salvador may have been used against the US Consulate General in October 2008, and again in January 2009, when Los Zetas also attacked a Televisa building in Monterrey.[50] A congeries of elements—weak institutions, low salaries, and few incentives to remain on the right side of the law—favored Los Zetas in Central America, especially Guatemala, El Salvador, and Honduras. Not every man was willing to take a bribe, but criminal bands needed only a few.

By early 2011, the intricacies of Major Espinoza's operation and the readiness of fellow military men to convey weapons to Mexican Mafias convinced Salvadorian authorities that Los Zetas posed an acute threat in their weak, corrupt nation. When members of the Eighteenth Street gang set ablaze a public bus in February 2011, intelligence officials concluded that the country's two largest outfits—the MS-13 and the Eighteenth Street gang—were in league with Los Zetas. The bus attack, they believed, was an initiation test for the Eighteenth Street gang.[51]

Salvadorian street gangs evolved in their relationship with Los Zetas, to the point that they began kidnapping migrants en route to the United States. They would then hand the captives over to Los Zetas in Mexico, where the paramilitaries would demand that the victims' families fork over cash to attain the liberty of their loved ones.[52]

Salvadorian authorities continued to piece together the threads linking Los Zetas and street gangs. Simultaneously, rumors began to circulate that the Mexicans had established a "little pathway," to impel smuggling operations through Chalatenango and Santa Ana provinces. *El caminito* provided a conduit from Honduras through El Salvador to Guatemala.[53] The contact with the local hired guns extended beyond corridors when, in early 2011, Salvadorian police discovered a Zeta training camp outside San Salvador, replete with a stash of $15 million. The DTO had hidden the facility in a coffee plantation, located on the edge of the Guazapa volcano. Its presence on a prominent feature of San Salvador's skyline suggested just how close Los Zetas had come to the country's capital and reminded some of the early 1990s, when guerrillas of the Farabundo Martí National Liberation Front had reached the same location just before peace negotiations began.[54]

In May 2011, pending cases, continuing investigations, and the undisputed existence of *el caminito* compelled President Mauricio Funes to confirm Los Zetas' presence in his nation.[55] The outsiders were less concerned about coercing local gangs and citizens than in obtaining recruits from MS-13 and Eighteenth Street gangs and carving out corridors. Of course, the longer Los Zetas remain in El Salvador, the ever-more powerful contractors may consider challenging their master, much like the Mexican paramilitaries turned on the Gulf Cartel. In 2012, however, Los Zetas pose a relatively minor threat in El Salvador compared to Guatemala.

Los Zetas Consolidate Hold on Guatemala

More than two years after the March 2008 murder of El Juancho, Guatemalan authorities amassed enough evidence to try Los Zetas for the crime. El Cachetes Pérez Rojas headed the list of fourteen suspects. At the time of their mid-2010 trial, the prosecution claimed to possess some five hundred pieces of evidence linking suspects to various murders committed on the day that Juan José León literally bit the dust. The prosecutors assembled 190 witnesses and experts to buttress their case. The PNC took no chances; it kept El Cachetes and an alleged Zeta associate in prison, allowing them to participate in the proceedings via video.[56] Three rings of security surrounded Pérez Rojas; the Guatemalan government went to similar lengths to protect the judges assigned to review the facts, determine guilt or innocence, and, if necessary, sentence the men. On the third day of the trial, the army placed a tank outside the tribunal's buildings.[57]

After hearing testimony, considering evidence, and deliberating for fifteen hours, the head magistrate, Judge Jazmín Barrios, sentenced the fourteen men to prison terms ranging from 43 to 313 years. The court found them guilty of crimes including murder, illegal transport of weapons, aggravated robbery, and the use of forged documents. El Cachetes and six other Mexicans remain in the Preventive Center for Men of Zone 18 in Guatemala City, which is still protected by a tank.[58]

The trial represented a triumph for the beleaguered Colom administration. Yet it failed to destroy that Los Zetas' blueprint for controlling the ancient Mayan country. In mid-October 2010, sixteen vehicles approached a police roadblock in northeastern Petén, south of the awesome Tikal Mayan ruins whose pyramids tower from the lush jungle canopy. The convoy rumbled to a stop, and the lead truck's front-seat passenger rolled down his window. He bellowed into a megaphone, "We are Los Zetas. We are going to pass through. We don't want any problems." To punctuate his last statement, several men fired a few rounds into the air. The display of force was more than enough to persuade the police to open the road barrier and allow the convoy to pass. In all fairness, the law-enforcement officers quickly alerted the military to the threat, leading to firefights between the Mexicans and the Guatemalan armed forces.[59]

Two months after this showdown, the Mexicans again demonstrated their prowess despite some arrests and the conviction of El Cachetes. On December 8, 2010, some twenty Zetas armed with AK-47s, grenade launchers, and pistols assaulted a prison in Malacatán, situated in the San Marcos department near the Mexican border. The attackers killed a guard and a passerby and wounded several others during a ploy to free one man. He was Élmer Aroldo Zelada Galdámez, who was suspected of murdering and subsequently dismembering Guatemalan soccer star Carlos Mercedes Vásquez—found dead ten days before the getaway.[60] Reports called the raid the first of its kind in Guatemala.[61] For Los Zetas, who had freed comrades in Mexico, the episode represented part of their operational and moral-building repertoire.

Colom responded by declaring a state of emergency in the Alta Verapaz, where Los Zetas had set up headquarters in Cobán—one of the three command posts denoted on El Cachetes' map. Just three hours by automobile from Guatemala City, control of this picturesque city blessed with caves, waterfalls, forests, and the rare Quetzal bird enabled the Mexicans to call the shots over crucial territory. Further, it provided access to the Petén and Izabal departments, the border with Mexico, and the Franja Transversal del Norte road system. Upon completion, this corridor will join the Atlantic to the Pacific along the country's north. Yet once they had moved into the city and made common cause with the Overdicks, the Mexicans had the upper hand. By the end of 2010, Zeta gunmen had taken up residence in San Marcos plaza, traditionally used for surveillance. Local residents decried the strangers for flaunting their weapons while sitting on park benches, swigging beer, and ogling women. Los Zetas allegedly installed a cordon sanitaire around the local McDonalds, while their commander tucked into a tasty "Combo Meal."[62]

The prison foray and other affronts to Guatemalan security, such as Los Zetas' ostentatious behavior in Cobán, compelled President Colom to impose a thirty-day state of siege on Alta Verapaz, beginning on December 19, 2010. Residents responded to the ukase with relief and dismay. Many citizens, tired of watching mysterious armed men zipping around in pickup trucks, hoped that the decree would restrict these maneuvers. During the one-month period, five hundred agents undertook twenty-one seizures of materials and equipment from sixteen safe houses.[63]

Local media portrayed the bold action as a declaration of war against Los Zetas, which by late 2010, controlled as much as 42,085 square miles in the country, roughly equivalent to the size of Ohio.[64] Other reports claimed that Los Zetas held sway over six of Guatemala's twenty-two departments and employed as many as eight hundred Mexicans throughout the country in 2010—a year when the Guatemalan authorities confiscated only 2 of the suspected 250 to 300 tons of pure cocaine that the DEA estimated entered the United States from Mexico.[65] Interviews suggested that the government played up Los Zetas' presence to garner international attention and financial support. After all, Los Zetas undermined public security, along with helpmates within indigenous crime families.[66]

As the clampdown stretched through the holidays and into January 2011, bomb threats kept citizens at home. A general fear, described as "psychosis," permeated the community, yet there were results. Crime nose-dived 30 percent, and the government seized weapons, fragmentation grenades, and forty-eight vehicles.[67] Such modest achievements did not satisfy Colom. His priorities remained the unrealistic objectives of governability in Alta Verapaz and security in Cobán. To show that he meant business, he extended the state of siege for another month because this was the "only measure that exists [to take] control of territory from drug traffickers."[68] Some 350 National Civil Police agents and fifty soldiers, down from seven hundred during the previous extraordinary action, remained encamped to secure the city.

Thirty days later, Colom returned to Cobán to proclaim the end of the state of siege. His administration announced a 55 percent reduction in homicides, which contributed to a 43 percent decrease in overall crime in the department. Agents had also seized a total of 478 weapons, but to what effect? For all the media coverage and bravado, many observers thought the exercise was just a publicity stunt. Several former government officials told one reporter that the whole emergency action, which was just one step removed from a declaration of war, had been a "show."[69]

The recrudescence of trafficking after the lifting of the state of siege indicated that the crackdown had failed to checkmate Los Zetas. Even while it applied, *sicarios* linked to the renegades killed a local businessman as he trained for the city's highly touted "half marathon." Shortly after the February 25 murder, gunmen emptied clips into a car shop, before igniting several vehicles six kilometers outside of Cobán.[70]

Los Zetas also continued trafficking. They received a drug shipment from Honduras in March 2011 near the Salinas River in Chisec, a municipality twenty-five miles northeast of Cobán. From Chisec, the consignment moved to the Raxruhá municipality, bordering the Petén. This variant of the several drug routes that Los Zetas operated in Guatemala's Alta Verapaz department remained open after the state of siege. So did their interest in corrupting, intimidating, or assassinating anyone who stood against them.

In a separate series of vicious events, Los Zetas demonstrated their dominance in the Zacapa, Alta Verapaz, and the Petén drug netherworld. On May 10, they initiated what appears to have been a carefully planned strategy by kidnapping Luis Carlos Bardales Chacón, who reportedly was traveling from Zacapa to the Petén to make a purchase. Later that day, Bardales' father, Luis Alberto Bardales Tobar, received a ransom command. The kidnappers demanded $58,000 and that the payment be made at kilometer 479 along the highway between Santa

Ana and Ciudad Flores in the Petén. With his daughter-in-law, Keiry Eunice Franco Salguero, the victim's father left the next day to pay the fee. They called family members in Zacapa at kilometer 476, and it was the last time anyone heard from them.[71]

On May 14, Los Zetas struck Los Leones by kidnapping and killing Haroldo Waldemar León, brother and replacement for El Juancho. The next day, police found the bodies of other victims, all of whom had been dismembered, a trade mark of the Mexicans' demonic behavior.

As the state of siege progressed in the Petén, investigators picked up the trail of Hugo "Comandante Bruja"/"Commander Witch" Álvarez Gómez Vásquez, a Zeta believed to be responsible for the atrocity. Commander Witch reportedly followed the orders of Z-200, the twenty-something nephew of a well-placed Zeta in Mexico.[72] Z-200 may have become the chief Zeta in Guatemala after Flavio "El Amarillo" Mendez Santiago, an El Cachetes sidekick, was arrested in Oaxaca in January 2011.[73] Speculation about the identify of Z-200 revolves around Roberto Rivero Arana, The Executioner's young nephew, who was taken into custody in late March 2010, and El 40, who spends a good deal of time in Guatemala.

Allan Stowlinsky Vidaurre, one of the attorneys responsible for the eventual capture of Comandante Bruja, went missing on May 23 only to show up the next day butchered and stuffed in five garbage bags, while his head was discovered in Cobán's central market. Local authorities attributed the fiendishness to Z-200.[74]

Fewer than fifteen years after the 1996 conclusion of Guatemala's thirty-six-year civil conflict, Los Zetas had brought a different kind of warfare to the country—one that the government was unprepared to wage. During the Colom's presidency, Los Zetas consistently resisted his every move. Even when he decided to use the military to control Alta Verapaz and then the Petén, the interlopers weathered the storm and organized surgical strikes to prove their invincibility.

Los Zetas' Guatemalan master plan depended on a route from Honduras to northern Mexico, fostering shipments across El Salvador, Honduras, and Guatemala. Alta Verapaz lay at the center of this scheme, with Izabal, Zacapa, and the Petén as important pieces in Los Zetas' overall scheme. When Los Zetas made their first independent incursion into Central America in March 2008, their success hinged on (1) dominating the eastern half of Guatemala, (2) capturing Zacapa by eliminating El Juancho, (3) allying with Overdick in Cobán, (4) shoving the Mendozas out of the Petén, and (5) delivering a crushing strike against Los Leones by murdering El Juancho's brother Héctor. Their thrust into El Salvador opened alternative corridors. For its part, Honduras furnished the receptacle for Colombian cocaine, possibly provided by Medellín Cartel descendants known as the Oficina de Envigado. A mélange of smaller groups comprised this body, which struck deals with street gangs to preserve a grip on their territory and businesses.[75]

Guatemalan intelligence officials confirmed the Honduras–Guatemala–Mexico trafficking thoroughfare as a lucrative and well-managed route. Notebooks gathered from a Los Zetas' safe house indicated that its Honduran operations included moving cocaine through Tela on the Caribbean coast approximately sixty kilometers northeast of San Pedro Sula. Receipts revealed that the Mexicans paid as much as $12,000 to boat operators to haul ashore cargoes arriving in the Caribbean Sea. They configured similar arrangements in Omoa, also on the coast and located some thirty-seven kilometers above San Pedro Sula. Between February and September 2009, Los Zetas dispatched 110 million dollars' worth of cocaine and heroin from Honduras, through Izabal into either Quiché or the Petén. Captured documents disclosed that Los Zetas' moved eight thousand kilos of cocaine through Central America during this seven-month period. The drug, which commanded $25,000 a kilo in Houston, Texas, generated upwards of $200 million in 2009.[76]

A Pérez Molina Solution?

As Los Zetas continued to flail at Álvaro Colom in May 2011, the ever-more stooped and fatigued chief executive faced a donnybrook in the political arena. He could not seek reelection, and his wife Sandra, who divorced him to run, failed to get on the ballot.[77] Retired General Otto Pérez Molina, sixty-one, the army's tough-as-nails intelligence director during the thirty-six-year civil conflict that ended in 1996, presented himself as a latter-day "Man on Horseback." He played a key role in the protracted internal strife—labeled "the dirtiest of Latin America's dirty wars"—in which more than 200,000 people died or disappeared. Paramilitary death squads with names like Eye for an Eye pursued counterinsurgency based on the adage "drain the sea to kill the fish," culminating in what a UN commission deemed acts of genocide.[78]

Pérez Molina argued that the inept Colom had permitted cartels to have the run of the country, and pledged to emulate Álvaro Uribe, who combated narco-trafficking and insurgencies in Colombia during his eight-year tenure. His vow to wield a "strong hand" against escalating lawlessness resonated with the public.[79]

"I regard it as an advantage that the thirty years I was in the army gave me the opportunity to know the whole country, to live inside, to be close to the problem," he told a reporter. "The training, discipline, [and] order are important attributes when you're in government and need to make decisions," he added.[80]

Although a popular plank in his platform, a militaristic approach against Los Zetas and DTOs will plunge Guatemala deeper into the regional "drug war."

Outgoing President Colom left a mixed legacy. In a BBC appearance, he admitted that the first two years of his presidency involved a "massive purge" of police. He claimed that he had thrown seven of Guatemala's ten most-wanted criminals behind bars, and, while Los Zetas still existed, they were "disarticulated" and "neutralized."[81]

Within days of the interview, explosions at the Fuentes del Norte bus station in Poptún demonstrated that the Mexicans were still out for blood. Poptún stands as the gateway to the Petén and, from Los Zetas' perspective, links Honduras and Belize with their access routes through the northern department to Mexico. This municipality ranks third in the organization's design for control of the Guatemalan criminal structure, with Cobán in Alta Verapaz and Sayaxché in the western Petén ranking first and second, respectively.

The September 14, 2011, attack on the terminal sent a clear message to the Mendoza family, which has aided El Chapo in transporting drugs through the Petén. One of owners of the firebombed building, Milton Oswaldo Mendoza Matta, is related to Haroldo Mendoza, a Petén businessman thought to be closely linked to the Sinaloans.[5] This attack was the latest in a series of events to drive the Mendoza family out of the Petén—a bully pulpit of venality they are loath to vacate.

As the title of an early October report suggested, Los Zetas will present a headache to Guatemala's new president. As a loosely constructed network of operators arrayed throughout the country, the Mexicans in late 2011 commanded vital corridors to Mexico and, since 2010, have benefited from surging revenues.[82]

Poptún could emerge as a hotspot for Pérez Molina. Not only is it Los Zetas' third most important Zeta plaza in Guatemala, it provides a regional base for remaining active-duty Kaibiles. Los Zetas strive to control real estate throughout the isthmus to export cocaine and other drugs to American consumers. The danger posed by Mexico's cartels precipitated meetings among Calderón and his Central American counterparts. In June 2011, the seven Central American nations convened an "International Conference in Support of the Central American Security Strategy" in Guatemala City. Colombia, Mexico, relevant international organizations, the United States, and other donor nations sent representatives. The conclave cited twenty-two projects, involving crimes against women and children, judicial and penal reform, and arms trafficking. At this gathering, rhetoric seemed to eclipse specific plans by extremely disparate ministates to forge an effective front against DTOs. Nevertheless, more parlays were scheduled.[83]

Notes

1. Quoted in "Inseguridad, el gran problema de Colom," *EFE*, February 14, 2008.
2. For this 2009 figure, see Department of Justice, FBI, "Crime in the United States," September 2010.
3. US Department of Justice, *World Development Report 2011*, as reported in "The Tormented Isthmus," *The Economist*, April 14, 2011.
4. Quoted in "Guatemala Election: Rising Crime Positions Otto Pérez Molina for Victory," *Christian Science Monitor*, September 11, 2011.
5. US National Drug Intelligence Center, December 1, 2008.
6. Eric Green, "Merida Initiative Would Help Mexico, Central America Combat Trafficking," *Mexidata.Info*, June 16, 2008.
7. Francisco Ancheyta, "Concidente. Otro fallo," *Siglo XI*, July 25, 2009.
8. Steven Dudley, "The Story of the Zetas in Guatemala: History and Modus Operandi," *InSight Crime*, August 31, 2011.
9. Elyssa Pachico, "Guatemala Massacre Points to Influence of Mexican Drug Gang," *Christian Science Monitor*, May 18, 2011.
10. Steven Dudley, "The Story of the Zetas in Guatemala: History and Modus Operandi," *InSight Crime*, August 31, 2011.
11. Julie López, "Las intrincadas rutas del narcotraficante," *Plaza Pública*, June 21, 2011.
12. "Balacera dejà 11 muertos en Santa Cruz, Rio Honda," *El Zacapeneco*, March 26, 2008.
13. Ibid.
14. Sylvia Gereda Valenzuela, "Masacre in Zacapa," *El Periódico*, March 27, 2008.
15. The numbers vary between six and sixteen.
16. "MP: capturado por caso de Zacapa, es uno de los líderes de los Zetas," *El Periódico*, April 15, 2008.
17. "Lanzan Zetas campaña para reclutar Kaibiles en Guatemala," *Notimex*, April 24, 2008.
18. Steven Dudley, "The Story of the Zetas in Guatemala."

19. "'Los Zetas' buscan el control del narco en Cobán," *El Periódico*, September 4, 2008.
20. "Guatemala, Arrest Warrant for Ex-Security Chiefs in Espionage Scandal," *Guatemala News*, September 7, 2008.
21. Luis Angel Sas, "Alta Verapaz, territorio ocupado por el narcotráfico," *El Periódico*, October 9, 2008.
22. Julie López, "Las intrincadas rutas del narcotraficante," *Plaza Pública*, June 21, 2011.
23. Ibid.
24. Coauthor (Logan) interview with Guatemalan journalist, October 15, 2009.
25. "Cae otro presunto Zeta in Guatemala con arsenal," *El Universal*, December 20, 2008.
26. "Guatemala, en jaque por Los Zetas y El Chapo," *El Milenio*, November 18, 2008.
27. Jill Replogle, "Mexico Exports Its Drug Wars to Guatemala," *Time Magazine*, December 12, 2008.
28. Ibid.
29. Lorena Seijo, "Tres jefes antinarcóticos son apresados en EE.UU.," *Prensa Libre*, November 16, 2005.
30. Based on the square kilometers of Guatemala, 108,890, and of Virginia, 110,785, and that Los Zetas controlled or operated across just over half of Guatemala, which could be "approximately half" of Virginia.
31. Luis Angel Sas, "Quien arma a 'Los Zetas' en Guatemala?" *El Periódico*, June 3, 2009.
32. "Guatemala: 'Los Zetas' amenaza de muerte al presidente Colom," *Info-LatAm*, March 1, 2009.
33. Quoted in David Grann, "A Murder Foretold," *The New Yorker*, April 4, 2011; Grann provides an in-depth analysis of a bizarre story that contains plots within plots.
34. Luis Ángel Sas, "CICIG presenta evidencias: Rosenberg planifico su crimen," *El Periodico*, January 13, 2010; and Grann, "A Murder Foretold."
35. Juan M. Castillo, "Localizan avioneta, carros y armas utilizadas por presuntos narcos," *El Periodico*, March 22, 2009.
36. Ibid.
37. Kevin Casas-Zamora, "'Guatemalastan': How to Prevent a Failed State in Our Midst," *Brookings Institution*, May 22, 2009.
38. Luis Ángel Sas, "Autoridades descubren finca de entrenamiento de 'Los Zetas,'" *El Periódico*, March 28, 2009.
39. Juan M. Castillo, "MP: Huehuetenango está tomado por el narcotráfico," *El Periódico*, November 4, 2009.
40. "Los Zetas entrenaron a doce MS salvadoreños," *El Diario de Hoy*, November 25, 2009.
41. Sergio Arauz, Óscar Martínez, Efrén Lemus, "El Cártel de Texis," *El Faro*, May 16, 2011.
42. Ibid.
43. Coauthor (Logan) interview with subdirector of organized crime division, National Civil Police, San Salvador, El Salvador, January 2011.

44. Coauthor (Logan) interview with intelligence officer, San Salvador, El Salvador, March 2011.
45. "Defensa: Los Zetas utilizan pandillas en el narcotráfico," *El Diario de Hoy*, January 20, 2010.
46. Coauthor (Logan) interview with intelligence officer, San Salvador, El Salvador, March 2011.
47. Daniel Valencia Caravantes, "Las 1,800 granadas y el mayor que esfumó," *El Faro*, June 28, 2011.
48. Ibid.
49. Ibid.
50. Ibid.
51. Coauthor (Logan) interview with intelligence officer, San Salvador, El Salvador, March 2011.
52. Ibid.
53. Tracy Wilkinson, "El Salvador becomes drug traffickers' 'little pathway,'" *Los Angeles Times*, March 22, 2011.
54. Coauthor (Logan) interview with former FMLN urban commander, San Salvador, El Salvador, March 2011.
55. "Los Zetas quieren entrar a El Salvador: Funes," *El Universal*, May 26, 2011.
56. "Guatemala Tries Mexican Massacre Suspects," *BBC*, July 29, 2010.
57. Hugo Álvarado, "Condenan a 14 Zetas por narcomasacre de Zacapa," *Prensa Libre*, September 10, 2010.
58. "Condenan hasta 313 años de prisión a integrantes de Los Zetas en Guatemala," *La Tercera*, September 10, 2010.
59. Myriam Larra, "Narcos mexicanos ganan terreno en selva de Guatemala," *Prensa Libre*, November 8, 2010.
60. "Los Zetas asaltan una cárcel en Guatemala y rescatan a un reo," *Excélsior*, December 8, 2010.
61. Francisco Cuevas, "Comando libera a presunto 'Zeta' preso en Guatemala," *Es Mas*, December 9, 2010.
62. Óscar Martínez, "Guatemala se escribe con zeta," *El Faro*, March 13, 2011.
63. "Decreta Guatemala estado de sitio en Alta Verapaz para combatir el narcotráfico," *La Jornada*, December 20, 2010.
64. Ibid.
65. "Los Zetas controlan seis regiones en Guatemala," *El Diario de Hoy*, December 25, 2010.
66. Coauthor (Logan) interview with Steven Dudley, coeditor, *InSightCrime*, July 14, 2011.
67. S. Nicolle, "Seguirá el Estado de Sitio en Cobán," *Siglo 21*, January 18, 2011.
68. Ibid.
69. Óscar Martínez, "Guatemala se escribe con zeta," *El Faro*, March 13, 2011.
70. "The Ghost of Los Zetas," *Plaza Pública*, April 22, 2011.
71. "Repudian muerte de empresario y nuera," *Prensa Libre*, May 15, 2011.
72. Steven Dudley, "The Story of the Zetas in Guatemala."
73. "Cae El Amarillo, fundador de los Zetas," *El Universal*, January 18, 2011.

74. "Matan a auxiliar fiscal de Cobán, Allan Stowlinsky Vidaurre," *Prensa Libre*, May 24, 2011.

75. "Nexos entre Ofician de Envigado y Cartel Mexicano de Los Zetas," *El Tiempo*, March 7, 2010; Envigado is the town where some narco-traffickers live.

76. "The Ghost of Los Zetas," *Plaza Pública*, April 22, 2011.

77. The Guatemalan Constitution bars family members of incumbents from seeking the presidency.

78. Grann, "A Murder Foretold."

79. "Quiero que alguien me demuestre que hubo genocidio," *Plaza Pública*, July 25, 2011.

80. Quoted in Nic Wirtz and Kara Andrade, "Guatemala Election: Rising Crime Positions Otto Pérez for Victory," *Christian Science Monitor*, September 11, 2011.

81. Ignacio de los Reyes, "Álvaro Colom: 'los Zetas están desarticulados, quizá replegados,'" *BBC World*, September 7, 2011.

82. "Los Zetas: el dolor de cabeza del próximo Presidente," *El Periódico*, October 1, 2011.

83. Comisión de Seguridad de Centroamérica (CSC), "Centoamérica define 22 proyectos de seguridad," September 7, 2011.

10

Zetas in the United States

A Mexican knelt on the floor in a Nuevo Laredo bar—he was sobbing, not praying; his captors and a boy stood around him. Everyone knew the individual's fate. The bound and bloodied man had experienced hours of torture and realized his time was limited, but he didn't know when or how he would meet his maker. Rosalio Reta was the thirteen-year-old boy in the Nuevo Laredo bar that night. He too didn't realize how the man would die until Treviño Morales told him to perform the execution. He handed over a .38 Super, a pistol whose handle was encrusted with diamonds that spelled out the Zeta leader's nomme de guerre, *El Cuarenta* or EL 40. With the conviction of a seasoned killer, the child pointed the handgun at his victim, pulled the trigger, and committed murder in cold blood. Such was the initiation for the youngest Zeta cadre.

Reta shot the man several times in the chest and head.[1] He felt like Superman and James Bond—the heroes he idolized when growing up in Laredo, Texas, where he was born. "I knew right then I was born to be a *sicario*," Reta said in a later interview.[2]

By the time Reta reached fifteen years of age, he had earned the right to join other recruits at a Zeta training camp in northern Mexico. Los Zetas snatched him in Laredo, jammed a hood over his head, and drove him south to a secluded ranch in northeastern Mexico.[3] Once he arrived at the destination, Reta fell in line with the rest of the inductees and focused on his training. Over the next six months, Reta would begin his days at 6:00 a.m. He dressed in military fatigues and, as part of his physical training, swam fully clothed with a backpack and assault rifle. The teenager learned the tactics and the skills necessary to avoid detection and to murder efficiently. He also came to understand what it meant to be a "Zetita," or "little Zeta." Instructors impressed upon him to leave no man behind. "If you go out with ten men and they get killed, you come home with ten corpses or not at all," Reta said in a 2009 interview.[4] By the time the teenager had completed his course, the peach fuzz-cheeked youngster had become a deadly tool that Miguel Treviño could use when and where needed. By the age of sixteen, Reta was ready to become American law enforcement's worst nightmare: a brazen assassin who hid in plain sight.

Back in Laredo, Texas, Reta joined the young man who had brought him into the fold, Gabriel Cardona. Only two years older than the *Zetita*, Cardona presided over a unit that, although trained to operate in Laredo, functioned on both sides of the frontier. In this border city, El 40 often needed to make good on death threats to keep his products penetrating the United States, while cash and weapons flowing southward. The young *sicarios* kept a low profile in a safe house on Hibiscus Street in Laredo, waiting for calls from Mexico that would put them to work.[5]

Cardona and Reta began cooperating in the run-up to one of the most violent periods in modern Mexico. Los Zetas would become a driving force behind the bloodshed across the country and beyond, but in mid-2005, they were on the defensive as they strove to safeguard Nuevo Laredo from Sinaloan hit men. Pitched battles between Los Zetas and their rivals often garnered striking headlines in the United States.[6]

Miguel Treviño was determined to maintain control over one of the most lucrative plazas in Mexico. Sitting atop the largest trading post between the United States and Mexico, the Nuevo Laredo–Laredo border crossing connected Los Zetas to the lucrative I-35 corridor inside the United States, which stretched from Laredo, Texas, to Duluth, Minnesota, and passed through Oklahoma, Kansas, Missouri, and Iowa along the way. From Laredo, Los Zetas' smuggling operations easily extended into such extremely hospitable markets as Atlanta, Chicago, Cincinnati, Dallas, Houston, Memphis, and Oklahoma City— each of which had satellite distribution cities. Metaphorically speaking, control of Nuevo Laredo represented a license to print money. El 40 had staked his reputation on his ability to stave off attackers, and part of that challenge had to be won inside the United States. At the zenith of that confrontation, Los Zetas number two activated his underage murderers.

After they received an order from Treviño's lieutenant, Lucio "El Viejón" Quintero, Reta, and Cardona homed in on their first target. On the night of June 8, 2005, they tracked down Bruno Orozco, a former policeman who was enmeshed in Nuevo Laredo's underworld. The two hit men watched the unsuspecting victim's movement for two days before acting. They shadowed him after he stepped out of an office building in an industrial park on the outskirts of Laredo. With Orozco's car just meters in front of their own, the boys placed a fake police light on the dashboard and forced their prey to pull over. With uncanny professionalism, the youngsters ordered Orozco to step out of the vehicle. They then spun him around, snapped handcuffs on the struggling man's wrists, and kicked him to the ground. Looking up from a supine position, Orozco's last sight was the coffin-black barrel of an AR-15 before the first muzzle flashed. Cardona unloaded the whole clip into the erstwhile cop, whose death was historic. It marked the first time that a Mexican DTO had used adolescents to carry out a hit inside the United States.

"I've killed men while they were tied and bound, but there is no thrill, no excitement in that for me," Reta later remarked to a filmmaker. "I prefer to stalk my targets, hunt them down, and then, after I know their moves front to back, I sneak up on them, look 'em in the eyes, and pull the trigger—now that's a rush."[7]

Treviño Morales also relied on teenagers to settle personal scores. Three weeks after Bruno Orozco's execution, Los Zetas' sadistic leader allegedly called for the death of Sergio Botello, who—he believed—was involved in his brother's death. The killers dumped their victim's body on the side of the road where it was found on June 29.[8] Soon after Botello's demise, El 40 summoned Cardona and Reta to kill again. The target, Moisés García, worked for the Mexican Mafia, an American-based prison gang with robust linkages to Mexican organized crime. Los Zetas needed to apprise the Mexican Mafia, who sometimes did contract work for them in the United States, precisely who was running the show. Garcia's death served as a powerful reminder. Reta didn't question or care why Treviño Morales wanted the man executed; the teenager's concern was performing the job and fattening his billfold.

When the day came to kill García, Reta found him at the Torta Mex taco stand in Laredo. It was just past 3:00 p.m. on August 12, 2005, and García was picking up a takeout meal. His pregnant wife and young son had come along for the ride. As García was leaving the parking lot on Corpus Christi Street, Reta pulled up in an SUV, blocking García's exit. With the practiced calm of a professional, the young assassin nonchalantly hopped out of his vehicle and approached the driver's side of García's white Lexus sedan. He looked his target in the eye, raised the pistol, and unloaded five bullets into García's face, instantly killing him and wounding the dead man's wife. Then, as if he had completed his work as a plumber or brick mason, the cold-blooded hit man slowly climbed back into his SUV and drove away—just another day's work.[9]

Reta and Cardona received $500 a week to respond to Treviño's beck and call. Killing García earned Reta $10,000 plus two kilos of pure cocaine as a bonus. For double murders, they received $50,000 and often additional perks in the form of cocaine worth tens of thousands of dollars.[10] The Zeta chief once rewarded Cardona with a Mercedes AMG, and later bragged that he had spent $8,000 on fog lights, rims, and other accessories.[11]

Money and drugs enabled Reta and Cardona to launch their own narcotics ring under El 40's watchful eye. Their loyalty earned them the trust of a man they called "El Comandante." He instructed the boys to follow shipments north, where they acted as Treviño Morales' eyes and ears for wholesale deals with Dallas and Houston distributors. The teenagers kept watch as El 40's couriers traveled south, transporting hundreds of thousands of dollars in earnings. Men like Moisés García, who had worked for the Zeta chieftain, were tempted to pocket some of the loot for their trouble, believing they could get away with it inside the United States. Reta and Cardona made sure that no one even considered betraying *El Comandante*.

Just after the New Year, Treviño Morales called on Reta again. The subject of interest had gotten involved with the wrong woman, one of El 40's girlfriends, and *El Comandante* wanted him dead. After days of surveillance in January 2006, Cardona and Reta crouched in a stolen vehicle parked on East Frost Street in Laredo, waiting for the culprit, Noé López Flores, to leave the house. When the front door opened, Cardona stepped out of the car, walked up to their prey, and discharged a clip of bullets into his torso.

When they reported the murder to Treviño Morales, he grew furious. The teenage assassins had made a mistake—they had killed the intended victim's brother-in-law. After the hit, Reta and his companion separated and lay low. Laredo detectives had already linked the string of deaths to Cardona. Before the botched job, police had arrested Cardona, but he was freed on bail. Still, after the mistake, Cardona needed to distance himself from the investigations. He slipped into Mexico, while Reta remained in Laredo.

Cardona wasn't south of the border long before El 40 demanded more blood. This time Jesús María "Chuy" Resendez, a Gulf Cartel apostate, had to die. Since his defection, Resendez had become a significant marijuana dealer in Laredo, and Treviño Morales wanted to send a message to others contemplating invading his turf. He allegedly offered $90,000 for the takedown.[12] On April 2, 2006, Cardona completed the lucrative assignment. He pulled up next to Resendez's truck at a stop light outside of Laredo to ask for directions. He and an associate opened fire, spraying more than one hundred rounds into the turncoat's truck.[13]

Commenting on the Jesús Resendez murder, Laredo Police Department Detective Roberto Garcia said that they "had never seen anything like it. There has always been violence, but . . . it doesn't spill over."[14] However, General McCaffrey told an *El Universal* reporter that Los Zetas operated in seventeen Texas counties.

Only days before he killed Resendez, Cardona was relaxing at Nuevo Laredo's Eclipse nightclub only to jump to his feet when he spied two boys—aged fourteen and nineteen—whom he had been told to kidnap. He abducted both youngsters at gunpoint and took them to an abandoned warehouse. Cardona tortured both boys and gutted them to let them bleed out before burning their bodies in fifty-five-gallon drums. The young murderer preferred working in Mexico, where police, on Los Zetas' payroll, would sometimes drive him to the location where he would seize and kill his quarry. The same cops would dispose of the body afterward.[15]

From a Laredo safe house, Cardona called Reta on April 10, 2006, to convey the details of the Nuevo Laredo slaughter. "You should have been there," he stated when his associate answered the call. Referring to the younger boy, Cardona reported that "he was crying and crying . . . and said, 'No, man, I'm your friend'" before the killer broke a bottle and slashed the boy's stomach. "I grabbed a little cup," Cardona recalled, "and I filled it with blood and . . . I dedicated it to the Santísima Muerte," the traffickers' patron saint alluded to earlier.

Neither *sicario* knew that Laredo police officers were eavesdropping on the call.[16] Investigators had found the stolen car the boys used during a previous killing. Forensic technicians lifted fingerprints from a cigarette pack that focused the investigation on the two teen assassins.

Detective Garcia was on Reta's trail. He visited a tattoo parlor frequented by him and left his card for Reta, who called a couple days later.

"This is Bart," he said, using his street name. "I heard you're looking for me."

"Yeah, I'm looking for you," Garcia responded to Reta's amused chuckle.

"Look, you need to quit these investigations," the youthful thug said with bravado, "or I'm going to kill you and your family. You do not know who you are messing with. Do you understand?" threatened the punk before cutting the call.[17]

Although not sufficient to arrest the hoodlums, the fingerprints persuaded a judge to authorize a wiretap. Still, Cardona's telephone confession gave Laredo SWAT team enough evidence to arrest Cardona, whom they found lounging in the safe house.

When he got word of Cardona's arrest, Reta hustled into Mexico. The young Zeta hit man had killed more than thirty people in Mexico and only four in the United States. He felt safer on the southern side of the border. Not long after his arrival, Reta received orders for another murder. In May 2006, he trailed his victim to Bar El Punto in Monterrey. As time passed, the young man grew impatient. He approached the hangout, yanked the pin from on a fragmentation grenade, and tossed it through the front door. Next, he kicked in the door and opened fire.

He reportedly killed four and wounded another dozen, but Reta had missed his target.[18] Again, El 40 was furious with his sloppy handling of an easy hit and banned the kid from operating outside the Laredo–Nuevo Laredo corridor.[19] Treviño Morales ordered other sicarios to find Reta. They kidnapped the boy and spent two days torturing him in Monterrey. Somehow Reta overpowered his captors, killing both of them, escaped, and called Detective Garcia. Convinced that he would be better off in an American jail than a Mexican one, the youngster expressed his willingness to cooperate.

Detective Garcia happily obliged and sought to have the tough extradited to a prison in Webb County, Texas, where Reta spilled the beans on his involvement with Los Zetas. For police in south Texas, it was the first time that they had obtained hard proof of the paramilitaries' criminality in the United States and the first time they had heard of Miguel Treviño.[20]

Safely ensconced in Nuevo Laredo, El 40 comprehended that he had made a mistake. The youthful assassins turned out to be as unreliable as they were counterproductive. Their impetuousness and lack of maturity not only landed them behind bars but exposed and endangered his organization. By the spring of 2007, US authorities learned Miguel Treviño's real name and knew that he was at least a *plaza* boss in Nuevo Laredo, but the DEA had neither tagged him as a kingpin nor placed a multimillion-dollar bounty on his head. After Reta's arrest, Treviño Morales focused on contracting labor to Latino street gangs.[21] These hardened criminals demanded more money for their time and were more difficult to keep in line, but they were generally reliable, so long as the pay was sufficient and they understood who was giving and who was taking orders.

The Mexican Mafia, also known as *La Eme* (Spanish for the letter "M"), a gang founded in California prisons in the 1950s, served as the perfect partner for Los Zetas. The Texas Syndicate, Mara Salvatrucha, and other groups also performed tasks for the Mexicans, but on the US side of the Rio Grande, the Mexican Mafia either did the bidding of Los Zetas or farmed out assignments to reliable partners.

Their ubiquitous presence appealed to Miguel Treviño and his high-level compatriots. *La Eme* cutthroats had recruited in US federal and state penitentiaries for more than six decades and had cadres in every major prison.[22] In most cases, Latinos entering a penal facility joined the resident Latino gang linked to the Mexican Mafia. Otherwise, they faced the prospect of living behind bars with no support. The Mara 18, the Mara Salvatrucha, and competing street ruffians became brothers-in-arms inside prison walls.

The Mexican Mafia extended its influence throughout the nation. When its affiliates gained release, they were sent back to their home country or returned to society. In both cases, many resumed a life of crime in service of their new masters.[23]

La Eme's members moved across the country as part of a floating labor force, often lured by opportunities in the construction industry. In the wake of Hurricane Katrina, mobile Latino workers flooded into southern Mississippi and Louisiana. Stretched along Interstate I-10 like an interlinked chain, Mexican Mafia loyalists followed their brethren to the Gulf Coast to take part in the reconstruction. While most of the Latinos found employment, worked hard, and were law-abiding, enough cadres of *La Emes* gravitated to Los Zetas, giving them presence east from Houston to Jacksonville, Florida.

La Eme and contractors helped Los Zetas enter markets across the United States. Although one investigation divulged that Los Zetas had operations in Baltimore, in 2005 and 2006 authorities had only a hazy picture of their activities outside the border. The November 2010 sentencing hearing for drug dealer James Bostic disclosed that he had been acquiring cocaine from Los Zetas since 2005 until February 2, 2010. Bostic made his cash payments as high as $589,000 at a hotel in White Marsh, Maryland, in exchange for previous shipments of cocaine and marijuana. Bostic admitted that he had distributed between 110 and 330 pounds of cocaine; yet his overall business may have been much more prosperous.[24]

By mid-2007, federal investigators concluded that Los Zetas were active in Tennessee and Oklahoma, conducting extortion, kidnapping, and drug trafficking. Individuals working on behalf of the cartel also targeted non-US citizens indebted to the paramilitaries, as well as foreign nationals involved in human smuggling.[25] A well-placed source described as having "excellent access," claimed in early 2008 that an inmate at the Bennettsville Federal Correctional Institution in South Carolina, while not a Zeta himself, boasted connections with the organization and purchased cocaine and marijuana from them in Texas for sale "anywhere inside the United States."[26]

A reported link between Los Zetas and another group, Los Tolles, enabled the desperados to penetrate markets in Atlanta and open routes into eastern Tennessee. As early as December 2007, Los Tolles received 100–150 kilograms of cocaine from the Mexicans "every two weeks to two months."[27] By the following April 2008, the paramilitaries expanded into Memphis and the northeast.[28] Even as the group pushed ever farther from their border comfort zone, access to the breadth of the US market hinged on dominating corridors passing through Texas, specifically in Dallas or Houston. From their position deep in the Rio Grande valley, Los Zetas initially focused on the Big D, a legacy territory "inherited" from the Gulf Cartel, which had been sending drugs through this channel for several years. The city straddled the important I-35 corridor, and connected with I-20, which ran across the country.

Dating to at least 2005, DEA wiretaps revealed that local drug retailers received cocaine from the Gulf Cartel.[29] FBI sources indicated that by November 2008, however, Los Zetas were monitoring Dallas to "determine whether drug trafficking in the region was composed of small, independent sellers or one specific organization."[30] Such intelligence on downstream cocaine markets would be useful if Los Zetas ever split from the Gulf Cartel. Entrée to US customers required a border crossing, which Los Zetas had in Nuevo Laredo. The next step was a staging ground for downstream distribution, and Dallas yielded an ideal location.

By October 2008, an FBI intelligence bulletin concluded that Los Zetas were "expanding their reach into Southeast and Midwest United States."[31] The bulletin outlined the Mexicans' extortion, kidnapping, and drug trafficking, and raised concern over their possible expansion into east Tennessee and Georgia. On October 17, the FBI's San Antonio Field Office dispatched a bulletin to Texas law-enforcement agencies, indicating that Los Zetas were "attempting to violently regain control of drug trafficking routes in the United States and [have] been ordered to engage law-enforcement officers to protect their operations."[32]

Three months later, Customs and Border Protection agents debriefed a confidential informant and member of the Hermanos Pistoleros Latinos. He confirmed that his gang received drugs directly from Los Zetas. According to the source, his criminal band transported and protected shipments from Nuevo Laredo to a stash house in Laredo, where the narcotics were prepared for marketing. The tipster indicated that Los Zetas had forged similar accords with the Texas Syndicate and *La Eme*.[33]

Los Zetas didn't always assign distribution to street hoodlums. Business is business, and even small-time Houston vendors who could pay the cash received product. Operation Gator Bait in October 2009 discovered that, at the height of his retail operation, Willie "Gator" Jones Jr. was purchasing upwards of $1 million a month of cocaine from Gulf Cartel contacts in Houston.

The illicit operation centered on an unprepossessing middle-class home on Magnolia Crest Place, a well-placed neighborhood be-tween I-45 and I-10 in northwest Harris County outside of Houston. A Bureau of Alcohol, Tobacco, and Firearms affidavit later described the residence as a "sort of satellite office for Mexico's Gulf Cartel and its partners . . . Los Zetas."[34]

The report read like a laundry list of items found in a safe house in Mexico, not the United States: "Body armor in the master bathroom, a 'machine gun' with a silencer on the floor by a bed, money-counting ma-chines, night-vision equipment, hundreds of plastic bags for packaging drugs in resale quantities, and machinery for packing the narcotics were found. Some of the twenty-seven high-powered weapons found in the dwelling were ready to fire, while others were disassembled to be smuggled into Mexico. Also, there was $500,000 worth of cocaine, nearly $100,000 in cash, and a duffle bag stuffed with documents."[35]

Investigators had come upon a cartel rest stop between Mexico, Houston, Louisiana, and points beyond. Drugs flowed east and north, while guns and cash entered Mexico. The case buttressed the belief that Los Zetas, the Gulf Cartel, and other Mexican DTOs had thrust their tentacles deep into the United States. By the time investigators had unraveled Gator's network, they had charged thirty-three suspects with weapons smuggling, drug-trafficking, and money laundering.

Authorities discreetly observed activity at the Houston stash house, even as they discovered that Los Zetas' network extended from south Texas to Cincinnati and Chicago. Coordinated raids in Laredo and San Antonio netted sixteen of twenty-five suspects on August 24, 2009. Authorities captured coconspirators in Chicago and Cincinnati, where $160,000 was believed to be awaiting shipment to Texas. They also seized drugs and arms.[36]

Another case broke just over a year later when the Mexican military arrested Joseph Allen Garcia, an American who was extradited to the United States on charges of murder and assault in Laredo. One report indicated that Garcia carried out assassinations for Los Zetas in Mexico and for the Mexican Mafia in the Rio Grande Valley.[37]

Several unsealed cases involving Los Zetas established that by 2010, the syndicate and their street gang allies had spread from the Rio Grande Valley across the country, focusing on the I-35, I-20, and I-10 corridors. Apart from killings in Laredo by Cardona, Reta, and other Zetitas, the cartel operates in other, more subtle ways such as purchasing real estate and opening legitimate businesses.

"They own used car lots on both sides of the border, restaurants, discotheques, liquor stores . . ." one Laredo detective said while describing Los Zetas' presence and growth on the US side of the border.[38] He and others in 2009 were convinced that Los Zetas, through the purchase of firms inside the Americas, sought to launder the money and invest "clean finances" in ventures on the northern side of the Rio Grande. "We could see them running for mayor, even governor, in the future,"[39] said one concerned politician in Nuevo Laredo, who knew that Los Zetas had a long way to go before they could run a political campaign. The organization's efforts at legitimization inside the United States depended on stability and an impregnable domain inside Mexico, which by late 2009 had fallen into doubt.

Notes

1. Jesse Hyde, "Young Guns," *Details* 27, (9) (June 2009): 130.
2. Rusty Fleming, "Drug Wars: The Next Generation," *Cable News Network,* August 5, 2009.
3. Ibid.
4. Ibid.
5. James C. McKinley Jr., "Mexican Cartels Lure American Teens as Killers," *New York Times,* June 23, 2009.
6. Madeleine Brand, "Warring Gangs Vie for Control of Nuevo Laredo," *National Public Radio,* August 8, 2005.
7. Fleming, "Drug Wars: The Next Generation."
8. Susan Carroll, Dane Schiller, and Lise Olsen, "Drug Cartel Suspect Wanted in Five Texas Killings," *Houston Chronicle,* July 21, 2009.
9. Hyde, "Young Guns."
10. Susan Carroll, "Case Offers Peek into Inner Workings of Hit Man Team for Mexican Drug Gang; U.S. Teens Carry Out Bloody Work for Cartel," *Houston Chronicle,* January 18, 2009.
11. Hyde, "Young Guns."
12. Michelle Roberts, "Jury Gets Case Against Alleged Cartel Hit Man," *Associated Press,* February 4, 2010.
13. Ibid.
14. Hyde, "Young Guns."
15. Ibid.
16. Jason Buch, "Mexican Teen Gets Life in Killings," *Laredo Morning News,* March 5, 2009.
17. Ibid.
18. Ibid.
19. Fleming, "Drug Wars: The Next Generation."
20. Coauthor (Logan) interview with Laredo Police Department Detective Roberto Garcia, December 2009.
21. Ibid.
22. Margaret Baker, "Mexican Mafia Entrenched in Mississippi, FBI Says," *McClatchy Newspapers,* September 27, 2009.
23. Ibid.
24. "Cocaine Supplied by Los Zetas Mexican Drug Cartel," *DEA News Release,* November 8, 2010.
25. "Los Zetas Expanding Reach into Southeast and Midwest United States," *FBI Intelligence Bulletin,* October 2, 2011. Accessed via Public Intelligence on June 26, 2011, http://tinyurl.com/3na224d.
26. Ibid.
27. Ibid.
28. "Los Zetas Expanding Criminal Activities and Influence in the United States," clipping of a FOUO FBI document, May 21, 2009.
29. "DEA Announced Gulf Cartel/Los Zetas Most-Wanted List," *Department of Justice Press Release,* July 23, 2009.
30. Ibid.
31. Quoted in "Los Zetas Expanding Reach into Southeast and Midwest United States," *FBI Intelligence Bulletin,* October 2, 2011. Accessed via Public Intelligence on June 26, 2011, http://tinyurl.com/3na224d.

32. Quoted in Sara A. Carter, "FBI Warns of Drug Cartel Arming," *Washington Times*, October 26, 2008.

33. "Los Zetas Expanding Criminal Activities and Influence in the United States," clipping of a FOUO FBI document.

34. Quoted in Dane Schiller, "Suburban Home Had a Secret," *Houston Chronicle*, January 31, 2010.

35. Ibid.

36. Guillermo Contreras, "Local, States, Fed Offices Make Multistate Drug Arrests," *San Antonio Express News*, August 25, 2009.

37. Grupo Savant, "Force Protection Analysis," October 1, 2010.

38. Quoted in Alfredo Corchado, "Mexico's Zetas Gang Buys Businesses Along Border in Move to Increase Legitimacy," *Dallas Morning News*, December 7, 2009.

39. Ibid.

11

War in the North

As discussed in chapter 1, increasing stains had afflicted the once-mutually-beneficial Zeta–Gulf Cartel marriage. Insiders knew about the troubles within the household, but their divorce became public only in 2010. Table 13 reveals the development of the Gulf Cartel and its evolving relations with Los Zetas.

Evidence of the nasty breakup became apparent after Mexico extradited Osiel Cárdenas to the United States in a scene reminiscent of the Keystone Kops. On January 20, 2007, Mexico's PGR dispatched the capo to Houston aboard a Boeing 727. The only problem was that the PGR had neglected to coordinate Osiel's transfer with their US counterparts in the Department of Justice. No US Marshals were on hand to receive the convict. As a result, air force fighters were scrambled with the possibility of taking out the aircraft from Mexico, whose pilot had not filed a flight plan. Once communications were straightened out, a DEA contingent rushed to the airport just as the inbound plane landed and took the prisoner to the nearest federal detention center. In a month, he would learn his fate at the hands of the US judicial system.

Judge Hilda G. Tagle granted the US government's request to bar the public from the kingpin's sentencing on February 24, 2010. As a result, these proceedings took place behind locked doors in a Houston federal courtroom fortified by additional armed guards. Only two members of Cárdenas's family and a handful of federal agents were present. Judges often seal particular documents in drug and terrorism trials to protect informants or continuing investigations, but it was highly unusual to close a penalty hearing for security reasons. The forty-two-year-old Osiel dutifully registered his mea culpa in what appeared as a choreographed scene. "I apologize to my country, Mexico, to the United States of America, my family, to my wife especially, my children,

Table 13 Chronology of Gulf Cartel and Los Zetas

Year	Event
1984	Juan García Ábrego takes the reins of Gulf Cartel after murdering a rival in a Mexico City hospital.
1986 (August)	Gulf Cartel offers a $100,000 bribe to an FBI agent.
1989 (October 4)	Authorities discover nine tons of cocaine in Harlingen, Texas.
1994 (August 12)	A court convicts two American Express bankers for laundering $30 million for the Gulf Cartel.
1996 (February 27)	Mexican authorities capture Juan García Ábrego and fly him to Houston, where he received eleven life sentences and a hefty fine.
1999 (February)	Lt. Arturo Gúzman Decena initiates recruitment of Los Zetas to protect Gulf Cartel chief Osiel Cárdenas Guillén.
1999 (November 9)	Cárdenas threatens two US law-enforcement agents in Matamoros—Joseph DuBois (DEA) and Daniel Fuentes (FBI).
2001	The Gulf Cartel extends its reach when $41 million is found hidden in Atlanta and $2.3 million in Houston.
2002 (November 21)	Elements of the army and UEDO kill Gúzman Decena in Matamoros, Tamaulipas.
2003 (March 14)	Mexican Army captures Cárdenas, who continues to run the cartel from prison.
2004	Los Zetas begin to distance themselves from the Gulf Cartel, now formally headed by Antonio Ezequiel "Tony Tormenta" Cárdenas Guillén and Jorge Eduardo "El Coss" Costilla Sánchez. Because of his key role in repulsing an attack by Sinaloans, Heriberto "The Executioner" Lazcano becomes an integral part of the Gulf Cartel's leadership.
2004 (January 5)	Commandos break into a prison in Apatingán, Michoacán, and free twenty-five fellow Zetas.
2004 (Late)	Miguel Ángel "El 40" Treviño Morales becomes Lazcano's number two in the Zeta command.
2005 (February 2)	The war between the Gulf and Sinaloa Cartels reaches its climax when Nuevo Laredo's police chief, Alejandro Domínguez Coello, is murdered hours after taking office, and La Barbie and the Sinaloans decide not to continue combat.

Table 13 (*Continued*)

Year	Event
2006 (November 25)	Zetas kill singer Valentín Elizalde along with his driver and manager.
2007 (January 20)	Mexico extradites Osiel to Houston; the capo is believed to be cooperating with the US authorities to get a lighter sentence.
2007 (February 6)	Several Zetas dressed in army uniforms kill five police officers and two administrative assistants in Acapulco.
2007 (April)	Los Zetas murder police chief in Chilpancingo, Guerrero, while he is eating with his wife and family in a restaurant.
2007 (Mid-year)	The Executioner dissents from the Gulf Cartel's entering into an alliance with the Sinaloa Cartel.
2008 (Mid-May)	The BLO breaks with El Chapo.
2008 (November 27)	GOPES capture Jaime "El Hummer" González Durán, Reynosa; The Executioner and El 40 object to the Gulf Cartel's replacing González Durán with its loyalist Héctor "El Karis" Manuel Sauceda Gamboa.
2009 (Mid-February)	"El Karis" is killed.
2009 (March 23)	The US government offers $5 million for the capture of Gulf Cartel leaders, including Osiel's brother, "Tony Tormenta."
2010 (January 18)	The schism between the Gulf Cartel and Los Zetas becomes patently clear when El Coss orders the execution of Zeta stalwart, Víctor "Concord 3" Peña Mendoza.
2010 (January 30)	El 40 retaliates for the murder of Peña Mendoza by abducting and executing sixteen Gulf Cartel loyalists in Reynosa.
2010 (February 24)	Federal Judge Hilda G. Tagle sentences Osiel to a twenty-five-year prison term; Osiel cooperates with US authorities by phoning José de Jesús "El Chango" Méndez, co-leader of La Familia Michoacana, and urging his organization to join the Sinaloa and Gulf Cartels in combating Los Zetas in Tamaulipas and Nuevo León.
2010 (August)	Wounded Ecuadorian claims that Los Zetas killed seventy-two migrants whose bodies were found in a mass grave.
2010 (November 5)	Mexican Navy kills Osiel's brother Antonio Ezequiel "Tony Tormenta" Cárdenas Guillén, leaving El Coss in control of the Gulf Cartel.

(*Continued*)

Table 13 (*Continued*)

Year	Event
2011 (Announced on May 20)	Federal Police captured Gilberto "el M 18" Barragán Balderas, who was Gulf Cartel plaza boss in Miguel Alemán, protector of drug-smuggling routes to the US and supervisor of brutal killings of Los Zetas, in a ranch outside of Reynosa; Mexican police also arrested other Gulf Cartel members Sergio Gutiérrez Costañon and Ramón Eduardo Mejía González.
2011 (June 3)	The Federal Police apprehend Jesús Enrique "El Mamito"/"Z-28" Rejón Aguilar, one of the most fearsome regional bosses of Los Zetas.
2011 (August 30)	Nuevo León attorney general Adrián de la Garza announces the arrest of five Zetas implicated in the August 25 firebombing of Monterrey's Casino Royale in which more than fifty-two people lost their lives.
2011 (September 2)	Discovery of the tortured and bound bodies of Flores Borrego and Eloy Lerma García points to an intracartel feud between El Coss's supporters, "Los Metros" led by Flores Borrego, and "Los Rojos" who are also called the *"Erres"* (name based on radio signals); the dispute arose when Juan "R-1" Reyes Mejía was overlooked for the post of plaza boss in Reynosa, which remained in the hands of Flores Borrego, who outranked Reyes Mejía; Rafael "El Junior" Cárdenas Vela, nephew to Osiel Cárdenas and the so-called heir to the Gulf Cartel, reportedly joined Reyes Mejía to eliminate Flores Borrego.
2011 (September 20)	*Matazetas* reportedly believed responsible for dumping the tortured corpses of thirty-five Zetas on a busy avenue in the Río Boca–Veracruz tourist zone.
2011 (Early October)	The navy killed eleven suspected Gulf Cartel members and captured thirty-six more, including an important financial operator, Gabriela "La Gaby" Gómez Robles, and a ranking capo, Ricardo Salazar Pequeño.
2011 (October 11)	Authorities discovered the body of César "Gama" Dávila García, Tony Tormenta's personal accountant, in an abandoned house in Reynosa.

Table 13 (*Continued*)

Year	Event
2011 (October 25)	US authorities apprehended Rafael Cárdenas Vela, nephew of Osiel Cárdenas, in Texas, where he owns property in South Padre Island, Texas, as well as homes in Brownsville and Río Hondo.
2011 (November 25)	As part of "Operation Northeast," Federal Police captured Ezequiel "El Junior" Cárdenas Rivera, son of Tony Tormenta, in Matamoros.

Source: US Department of Justice; various articles from *The Monitor* (McAllen, Texas); telephone conversations and e-mails with Ildefonso Ortiz, a top journalist for *The Monitor*; US Department of Justice, *Reforma* newspaper; and www.enotes.com/topic/LosZetas.

for all the mistakes I made," Cárdenas said, while also adding, "I am remorseful."[1] Tagle sentenced him to a twenty-five-year sentence and the forfeiture of $50 million in illegal gains from a US federal court whose proceedings were closed to the media.

This sanction appeared like a slap on the wrist compared with the huge fine and eleven life sentences that García Abrego is serving in a Colorado prison, especially since the seven years that Cárdenas Guillén, then forty-two, had served in Mexico reduced his confinement in the United States to eighteen years—with the prospect of even earlier release for good behavior. Model federal prisoners can win freedom after serving 80 percent of their time. Thus Osiel was looking at no more than fourteen—probably fewer if he helped bring down The Executioner and El 40. The relatively light punishment intensified the belief that Osiel had given sensitive information about Los Zetas and Gulf Cartel members to US law-enforcement agents to obtain leniency, to destroy his enemies in the underworld, and to boost the ascent of his law-breaking allies.

Indeed, at the behest of US authorities, he communicated by cell phone from prison with José de Jesús "El Chango"/"The Monkey" Méndez Vargas, co-leader with Nazario "El Más Loco"/"The Most Crazy" Moreno González, of La Familia Michoacana. Cárdenas had told El Chango, in effect, "Nazario is unstable; his erratic behavior jeopardizes La Familia. You would be wise to cast your lot with the Sinaloa and Gulf Cartels against Los Zetas." That's exactly what he did.

News of Osiel's sentence intensified the animus between Gulf Cartel and Los Zetas. "Osiel was looked on as an extraordinary leader," said one US law-enforcement agent. After he was flown to the United States, "there was enough leadership there to maintain the organization, but Osiel was the glue that held everything together."[2]

This shift in the command structure was the beginning of a string of events that set Los Zetas on a path toward independence, eventually posing a menace to the continued existence of the Gulf Cartel. By January 2007, Los Zetas had already established themselves as a formidable DTO. A focus on extortion as a new revenue source vouchsafed their newly achieved freedom of action. The ex-GAFES targeted casinos in Nuevo Laredo, Veracruz, Coahuila, and Baja California, likely for lucrative extortion contracts. In mid-2007, outside observers indicated that Los Zetas were positioned for a "classic coup" against their masters.[3]

The CDG–Los Zetas relationship evolved from a master–bodyguard footing to an "uneasy truce" in early 2007. The Executioner had been admitted to the troika that headed the Gulf Cartel by "Tony Tormenta" Cárdenas Guillén, Osiel's elder brother, who considered himself the heir-apparent of the organization, and El Coss Costilla Sánchez, who functioned as the operational chief. Authorities referred to Tony Tormenta as "Tango Tango" and knew that he had a raging temper fueled by his cocaine habit. Members of this loose triumvirate were not personally close, generally communicated by telephone, and during their infrequent meetings stuck to the business—payments to mid-level managers and prices charged for cocaine and marijuana. Observers noted that the three capos primarily kept the organizations together to manage downstream drug sales in the Texas market.[4] The October 2007 seizure of a thirteen-ton shipment of cocaine in Altamira, Tamaulipas, intensified misgivings that The Executioner and his lieutenants had about their partners' "trustworthiness."[5] This seizure might have also prompted Lazcano to look more intently at ways to diversify Los Zetas' revenues.

Mexican police reported that at one time the syndicates shared "gatekeepers"—those men and women responsible for bribing customs agents, military personnel, customs officials, policemen, and lookouts, while lining up truckers and other mules to carry drugs across the sector of the border for which they were responsible. These trafficking facilitators reportedly earned $200 for every kilogram of drug handled—with shipments averaging five hundred to three thousand kilograms.

The three men met in person only a half-dozen times during the summer of 2007 to discuss the merits of a nonaggression pact with the Sinaloa Cartel. El Coss and Tony Tormenta were interested in letting bygones be bygones between the two organizations, considered the country's most powerful DTO at the time, but The Executioner dissented. The mid-year parlays crystallized the personal differences between Lazcano and Costilla Sánchez, which portended the end of the bilateral alliance. "The Gulf Cartel created the lion, but now the lion has wised up and controls the handler," stated a US official. "The Zetas don't ask the Gulf Cartel for permission for anything anymore. They simply inform them of their activities whenever they feel like it."[6]

The crack in the decade-old association widened after the late 2008 arrest of "El Hummer" González Durán, an intriguing case described in chapter 2. The Gulf Cartel soon replaced El Hummer with one of its own loyalists, Héctor "El Karis" Manuel Sauceda Gamboa. Los Zetas mounted a raid to remove El Karis and resume control over this vital *plaza*. On February 17, 2009, The Executioner reportedly made his move. Roads in and out of the city were all blocked, and the renegades "practically kidnapped" the city for hours while they searched for El Karis, who wound up dead before Lazcano's men completed their assignment.[7]

Reynosa quickly—and quietly due to a lack of national media coverage—became the modern version of a mini-Armageddon as Los Zetas and the Gulf Cartel lunged for each other's collective throats. El Coss' troops mounted one unsuccessful assault after another. In December alone, the Tamaulipas public security office recorded more than three shoot-outs a week.[8]

Emboldened by the assistance of El Chapo's Sinaloans and the final push Osiel had provided to seal a pact with La Familia Michoacana, El Coss resolved to banish Los Zetas from Tamaulipas. The attackers sought to control drug flows across the Rio Grande at Nuevo Laredo and other crossing points. In a matter of weeks, Los Zetas found themselves bereft of strong allies, with the exception of the various policemen who cooperated with the paramilitaries in Nuevo Laredo, Reynosa, and Matamoros, as well as the Frontera Chica or Small Frontier made up of such municipalities as Miguel Alemán, Camargo, Ciudad Mier, Nueva Ciudad Guerrero, and Díaz Ordaz.

The event that splintered the alliance took place on January 18, 2010 when Gulf Cartel operators kidnapped Víctor "Concord 3" Peña Mendoza—a confidant of El 40—and sought to convince Reynosa's ranking Zeta to switch allegiance. When Concord 3 refused to change sides, he was tortured and executed, presumably by Samuel "Metro 3" Flores Borrego, a former state judicial policeman who once protected Osiel and later became El Coss' right-hand man and plaza boss in Miguel Alemán, Tamaulipas. Before signing on with the Gulf Cartel, Flores Borrego had served as a judicial policemen under Governor Tomás Yarrington Ruvalcaba (1998–2004)—the heyday of the Gulf Cartel.

Upon learning of his comrade's ghastly demise, Treviño Morales issued an ultimatum to El Coss: "Hand over the assassin of my friend, you son of a bitch . . .. You have until the 25th, if you don't comply, there will be war."[9] The Gulf Cartel honcho ignored the command, and Treviño Morales did not wait long to take revenge. On January 30, his men abducted and executed sixteen Gulf Cartel loyalists in Reynosa[10]; the slaughter marked the beginning of several months of firefights across Tamaulipas and, eventually, Nuevo León and Veracruz.[11] SUVs driven by Gulf Cartel hitmen appeared with the letters "CDG" stenciled on white poster board paper and taped to the vehicles' front door panels. Previously, there had been no need to identify Cártel del Golfo trucks so boldly. Escalating violence meant that CDG members did not want to be targeted by friendly fire.

A mass e-mail distributed on February 17 threatening widespread violence emptied Reynosa streets, businesses, and schools. The US Consulate closed until further notice. Less than twenty-four hours later, the local government confirmed an attack on a Zetas' redoubt in Valle Hermoso, twenty-five miles southwest of Matamoros.[12] Entire villages near the border hemorrhaged citizens overnight, and the only information emanated sporadically from the Internet, *Twitter*, *Facebook*, and *narcomantas*.

On February 21, the Gulf Cartel posted banners throughout Reynosa in a ploy to turn the population against Los Zetas. One observer claimed that the message evinced the possible arrival of La Familia Michoacana, to join forces with the Gulf Cartel, inasmuch as the LFM had used similarly worded banners in Michoacán. "Nothing is happening, nothing will happen. Continue with your normal life. We are part of Tamaulipas, and we do not get involved with civilians, sincerely, CDG."[13]

Subsequent accounts indicated that a torrent of violence had convulsed the Tamaulipas border zone, affecting Camargo, Xicoténcatl, Valle Hermoso, and Miguel Alemán. In Valle Hermoso, a reported one hundred vehicles entered the city early on Wednesday, the twenty-fourth, and Gulf Cartel men prowled the streets in search of Zetas. For two days, residents were too frightened to leave their homes as people in Valle Hermoso interviewed over the phone claimed that the CDG had deposited bodies of Los Zetas in the town plaza. "No one wants to go out," the interviewee said. "Many of us need to get supplies, but we're very scared, and we don't see any authorities in the street to offer us protection. The army disappeared on Wednesday; they're not in the streets. It looks like they left the bad guys alone to arm their war, leaving us to our luck."[14]

In the last week of February 2010, five face-offs between Los Zetas and Gulf Cartel rocked Nuevo Laredo. El Coss's gunmen set upon Los Zetas on as many fronts as possible. The series of swift, effective attacks drove the defenders into a tactical retreat, ceding most of Tamaulipas to the FACZ.[15]

The viciousness of the collision and Los Zetas' threat of massacres spurred the exodus of local residents from San Fernando, Ciudad Mier, and other towns along the *frontera chica*. "There is not a house that doesn't have broken windows," said a native of Ciudad Mier, taking refuge in Reynosa. "The authorities do not go there. There are no soldiers there. There is nobody. The mayor is not there anymore, there is no police, no traffic authority—nobody. It's a ghost town. All the businesses are closed. If you want an aspirin, you have to travel to Miguel Alemán, and by bus, because if you drive, they take away your car. They have strangulated my town."[16] Some estimates claimed that up to 90 percent of the town's inhabitants fled to Miguel Alemán in the wake of fighting.[17]

By the end of February, authorities listed at least fifty narco-related homicides in Nuevo León and Tamaulipas, while the same two states registered only 198 such fatalities in all of 2009.[18] Ironically, the stormiest year before 2010 was 2007, when the Sinaloa Cartel had assailed Gulf Cartel holdings in the northeast. Three years later, the erstwhile enemies had closed ranks against the crew spawned to protect Osiel and his organization.

On March 3, 2010, news circulated of a raid on Camargo, located across from Rio Grande, Texas, and the alleged site of a Los Zetas training camp. A six-minute *YouTube* video exhibited damaged vehicles and accentuated the eerie silence that haunted the municipality.[19] The military discovered only two corpses, though the strife had involved enough men to fill twenty-two trucks, and two thousand shell casings carpeted the battle zone.[20] Bloodstains and body parts found in abandoned vehicles suggested that gunmen were carrying off their dead and wounded.[21]

From Valle Hermoso to Camargo, more than eighty miles away, the antagonists had proven their readiness to fight for Tamaulipas, *plaza por plaza*. On March 3, 2010, when El Chapo, La Familia Michoacana, and the Gulf Cartel publicly announced their joint venture, banners reinforced news of the continuing struggle against Los Zetas. Internet and Mexican media teemed with photos of dismembered bodies, decapitated heads, and other frightening images in Tamaulipas and Nuevo León; the events in Matamoros and Reynosa diffused southward; and despair hung over northern Mexico like a shroud. Mainstream media coverage was equally opaque, and journalists were warned to steer clear of Tamaulipas, or face reprisals.[22] Those who ventured into the state were muzzled, disappeared, or killed. Reporters on the outside looking in depended on *narcomantas* for information, and their content was consistently menacing.[23] Banners gave notice of the formation of the "Fusion of Anti-Zeta Cartels." Their purpose was simple—eliminate Los Zetas. This three-party amalgam dispatched a message to President Calderón in early March, asking him to remove the army and the marines to give them space to excise the "cancer" of Los Zetas.[24]

In turn, Los Zetas introduced *narcomantas* that mocked the Gulf Cartel in Veracruz, Monterrey, Quintana Roo, Tabasco, and Puebla: "Poor innocents, your desperation is so [great] that you don't know what to do, it's an embarrassment that you're now announcing alliances, which tell the country that you're beaten, such a disgrace, here comes the monster."[25]

National media related the theft of SUVs in broad daylight from dealerships in Monterrey—with a marked increase from February through August.[26] Caravans of CDG-marked trucks rumbled through Matamoros and Reynosa. Meanwhile, well-compensated local cops supposedly kept watch on Gulf Cartel turf. Los Zetas hunkered down in Nuevo Laredo, the crown jewel of their border *plazas*, and in smaller outposts. Texas officials voiced concern that the inter-cartel battles would cross the border. On May 8, 2010, a Spanish-language flyer appeared on a vehicle in Brownsville with a disturbing notice: May 15–17 would be one of the "most violent weekends in all of Mexican history." The communiqué advised the public to be cautious and avoid dressing in black, the color that combatants would be wearing.[27] This prophecy came true with the execution-style murder of Alberto "El Beto Fabe" Castillo on May 17, 2010. A Gulf plaza boss in Matamoros, Castillo was apparently knocked off for allowing his brother Arturo "El Apache" Castillo Flores, thirty-three, to switch sides and work for Los Zetas. After El Beto Fabe's death, fifteen corpses, bearing large "Z"s carved on their tortured bodies, turned up on the Matamoros–San Fernando highway. Authorities believed they were members of the team of El Apache, who was later arrested on July 24. Also apprehended were Castillo Flores along with two cohorts. Alberto "El Pelochas" Blanco Flores and José Ezekiel "El Niño" Galicia Gonzálezwere seized when they attempted to flee by swimming to Texas. Blanco Flores made headlines after crying in open court at the sight of his mother. While under custody of the US Marshal's Service, Galicia used a shard of plastic cutlery to slash his wrist and slit his throat. He survived.

Two months later, El Apache's younger brother, Omar "Omarcillo" Flores, twenty-five, and an accomplice showed up inside a bullet-riddled gray Dodge Ram. The pickup was parked along a state highway in a secluded area, approximately three hundred yards from the Cameron County Sheriff's Office and the adjacent jail that held El Apache. The gunmen had used silenced Beretta pistols and had tracked their prey waiting for the right time and place. Brownsville Police Chief Carlos Garcia confirmed that the murder had been a hit presumably at the behest of the Gulf Cartel. Although identified by Brownsville and federal authorities, the assassins managed to escape. A source with firsthand knowledge of criminality in the area stated that both Oscar and his group belonged to a cell called "Grupo L," which was believed to have betrayed the Gulf Cartel and cast its lot with Los Zetas.[28] Despite rumored appearances of armed Mexican felons on American soil, relatively little overt violence against prominent figures has "spilled over." Table 14 indicates the disparity of drug-related murders in five twin cities.

The US government officially recognized the Los Zetas–Gulf Cartel split on April 11, 2010, when the DEA special agent in charge in McAllen, Texas, explained the alliance formed against the paramilitaries in simple terms, "It's an issue of a common enemy . . .. It's been well-documented that the Gulf cartel has formed alliances with the Sinaloa cartel and [La Familia] to wage war against the Zetas."[29]

After a manhunt across Nuevo León and Tamaulipas, the FAZC concentrated on Treviño Morales' stronghold, Nuevo Laredo. That city also drew the attention of the armed forces. At the end of July, marines

Table 14   Murders in Border Cities, 2010

US City	Murders	Mexican City	Murders
El Paso	5	Ciudad Juárez	3,951
Brownsville	5	Matamoros	85
Laredo	17 (2009)	Nuevo Laredo	109
Nogales	15 (Santa Cruz County)	Nogales	165
San Diego	29	Tijuana	800

Source: Elizabeth Findell, "McAllen Saw Less Crime in 2010, Police Say," *The Monitor*, January 14, 2011; www.city-data.com/city/Laredo-Texas.html; Fiscalía: 11 homicidios diarios en Juárez Mexico, *Tiempos de Angustia*, March 14, 2011; Julieta Martínez, "Suman 800 homicidios en Tijuana en 2010," *El Universal*, December 22, 2010; Kristina Davis, "Murders in San Diego at Lowest Level Since 1968," *SignOnSanDiego*, January 17, 2011; and Presidencia de la República, "Base de Datos Fallecimientos," http://www.presidencia.gob.mx/base-de-datos-de-fallecimientos/.

and army soldiers engaged in a firefight with El 40's gunmen that ended in a stalemate. Reports suggested that the military retreated after encountering a barrage from rocket-propelled grenades.[30] So spectacular was the showdown that a small crowd gathered on the US side of the Laredo International Bridge 1 to watch the dazzling explosions and listen to a cacophony of automatic gunfire.[31] Ultimately, however, the three-cartel coalition was unable to kill Treviño Morales.

The first case of collateral damage came to light in late March, when stray bullets felled two students from the prestigious Monterrey Technological Institute.[32] Errant shots killed several more Monterrey citizens, but the students' highly publicized deaths represented, for many, the dividing point between a previously peaceful Monterrey and a metropolis under siege.[33]

Since the summer of 2005, Treviño Morales had entrenched himself in his well-protected Nuevo Laredo hideouts. Through the alliance that they had cemented with the BLO, Los Zetas operated from a position of strength in Monterrey, where the Beltrán Leyvas had controled a major enclave for several years. The attempt of the CDG and its allies to displace the paramilitaries from these cities ignited a protracted conflict in Monterrey, which most analysts agreed would be the last urban center to succumb to the cartels. After a year of fighting, one businessman observed in 2011 that "if Monterrey is lost, all is lost."[34]

In August 2010, the Mexican government responded to the nightmare in the north by steadily increasing the number of soldiers patrolling Nuevo León and Tamaulipas. Clashes between troops and criminals elevated the body count. Ultimately, the military's presence did not stop the intercartel mayhem, but further destabilized Tamaulipas, many of whose residents migrated south or to the United States.

Human rights abuses committed by the armed forces prompted academics and analysts to lambast Calderón's strategy. "To put the army in this situation without any exit strategy is to waste one of the few assets in which Mexican society has any confidence," a public security expert at the University of Monterrey told a visiting reporter, adding that "the urban deployments are putting new stresses on the traditionally opaque military hierarchy, and exposing shortcomings of the troops, many of whom have only a primary school education and enlisted more for a paycheck than a vocation."[35]

Los Zetas employed roadblocks, kidnappings, extortion, and daytime skirmishes to defend themselves from the military and the FAZC offensive. The imperative for El 40 and The Executioner to generate more cash for the war boosted shakedowns of professionals and small business owners. In 2010, they spent as much as $4 million a month to fend off the Gulf Cartel and its confederates.[36]

Resourceful kidnappers, Los Zetas began abducting even more poor Central and South American migrants who passed through Guatemala in hopes of reaching El Norte. As discussed earlier, the extremely cruel brigands milked money from captives and their families, put some of them to work on behalf of the cartel, and impressed a few into auxiliary combat roles.

In August 2010, one itinerant—lucky or smart enough to survive her initial encounter with Los Zetas—who won their confidence, first as a cook, and later as a housekeeper, recounted the Los Zetas' fiendish handling of their quarry. The thuggish operators had kidnapped Marisolina from the train in Coatzacoalcos, Veracruz, and charged $3,000 for her freedom. She had no family in the United States or El Salvador. Rather than execute the prisoner, they allowed her to prepare meals for the men who supervised the kidnapped migrants awaiting word and money from family members abroad. As a "slave for Los Zetas," she cooked and cleaned for the evildoers charged with executing migrants; she even prepared the last meal for the hapless men and women destined to die.[37]

After several days, the head of the safe house invited Marisolina to chat. He was high on alcohol and cocaine when he asked if she knew why his clothes were always dirty. Afraid for her life, Marisolina suggested that perhaps it was because he repaired trucks that transported the migrants. He laughed before saying, "I am the butcher. I don't have anything to do with being a mechanic. My job is to get rid of the trash that doesn't pay."[38]

The inebriated Zeta continued, "First I cut them into pieces so they fit in the drums and then I set them on fire until there's nothing left."[39] Marisolina said that she had repeatedly washed the blood of these victims from garments, and when she shook out the clothes before washing them, chunks of flesh would fall from their folds. The smell of soot reminded her of death. After three months, she managed to escape only to find out that authorities were less concerned with her story of the safe house butchers than they were that she might be a Zeta herself.

Former CIA contract pilot William Robert "Tosh" Plumlee reported that Los Zetas captured a grandmother along with her granddaughter as they were driving from Deming, New Mexico, into Mexico. The elder brother of the nine-year-old girl was apparently selling arms to a rival cartel. Plumlee believes that the grandmother, who was later found decapitated a mile away, was forced to watch the burial of the little girl without killing her first along with her two-year-old Labrador dog and teddy bear.[40]

As if events in the north were not bloody enough, in mid-September officials discovered seventy-two bodies.[41] The deceased were not gunmen but innocent migrants, who, traveling without the support of a coyote network, had been kidnapped. Family and friends who were unable to pay the ransom would never see their loved ones again. Rather than taking the time to "disappear" the migrants, Los Zetas simply dumped their corpses in a mass grave. Their barbarity soared to new heights in late April 2011, when 193 bodies were pulled from forty deep pits near San Fernando, a once-sleepy Tamaulipas farming and ranching community of 60,000, which some observers have now labeled the "anteroom to hell." The Gulf Cartel has driven Los Zetas out of San Fernando, prized for its spiderweb of roads that connects the municipality with a dozen or more others. The PGR later indicated that Los Zetas may have perpetrated the murders to intercept La Familia stalwarts who might have been trying to sneak into the north to aid the Gulf Cartel.

The killers used a sledgehammer or a similar blunt instrument to crush their victims' skulls. The navy took into custody Omar Martín "El Kilo" Estrada and other alleged Zetas believed to be involved in the mass murders.[42] They later alleged that the barrel-chested El Kilo reported to Édgar "El Wache" Huerta Montiel, twenty-two, captured in Fresnillo, Zacatecas, on June 16, 2011, who—in turn—was the right-hand man of Salvador Alfonso "La Ardilla" Martínez Escobedo, a Zeta regional chief in Tamaulipas. El Wache claimed that some six hundred more bodies were still buried in Tamaulipas.[43]

Fear engulfed the state, even as coroners and other personnel in overcrowded morgues sought to identify the scores of nameless victims who were placed in a refrigerated truck before being taken to Mexico City. Flies buzzed over the blood stains on the pavement. "This is frightening. It's horrible," said a tortilla vendor. "It smells like death. I vomited," his friend added.[44]

In light of the dreadful conditions, the Public Security Ministry dispatched an additional five hundred soldiers, raising to 3,500 the troop level in the state by mid-May 2011.[45] Meanwhile, the army brass took advantage of the Gulf/Sinaloa/La Familia union. Rather than participating in the initial engagements, the armed forces often came in after the heaviest fighting to bury the dead and arrest the wounded, the majority of whom were Zetas. There was no accord between Defense Secretary Guillermo Galván, on the one hand, and El Chapo and El Coss, on the other, but mutual interests engendered coordination.

On September 17, 2010, fighting again erupted in Matamoros, the nerve center of the Gulf Cartel. Tony Tormenta led a group of FACZ gunmen in a foray against a Zeta stash house located in the Expofiesta Sur neighborhood in southern Matamoros. Returning from the fire-fight, the CDG men engaged a patrol of marines near the municipal police station. The running battle engulfed much of the city, ending in Las Arboledas neighborhood near the border. Tony Tormenta managed to escape the onslaught as Gulf Cartel reinforcements flooded the area to hold off the military offensive. There had been three separate engagements and several bodies had been scattered across the city. Officials did not issue a count of dead and wounded.[46]

The struggle for Monterrey simmered but didn't boil over into daylight street fights. Still, it resulted in the deaths of at least four area mayors, numerous policemen, and poorly trained gunmen from both sides.[47]

After eight months of holding out against their adversaries, the tide appeared to be turning for The Executioner's men. On July 29, 2010, the army killed Nacho Coronel Villarreal, a veteran powerhouse in the Sinaloa Cartel who ran the syndicate's methamphetamine operations and held sway over Jalisco and neighboring areas. Rumors spread that El Chapo believed his longtime ally had gotten too big for his pants. As a result, he may have tipped the military to the location of the local "capo de los capos" mansion in an affluent neighborhood of Zapopan, which forms part of the Guadalajara metropolitan area and is home to renowned Chivas team. Los Zetas again rejoiced on August 30 when the army arrested their bitter enemy, La Barbie. As noted in chapter 1, Valdez Villarreal had fought the paramilitaries on behalf of the Sinaloa Cartel, switched his allegiance to Arturo Beltrán Leyva, only to turn against the BLO when he formed the Independent Acapulco Cartel (CIDA) in late 2009. CIDA specialized in kidnappings, extortion, and murders in Acapulco and throughout Guerrero state. His animus toward Los Zeta's top man became evident after Barbie was behind bars. The baby-faced assassin said little except that he regretted getting caught before he could kill The Executioner.[48]

On November 5, 2010, another Zeta antagonist bit the dust when marines surrounded and killed Tony Tormenta in Matamoros. This take-down followed an eight-hour exchange of fire that necessitated closing three international bridges, shuttering dozens of schools, and freezing public transport. Dozens of CDG gunmen went to great lengths to shield their chief by blocking roads and confronting the military throughout the city. With at least 150 marines, and 660 soldiers and police, as well as 17 vehicles and three helicopters, the Mexican government finally killed the longtime fugitive.[49] The death of Osiel's elder brother enabled El Coss and his "Metros" to dominate the cartel, which faced internal opposition from "Los Rojos." Although an examination of the inner workings of the Gulf Cartel lies beyond the purview of this book, the table below provides an aperçu into recent strife within the syndicate.

Less than a year after El Coss failed to eliminate The Executioner, he had lost territory and cadres. By the end of 2010, Los Zetas had once more expanded their activities and regained solid footholds in many areas that they had controlled before the outbreak of the war in the north.

The initial phase of this conflict began in mid-January 2010 with the torture and execution of Concord 3 and lasted until the navy killed Tony Tormenta ten months later. Significant battles remain to be fought, namely, for the definitive control of Reynosa, Matamoros, and Monterrey. Nevertheless, Los Zetas survived the initial onslaught and have rebounded to fashion an offensive strategy, possibly designed to cut the country into four squares.

The Casino Royale Firebombing

A tragic event in mid-2011 marked a tectonic shift in the campaign to eradicate Los Zetas. On August 25, 2011, a fist of Zetas entered the Casino Royale in Monterrey and ordered everyone out as they doused the ground floor with accelerant and set the building ablaze. Many people escaped, but fifty-two victims, who in their terror fled deeper into the betting parlor, ascended to the second floor, or tried to escape through locked doors. From the scene of the crime, President Calderón condemned the tragedy as an act of "narco-terror"—the first time he had applied the term to Los Zetas. He also berated Uncle Sam for the bloodshed, avowing that "[t]he economic power and firepower of the criminal organizations operating in Mexico and Latin America come from this endless demand for drugs in the United States. We are neighbors, we are allies, we are friends, but also, you are responsible."[50] Mexico City Cardinal Norberto Rivera Carrera castigated the carnage as a "diabolical act" and warned against legalizing "the law of the jungle." These denunciations aroused national and international media attention. The scrutiny also exposed gaming centers as magnets for underworld groups because of opportunities for extortion and money laundering. *Proceso* magazine reported that the number of legal and illegal gambling businesses mushroomed from one hundred in 2000 to eight hundred in 2011; during the same period, Nuevo León State has witnessed an increase in such establishments from five to fifty-seven. Thus, it is possible that either the Zetas or the Gulf Cartel operated the Casino Royale and its rival sought to put it out of business.

Francisco "El Quemado: Medina Mejía, Zeta chief in Monterrey and the northern region, and Baltazar "El Mataperros" Saucedo Estrada Santa Catarina (Nuevo León) plaza boss, apparently masterminded the conflagration. Although El Quemado remained at large, authorities arrested El Mataperros and his ally, El Pepito Sarabia, in early 2012. The previous August, they had collared five of their subordinates: Luis Carlos "El Chihua" Carrasco Espinosa, Javier "El Javo" Jonathan Jair Reina Gutiérrez, Juan Ángel Leal Flores, and Julio Tadeo "El Julio Rayas" Barrones Ramírez. Later, authorities took two other suspects into custody: Jesús Rafael "El Colitas" Torres Bautista and José Alberto Loera Rodríguez. The latter, who went by the sobriquet "Voltaje Negro," was both a policeman and a professional boxer. Arrest warrants were also issued for Monterrey area plaza bosses Héctor Javier "La Rana" Montoya Chávez, Miguel Ángel "El Barraza" Barranza Escamilla, and Carlos "El Toruño" López Castro.

Many dignitaries in Monterrey's business, political, religious, and cultural hierarchies had continually chastised the Calderón administration for not protecting their metropolis, which six years earlier had been named "the safest city in Latin America." *Nuevoleoneses* reeled from what appeared to be the beginning of a new level of violence, and the tragedy catalyzed a no-holds-barred pursuit of culprits—with the first major operations in the Zeta bastion of Veracruz.

Like their Semper Fi! US counterparts, Mexico's marines stationed in Veracruz were especially eager to take on The Executioner's men. They still smarted over Los Zetas' having executed the family of Marine Meiquisedet Angulo Cordova after the late 2009 killing of Arturo Beltrán Leyva. El Lazca may have orchestrated the assassination of several other of their comrades in the state.

On September 8, the navy and marines dismantled 12 antennae configured to support Los Zetas' communication networks in ten municipalities in northern Veracruz. The Mexican government struck twice more against the paramilitaries' communications: in Torreón in mid-November and again in Veracruz in late November when it seized 167 antennas, 155 repeaters, 166 power sources (some solar), 1,466 radios, and 71 computers.[51]

El Chapo also landed a blow against The Executioner's men. He is believed to have paid the *matazetas*, freebooting mercenaries available to the highest bidder and linked to the New General Cartel of Jalisco (Cártel de Nueva Generación Jalisco—CNGJ), to kidnap and execute thirty-five Zetas and their allies. On September 21, the masked contract killers disposed of the mutilated bodies on a busy thoroughfare in the Veracruz–Boca del Río tourist zone. El Lazca and El 40 could no longer consider the state a secure citadel for their criminal enterprise. They may have been able to hold their own with government foes, but the Sinaloa Cartel and its gunmen were an entirely different enemy. Guzmán Loera demonstrated that his troops could conduct dramatic strikes inside what had been considered Los Zetas territory.

In late October, shadowy international cyber-pirates called "Anonymous" threatened to publicize the names, photos, and properties of Los

Zetas' toadies among police, journalists, and taxi drivers if, by November 5, the killers failed to release a computer activist abducted in Veracruz. In a *YouTube* transmission, the movement rebuked the extortion, kidnapping, and robberies committed by the renegades, emphasizing, "You committed a huge error in seizing one of us." Reuters related that the hackers canceled their plans, explaining that Los Zetas had released their ally and warned that dissemination of information would trigger retribution against his family and ensure the death of ten people for every contact exposed. Stratfor indicated that Los Zetas has its own computer experts, who keep tabs on "anticartel" campaigns online. This capability may explain the high number of journalists murdered.

Seven weeks after the September massacre, The Executioner's men fired shots at the Veracruz–Boca del Río Intermunicipal police force headquarters but lost three sicarios in the attempted revenge. *Reforma* reported that eighty-eight corpses turned up in Veracruz state in September and October—with the number for the year exceeding 325.

Los Zetas then shifted their gaze to Jalisco and Sinaloa.

Eleven thousand police and soldiers participated in the "Secure Veracruz Operation" to safeguard Guadalajara, which hosted the October 14–30 Pan American Games. The relative peacefulness during the international competition represented the veritable lull before the storm. In the wake of his Nacho Coronel's death, his Jalisco organization splintered, with the pro-El Chapo CJNG arising from the remnants of Coronel's supporters. The Sinaloans had other allies in the nation's second-largest city: Gonzalo Araujo "Macho Prieto" Inzunza, El Mayo Zambada's ace gunman, who commanded forty pistoleros; elements of the Knights Templars; and Los Güeros headed by the Rodríguez Olivera brothers.

Arrayed against it were The Resistance (La Resistencia), a loosely organized contingent that emerged from a May 2010 split between the Sinaloa and Milenio Cartels; Los Zetas, outsiders who received backing and resources from the locally based Resistance; and the Beltrán Leyvas.[52]

For months, Los Zetas had been moving cautiously into Jalisco from their strongholds in neighboring Zacatecas state. On February 1, 2011, they began by closing off streets and burning vehicles in Zapopan, the first *narcobloqueos* in the Guadalajara region. In nearby Tonalá, motorcyclists hurled fragmentation grenades at the headquarters of the Municipal Police.

On February 26 Los Zetas and their cohorts launched a grenade attack that killed four law-enforcement personnel in a restaurant located a block away from state police headquarters in Puerto Vallarta. The killers made two other assaults on state police agents in Zapopan, in the Guadalajara and its vicinity. On November 21 and 22, they carried out abductions before depositing twenty-six cadavers in two vans and a pickup truck at the golden *Arcos de Milenio*, a signature sculpture in an extremely busiest intersection, on November 24. The next day Los Zetas unfurled a banner near the arches in which they denied any "dispute with the local population." They stressed that the conflict was with El Chapo, Maya Zambada, Vicente Zambada, Noel "El Flaco" Salgueiro Nevarez (CJNG founder), and the CJNG who are "informants for the American government" and that the Jalisco and Sinaloa governors were friends of the Sinaloa Cartel big shots. In light of the mayhem, Guadalajara's cardinal, Juan Sandoval Iñiguez, called for army units to patrol local streets. In one stroke, the Los Zetas leader alerted the government of the vulnerability of even its "safest" city.

For several years, the paramilitaries had been infiltrating Sinaloa. Instead of engaging in hostile acts, they contented themselves with recruiting men and suborning police, judges, and prosecutors. They enjoyed the support of the BLO, which—in turn—collaborated with Los Mazatlecos, to carry out ambushes against law-enforcement agents in the Sinaloan municipalities of Gusave, Ahome, Los Mochis, and Mazatlán. The leader of this Mazatlan-based gang, Santiago "El Chaquín" Lizárraga Ibarra, is believed to have kidnapped and murdered El Nacho's sixteen-year-old son in April 2010. The Executioner's men showed their colors only in late 2011 when, in concert with the BLO and Los Mazatlecos, they kidnapped and killed at least twenty-four Sinaloa Cartel members, burned their bodies, and dumped them outside of Culiacán on November 23, just one day before the Guadalajara "message." On November 24 twenty-six additional corpses appeared in Sinaloa's capital.

Los Zetas' exploits in Jalisco had five goals: to revenge the bloodshed suffered in Veracruz, to distract foes from their scorched earth campaign in Veracruz, to strengthen bonds with The Resistance in hopes of garnering a beachhead in a traditional Sinaloan fiefdom, to enter the methamphetamine trade, and to emphasize their ability to absorb a battery of punches and remain standing. Some of these factors explain Zeta initiatives in Sinaloa. Above all, they wanted to notify El Chapo that they could strike in his backyard.

The skillful tactical planning and execution of the Guadalajara and Sinaloa forays suggests El Lazca devised the operations himself. Although the paramilitaries have endured losses that would have hobbled other groups, the organization's command and control structure was battered but intact in early 2012. Meanwhile, instruction became less a top-down exercise than a city- or municipal-based rush job managed by mid-level operatives determined to keep hot guns in the hands of warm bodies. This change produced poorly trained young men with whom the renegades constantly harassed their adversaries during the deadly on-the-job training. Successful recruits rose rapidly through the ranks, and some even wound up as bosses of small plazas. Their superior strategy might be the single asset that keeps Los Zetas one step ahead of swarming enemies. Zeta strategists have a sound idea of how far they can go against the Sinaloa Cartel and its comrades-in-arms. They realize that at this point a concerted offensive to takeover Guadalajara and Jalisco would be the group's Waterloo.[53] Whatever may be Los Zetas' next objectives for expansion in Mexico and abroad, few observers question the organization's strength.

In early December 2011, Treviño Morales released a communiqué to "the nation, the government and all of Mexico and to public opinion." In this challenge, the treacherous boss advised that "[n]ot the army, not the marines nor the security and anti-drug agencies of the United States government can resist us. Mexico lives and will continue under the regime of Los Zetas."

Notes

1. James C. McKinley Jr., "Mexican Drug Kingpin Sentenced to 25 Years in Secret Hearing," *New York Times*, February 25, 2010.
2. Quoted in "Authorities: Gulf Cartel, Zetas Gang Up On Each Other as Arrangement Dies," *The Monitor*, March 10, 2010.
3. Alfredo Corchado, "Cartel's Enforcers Outpower Their Boss," *Dallas Morning News*, June 2007.
4. Jeremy Roebuck, "Criminal Cooperation," *The Monitor*, July 1, 2009.
5. Ibid.
6. Quoted in Corchado, "Cartel's Enforcers Outpower Their Boss."
7. Quoted in "Narco: infierno en Tamaulipas," *Proceso*, February 27, 2010.
8. Ibid.
9. Nick Miroff and William Booth, "Mexico's Drug War Intrudes on Monterrey, a Booming Metropolis," *Washington Post*, March 11, 2011.
10. Raymundo Riva Palacio, "La batalla de Tamaulipas," *Vanguardia*, March 1, 2010.
11. "Guerra entre cartels del Golfo y Los Zetas augura baño de sangre en México," *Terra*, February 25, 2010.

12. Jeremy Roebuck, "Criminal Cooperation," *The Monitor*, July 1, 2009.
13. Quoted in Gustavo Castillo García, "Opera ya La Familia en apoyo al cartel del Golfo en Tamaulipas," *La Jornada*, February 27, 2010.
14. Quoted in "Estado de Sitio," *Proceso*, March 1, 2010.
15. "El cartel del Golfo echa a Los Zetas de Tamaulipas," *El Milenio*, April 5, 2010.
16. Quoted in "Ciudad Mier Evacuates After Zetas Threaten to Kill Residents," *The Monitor*, November 9, 2010.
17. Mark Stevenson, "Drug Battles Create Border Ghost Towns," *Washington Times*, December 27, 2010; figures on death toll appeared in *Reforma*.
18. Gustavo Castillo García, "Guerra por territorios dispara la cifra de ejecuciones en Tamaulipas y NL," *La Jornada*, March 6, 2010.
19. See http://www.youtube.com/watch?v=8VCEU9r4FQs.
20. Benito Jiménez, "Atribuyen militares choque en Camargo a un presunto ataque del Cártel del Golfo," *Reforma*, March 3, 2010.
21. Gustavo Castillo García, "Suman 4 días de balaceras en Tamaulipas," *La Jornada*, March 3, 2010.
22. Ibid.
23. "Fusión de carteles 'antizetas' piden al 'senor Calderón' retire al Ejército," *Proceso*, March 3, 2010. See: http://tinyurl.com/y8ess68.
24. "Cárteles ofrecen a Calderón 'terminar' con Los Zetas," *El Milenio*, March 9, 2010.
25. D. Casas and J. Martínez, "En mantas, Zetas se burlan de alianzas para combatir el narco," *La Crónica* de Hoy, February 24, 2010.
26. "Semáforo delictivo," *Iluminemos Nuevo León*, July 7, 2011.
27. "Officer Awareness on the Border: Narcomessage in Texas," *Intelligence Bulletin*, Texas Department of Public Safety, Intelligence and Counterterrorism Division, May 10, 2010.
28. "Arrestan a 'El Apache,'" *El Nuevo Heraldo*, August 4, 2010; and "Authorities: Murders Related to Mexican Cartels," *The Monitor*, October 2, 2010.
29. Quoted in "Mexico Drug Cartels 'Join Forces,'" *Al Jazeera*, April 13, 2010.
30. J. Jesús Esquivel, "El 'show' de la sangre," *El Diario de Coahuila*, August 15, 2010.
31. Ibid.
32. Víctor Salvador Canales and José Plata, "Sicarios mataron a los estudiantes, sugiere la SEGOB," *Milenio*, March 23, 2010.
33. Coauthor (Logan) interview with chief security officer for Monterrey, Fortune 500 Company (name withheld), August 2010.
34. Miroff and Booth, "Mexico's Drug War Intrudes on Monterrey."
35. Quoted in Tim Johnson, "In Mexico's Drug War, Military Has to Defend Reputation, Too," *McClatchy News Service*, May 4, 2010.
36. Coauthor (Logan) interview with Department of Defense employee (name withheld), July 2011.
37. "Esclava de 'Los Zetas': una historia desde adentro," *El Universal*, August 28, 2010.
38. Quoted in "Esclava de 'Los Zetas': una historia desde adentro," *El Universal*, August 28, 2010.
39. Ibid.

40. Tim King, "Mata Zetas—Has Los Zetas Cartel Met Its Own Murderous Match?" *Salem-News.com* (Oregon), September 30, 2011.

41. "El terror y el grito ahogado," *El Diario de Coahuila*, September 5, 2010.

42. Nick Miroff and William Booth, "At Mexican Grave Site, a New Level of Barbarity," *Washington Post*, April 25, 2011; the other possible Zetas taken into custody include Esvin "El Gato" Leonel Batres Hernández, Johnny "La Sombra" Torres Andrade, and El Kilo's girlfriend, Saray Fabiola "La Muñeca" Díaz Arroyo; see Alberto Morales, "Poiré: está Tamaulipas bajo control," *El Universal.com.mx*, April 27, 2011.

43. Benito Jiménez, "Cae coordinador de massacre de migrantes," *Reforma. com*, June 17, 2011.

44. Quoted in E. Eduardo Castillo, *Huffington Post*, August 26, 2010.

45. Dudley Althaus, "Mexican Victims Overwhelm Border Morgues," *Chron. com*, April 15, 2011; and Alberto Morales, "Van a Tamaulipas 500 soldados más," *El Universal.com.mx*, May 13, 2011.

46. "Multiple Shootouts Reported in Matamoros," *Brownsville Herald*, September 17, 2010.

47. Tracy Wilkinson, "Fourth Mexican Mayor Killed in under Six Weeks," *Los Angeles Times*, September 25, 2010.

48. "No dejaron chingarme a mis rivales," *Milenio*, September 1, 2010.

49. Gustavo Castillo, Jesús Aranda, and Alonso Urrutia, "Muere Tony Tormenta luego de ocho horas de tiroteos con efectivos federales en Matamoros," *La Jornada*, November 6, 2010.

50. Quoted in William Booth, "Mexico Blames U.S. Drug Culture, Guns for Casino Massacre," *Washington Post*, August 26, 2011.

51. Corchado, "Cartel's Enforcers Outpower Their Boss."

52. "Desatan cárteles guerra en Jalisco," *Reforma*, November 25, 2011; and Steven Dudley, "RawFeed: Decoding the Violence in Jalisco," *InSightCrime*, February 7, 2011.

53. Raymundo Riva Palacio, "La batalla de Tamaulipas," *Vanguardia*, March 1, 2010.

12

Conclusions

On July 1, 2011, marines opened fire on Los Zetas in Fresnillo and pinned down their quarry long enough for other military units to ensnare the criminals inside a noose. After five hours, and at least fifteen deaths, the bloody competition ended with the paramilitaries still in catbird's seat. After all, The Executioner's men have purchased local and state police, and the military conducts only desultory maneuvers. Fresnillo, and the state of Zacatecas, may form part of a blueprint to complete an east–west corridor from Tampico to Durango, passing through San Luis Potosí and Zacatecas, and a north–south thruway from Nuevo Laredo south through Zacatecas into the states of Jalisco, Colima, and Nayarit, where the outlaws could detonate their next major offensive.

This "Zetas-Cross" theory, developed by Southern Pulse investigators in Mexico, holds that consolidation of both corridors would isolate the Gulf Cartel, ensconced in Matamoros, and what remains of La Familia and the Knights Templars, well positioned in Morelia. By drawing a line from Monterrey south to Colima on the Pacific Coast, and examining Los Zetas' move to dominate each *plaza* along the route, including Zacatecas, Aguascalientes, and Guadalajara, one official suggested that the renegades seek to cut off the Knights Templars' geographical link to the border to marginalize and strangle its longtime rivals, once considered the third strongest criminal organization in Mexico.[1]

The Executioner's men have weathered assaults that would shake the foundations of many sturdy corporations. They have survived an onslaught from powerful enemies only to emerge stronger than they were in mid-2009. More than two years later, Los Zetas counted a presence in seventeen of the country's thirty-one states and the federal district; the cutthroats pose a growing threat in Central America, especially Guatemala; and its tentacles plunge into Colombia and beyond, perhaps east into Africa and Europe.

Los Zetas have profited from a complex mixture of (1) good timing and luck, (2) poor decisions by the government and other adversaries, (3) the counterproductive kingpin strategy, (4) strong, diabolical leadership, (5) an enduring paramilitary model that places command, control, and accounting above all else, and (6) PSYOPS.

The arrest of some two thousand employees in La Familia's network inside the United States in July 2011[2] underscored a level of law-enforcement prowess not present in Mexico, where corruption prevails and anticartel plans seep into the underworld.[3] Faults such as the "Fast and Furious" program aside, the US Department of Justice and other federal agencies achieve successes because they arrest suspects in several dozen cities simultaneously and, more important, conduct their business without leaks. Until Mexico develops professional, honest law-enforcement agencies, it will not be able to pull off such strikes. The Mexican government has delivered blows against individuals or smaller groups, but tends to home in on *capos* one at a time. This approach augments violence as lieutenants, who may be less skilled than their dethroned boss, vie to replace a fallen don, and other cartels poach on the turf of the decapitated número uno. At the same time, gangs associated with the syndicates lunge for more power.

Its relationship with the BLO enabled Los Zetas to expand rapidly into Monterrey and Zacatecas. And it may be links with La Línea that throw open the gates to Juárez. Reports suggest that La Línea is the tail that wags the dog of the debilitated Juárez Cartel. In light of the possible retirement of Vicente Carrillo Fuentes and arrests of his comrades, this brutal gang could make common cause with Los Zetas by exchanging tactical support for access to the lucrative Juárez corridor.[4]

Such alliances explain why Interpol listed the Los Zetas as one of the "most active" DTO in the world.[5] Still, the paramilitaries' core strength constitutes its principal weakness. The Executioner and El 40 have preserved the syndicate's cohesion amid extraordinarily difficult times. Both men surround themselves with platoons of bodyguards. Yet there is the possible wild card; that is, a girlfriend, veterinarian, or some other noncombatant could inadvertently talk out of school and furnish information that might allow enemies to track down the sadists.

Los Zetas' leaders now figure prominently on the Washington's and Mexico City's "most wanted" lists along with El Chapo, the proud father of twins born to his wife in California in September 2011, and fellow Sinaloan El Mayo Zambada.

Although Los Zetas continue to bring into their ranks soldiers and policemen, they increasingly recruit indolent teenagers who are prone to "spray and pray" rather than follow the methodical style of highly trained shooters. If their rumored alliance with La Línea materializes, Los Zetas would benefit from the services of seasoned hit men—ex-cops abound in the Ciudad Juárez/El Paso gang—rather than depending heavily on lower-class neophytes.

No matter the outcome of fighting in the north, in Veracruz, in Jalisco, and in Sinaloa, the Colombian experience demonstrates that results occur only when the economic, social, and political elite commit themselves to combating organized crime. This has happened only in northern Mexico. Of course, it took place in Colombia when Pablo Escobar moved from drug-trafficking to terrorism. But does the Mexican situation require such extremes before all stakeholders have reached consensus? Assuming the PRI wins the July 1, 2012, presidential election, it will have a strong incentive to conduct a more astute drug war with better intelligence drawn from wire-taps, informants, drone overflights, scrutiny of bank accounts, reliable cooperation with the United States, and more to manage an effective "drug war" and, in doing so, also likely expose corruption engendered during the twelve years of PAN rule. Although Mexican drug-war violence exists in the United States, it is on a small scale compared with Mexico's woes and, indeed, has not crossed over according to one study.[6] Assuming that the PRI configures an effective approach that leads to the capture or death of The Executioner and El 40, Los Zetas will survive, even if little more than a criminal brand and a new way of conducting criminal business in Mexico. "Nothing will change if the military completely exterminates the founders of Los Zetas, their school and their teaching [will] remain."[7]

Mexico's DTOs are sufficiently pragmatic to avoid provoking the consignment of US troops south of the Rio Grande. Yet if the cartel escalate their criminality above the border, pressure will mount for US armed action in Mexico, as proposed by Texas Governor Rick Perry. Closer relationships between Los Zetas and US-based street gangs would serve as an omen of such activities. So too would attacks on prominent US officials, bases, buildings, and infrastructure.

In terms of political consequences, the Monterrey tragedy further weakened the Calderón administration. Meanwhile, the PRI, whose candidate, former Mexico State Governor Enrique Peña Nieto, enjoyed a double-digit lead over other presidential hopefuls at the time of the firebombing, and the public's desire for both security and change invest him with an excellent chance to recapture Los Pinos in the July 1, 2012, contest.

The unprecedented bloodshed appears without reason or form and directly affects the country's political landscape. Nonetheless, Los Zetas and other cartels do not want Mexico to fail as a state. Rather, they are eager to do business with impunity—that is, to establish parallel government along key trafficking routes. Such "dual sovereignty," as illuminated above, already exists in the Tierra Caliente, the Golden Triangle, much of Michoacán, areas of Guerrero, Chiapas, and Oaxaca, and sectors of northern cities such as Ciudad Juárez, Matamoros, Reynosa, and Nuevo Laredo.

If a miracle should occur and authorities curbed drug activities, the cartels would continue their criminal pursuits—extortion, kidnapping, murder-for-hire, smuggling, contraband, prostitution rings, and so on. Thus, to ensure legitimacy amid widespread criminality, Mexico's establishment must improve educational, health-care, and employment opportunities for the third of the population who lived as ragpickers in fetid slums or on unproductive, sun-baked *ejidos*. Reforms should include the following: breaking the back of the SNTE teachers union; overhauling the Petróleos Mexicanos monopoly to continue exporting hydrocarbons; boosting tax collections, now only about 10–12 percent of GDP; rationalizing the provision of health care, now spread among a half-dozen or more state agencies; smashing monopolies and bottlenecks in petroleum, electricity, telecommunications, cement, and so on; launching job creation and regional development programs; and, above all, adopting re-election, at least at the municipal level, to allow the now-impotent citizenry an opportunity to influence public policy. Rather than expecting deliverance from Washington, Mexico's leaders must recognize that the future of their resource-rich country lies in their hands.

Notes

1. Coauthor (Logan) interview with a Mexican government official (name, position withheld), July 2011.
2. Geoffrey Ramsey, "US Arrests Nearly 2,000 'Members' of Mexico Drug Gang," *InSight Crime*, July 25, 2011.

3. Samuel Logan and James Bosworth, "Mexico's Criminal Organizations: Weakness in Complexity, Strength in Evolution," *Southern Pulse*, June 24, 2011.

4. Steven Dudley, "Zetas-La Linea Alliance May Alter Balance of Power in Mexico," *InSight Crime*, June 3, 2011.

5. "El cartel del Pacífico y Los Zetas, los más actives en el Mundo: Interpol," *Proceso*, July 12, 2011.

6. Alan Gomez, Jack Gillum, and Kevin Johnson, "U.S. Border Cities Prove Havens from Mexico's Drug Violence," *USA Today*, July 18, 2011.

7. Quoted in Ricardo Ravelo, "El poder y la estructura de 'Los Zetas,' intocados," *Proceso*, July 18, 2011.

Appendix 1

Original Zetas, Their Specialties, and Status

Original Zetas	Military ties	Specialty and area of operations	Status
Arellano Domínguez, Braulio "El Gonzo" or "El Z-20" or "El Verdugo"/"The Hangman"	Joined the army Feb. 22, 1993; deserted June 21, 1999	Sharpshooter; in charge of the main *plazas* in Quintana Roo and Veracruz	Marines killed him in Soledad de Doblado, Veracruz, Nov. 3, 2009
Betancourt, Alejandro Lucio Morales "Z-2"	Second Lt. in army	Developed a close relationship with Osiel; once arrested, he provided intelligence to help accomplish the kingpin's arrest	Captured Nov. 17, 2001; in witness protection program; referred to as "Geraldine" in official documents
Castrejón Peña, Víctor Nazario	Joined the army Sept. 1, 1988; resigned from active duty Sept. 30, 1999	Assassinations; hit man for Cárdenas Guillén	Captured
Dávila López, José Ramón "El Cholo" Alias: Antonio Torres Hernández and David Rubio Conde	Joined the army April 16, 1995; reached the rank of sergeant in GAFES; Feb. 16, 2001, resigned from active duty and entered the reserves; former member of the Pan American Protective Service	Excellent marksman; suspect in the kidnapping of a married couple, Ricardo González and Nelly Peña; worked directly under Omar Lorméndez Pitalúa and Heriberto Lazcano	Tamaulipas police captured him in Ciudad Victoria, Tamps, Feb. 9, 2007

Name	Military background	Role/description	Status
Díaz López, Mateo "Comandante Mateo"/"Z-10"	In 1996, joined the army's XV Motorized Cavalry Regiment and then the GAFES; deserted Sept. 20, 1998	Recruiting and training; graduated from the Conalep in Tabasco in electromechanics; in charge of Nuevo León plaza until being moved to Cunduacán, Tabasco, in early 2006; in his new post, he killed members of the competing Flores Torruco and Guizar Valencia families; known as the most bloodthirsty of Los Zetas	Local police captured him in Cunduacán, Tabasco, July 15, 2007; he provided testimony about Los Zetas to authorities
Escribano, Jerezano Gonzalo "El Z-18" or "El Cuije"	Joined the army April 25, 1992; deserted May 11, 2000		At large
González Castro, Gustavo "El Erótico"	Joined the infantry march 22, 1990; promoted to corporal in 1995; resigned from the army and joined the reserves August 1, 1998; and served in the Ministry of National Defense (SEDENA)	Trained in assault operations during seven years in the military; extremely dangerous; helped free twenty-five fellow narco-traffickers from a prison in Apatzingán, Mich.	Captured

(Continued)

Original Zetas, Their Specialties, and Status (*Continued*)

Original Zetas	Military ties	Specialty and area of operations	Status
González Dúran, Jaime "El Hummer"	Born January 22, 1976, San Luis Potosí; joined the army November 15, 1991; deserted February 24, 1999	Accused of killing popular entertainer Valentín Elizalde in November 2006, after the so-called Gallo de Oro had sung "A Mis Enemigos" ("To My Enemies"), which Los Zetas considered a warning to them from El Chapo; also wanted in the US for conspiracy, importation, and distribution of cocaine and marijuana as well as money laundering; extremely violent; active in plazas in Nuevo León, Tabasco, Michoacán, Tamaulipas (Reynosa and Miguel Alemán), DF, and Mexico State; extremely dangerous	Federal Police and COPES captured him in Reynosa, November 7, 2008
Guerrero Silva, Óscar Eduardo "El Winnie Pooh" or "Winnie" or "El Amarillo"	Joined Seventieth Infantry Battalion, January 28, 1992; ex-member of General Services Group (EMP); promoted to corporal in 1993; deserted November 26, 1999	Lieutenant of Cárdenas Guillén	Committed suicide by shooting himself in the head with a 9 mm pistol, at his girlfriend's home, Guadalupe, NL, February 1, 2001

Name	Military career	Activities	Fate
Guerrero Reyes, Luis Luis Alberto "El Guerrero"/"Z-5"	Joined Seventieth Infantry Battalion, March 1, 1987; promoted to corporal, November 1, 1990; became member of the Parachute Brigade of Marksmen (BFP), the elite unit before formation of GAFES, June 17, 1988; promoted to sergeant March 1, 1992; left army January 4, 1999; expert in explosives, martial arts, and grenade launchers	Matamoros plaza; known for his arrogance	Killed by four hit men riding in a white taxi and possible members of a rival cartel, Matamoros, May 10, 2003; it took local police eight hours to deactivate a hand grenade in dead man's hand
Guerra Ramírez, Rogelio "El Guerra"	Joined the army August 25, 1989; resigned April 18, 1999		At large
Guzmán Decena, Arturo "Z-1"	Born in Puebla, January 13, 1976	Trained in combat by Mexican and Israeli instructors; distinguished himself in the army and rose to the rank of lieutenant in the GAFES; helped recruit military personnel for Osiel Cárdenas	Killed by elements of the army and UEDO, Matamoros, Tamps, November 21, 1992
Hernández Barrón, Raúl "The Dutchman I" or "Flander I" or "Flandes"	Enlisted in the army September 1, 1993; left active duty September 1, 1999, and joined the reserves	Trafficking drug shipments into the US through the northern region of Veracruz; likely involved in the assassination of Valentín Elizalde	Elements of the army and PGR captured him in Coatzintla, Veracruz, March 21, 2008

(Continued)

Original Zetas, Their Specialties, and Status (*Continued*)

Original Zetas	Military ties	Specialty and area of operations	Status
Hernández Barrón, Víctor Manuel "El Flander 'II'"			Army special forces captured him in Matamoros, March 14, 2003; sentenced to twenty-nine years in prison
Hernández Lechuga, Raúl Lucio "El Lucky" or "Z-16" or "El Lucky"	Joined the army September 6, 1996; resigned October 24, 1997	Chief of Los Zetas in Puebla	At large
Ibarra Yepis, Prisciliano			At large
Lazcano Lazcano, Heriberto "El Lazca" or "The Executioner" or "El Z-3" or "El Verdugo"	Joined the army June 5, 1991 at the age of 28; promoted to corporal July 5, 1993; selected for GAFES; resigned March 27, 1998	Leader of Los Zetas; ex-policeman; believed to have killed Francisco Ortiz Franco; the courageous coeditor of the Tijuana weekly, *Zeta* (no relation to paramilitaries); current leader of Los Zetas; trained by GAFES in combat, intelligence, and counterinsurgency	At large
Lechuga Licona, Alfonso "El Z-27" or "El Cañas"	Joined the army December 1, 1991; deserted August 19, 1994	Kidnapping; border region of Tamaulipas	Captured by state police, May 25, 2006
Lorméndez Pitalúa, Omar "El Z 10" or "El Chavita" or "El Pita"		Controlled the Nuevo Laredo plaza along with Iván Velásquez Caballero, Mateo Díaz López, Héctor Sauceda Gamboa y Miguel Ángel Treviño; one of top four commanders at time of his arrest	Thanks to an anonymous tip, police captured him in Lázaro Cárdenas, Mich., September 21, 2005

Name	Service record	Activities	Status
López, Jorge "El Chuta"	Joined the army October 1, 1979; deserted September 17, 1981	Martial arts, explosives, ambushes, guerrilla tactics; instructs new Zetas	At large
López Lara, Isidro "El Colchón" or "Adrián Rodríguez Alarcón" or "Isidro Lara Flores" or "El Interno" or "El Colchas"	Enlisted in the army August 16, 1996; May 16, 2001, resigned from active duty and joined the reserves	Specialist in kidnapping and murder	Captured Ciudad Victoria, Tamps, September 11, 2005
López Lara, Eduardo Salvador "El Chavita" or "El Z-48"		Helped free Ramón "El Cholo" Dávila López from the Matamoros police; facilitated the landing of cocaine shipments at a clandestine airfield in "Las Amarillas" ranch in China, Nuevo León (now a Zeta training camp); and participated in murders and kidnappings	Captured and sentenced to twenty years in prison in late February 2008
Márquez Aguilar, Daniel Daniel Enrique "El Chocotorro"	No information is found for Aguilar at SEDENA		At large
Mellado Cruz, Galindo "El Mellado" or "El Z-9"	Joined the army September 1, 1992; resigned May 1, 1999		At large
Méndez Santiago, Flavio "El Amarillo" or "El Z-10"	Joined the army October 16, 1993; resigned July 4, 1997	Human trafficking from Central and South America; and drug shipments in the Southeast of Mexico	Captured by Federal Police in Villa Etla, Oaxaca, January 17, 2011

(Continued)

Original Zetas, Their Specialties, and Status (*Continued*)

Original Zetas	Military ties	Specialty and area of operations	Status
Pérez Rojas, Daniel "El Cachetes"	Joined the army May 23, 1997; deserted November 26, 1999; kidnapped by Zetas, who admired his skills	Expert in moving contraband across the border	Captured by antinarcotics agents in the western part of Guatemala City, April 9, 2008
Rejón Aguilar, Jesús Enrique "El Mamito"/"El Z-8"	Born June 9, 1976; Temapache, Veracuz; joined the army April 5, 1993; defected November 26, 1999; another version indicates that he joined the infantry August 1991; promoted to corporal in 1993; deserted on September 13, 1998	Munitions; sharp shooter; has been in charge of two Tamaulipas plazas with Efraín Teodoro Torres; active in Quintana Roo, Veracruz, and Tamaulipas (Ciudad Miguel Alemán and Ciudad Camargo); later, ran the western part of the country from San Luis Potosí. The US ($5 million) and Mexico ($2.3 million) offered rewards for information leading to his arrest	Captured by Federal Police while on his way to visit his mother; apprehended in Atizapán de Zaragoza, Mexico State, July 3, 2011
Reyes Enríquez, Luis "El Rex"/"Z-12"	Joined army January 30, 1990; on March 1, 1999, dispatched as a member of the PJF as a delegate of the Attorney General's Office to Tamaulipas	Close to Osiel Cárdenas; at one point in charge of Mexico City area operations	Elements of the army and the PGR captured him in Atotonilco, Hidalgo, along with ten accomplices, June 24, 2007
Ruíz Tlapanco, Sergio Sergio Enrique "El Tlapa"/"Z-44"	Joined the army March 6, 1988; resigned November 16, 1999	Mountain operations; and municipality of Cárdenas, Tabasco, and, possibly, Campeche	Captured

Soto Parra, Miguel Ángel "El Parra"	Joined the army May 2, 1994; resigned May 1, 1999; head of the Federal Judicial Police in Tamps	Former head of the Federal Judicial Police in Tamaulipas; assisted Osiel Cárdenas Guillén in drug trafficking as a dirty cop in Tamps	AFI arrested him in Coyoacán in southern DF, January 2, 2009
Torres, Efraín Teodoro "El Efra" or "El Z-14" or "La Chispa"	Joined an infantry division August 1, 1991; promoted to corporal in 1993; deserted September 13, 1998	Controlled two plazas in Tamaulipas with Jesús Enrique Rejón Aguilar Jesús Enrique (Ciudad Miguel Alemán and Ciudad Camargo)	Shot in dispute over winner of a clandestine horse race in rural Villarín, Veracruz, March 3, 2007
Torres Jiménez, Germán "Z-25"/"El Tatanka," as well as Leonardo Villarreal Zaragoza and/or Javier and/or José Luis	Instructor of Los Zetas; close to Osiel Cárdenas	Executed five members of La Familia Michoacana	Federal Police captured him in Poza Rica, Veracruz, March 2009
Trejo Benavides, Raúl Alberto "El Alvin" or "El Z-6"	Joined the army May 3, 1991; resigned March 16, 1999	Accused of participating with Raúl Hernández Barrón in the murder of singer Valentín Elizalde	Shot by rivals and abandoned by his own men; for lack of medical attention, he died in a seedy Matamoros hotel, May 2002; the La Paz funeral home returned his remains to his native Villahermosa
Treviño Morales, Miguel Ángel "El 40" claims to have been a GAFE, but never was in the military	Born November 18, 1970, Nuevo Laredo, Tamps	Performed odd jobs for the Gulf Cartel before working his way to number two in Los Zetas; controls the Nuevo Laredo plaza; sadistic	At large

(Continued)

Original Zetas, Their Specialties, and Status (*Continued*)

Original Zetas	Military ties	Specialty and area of operations	Status
Vargas García, Nabor "El Debora"	Joined the army June 28, 1995; on July 1, 1999, he resigned from active duty (and the Presidential Guard's assault battalion); joined the reserves	Ran a Zeta unit in Tabasco, Campeche, and Chiapas	Captured with twenty of his henchmen after a gunfight in Ciudad del Carmen, Campeche, April 18, 2007
Vera Calva, Carlos "El Vera" or "El Z-7"	Enlisted in army October 11, 1989; deserted November 16, 1999		At large
Zatarain Beliz, Ernesto "El Traca"/"El Z-10"	Joined the army May 1, 1993; on February 16, 1998, resigned from active duty and joined the reserves	Communications and radio interceptions	Committed suicide in December 2001

Source: "Problema de seguridad nacional en México, los 'Zetas' (desertores del Ejército Mexicano)" "Soluciones de Seguridad Global," *Belt Ibérica www.belt.es*; "El poder de los 'zetas'," Presidencia de la República, "Suma cártel del golfo 5 golpes en su contra," October 30, 2004; "Acorralan a 'Los Zetas,'" *Zeta* weekly no. 1689; Miguel Ángel Pérez López, "Asesinos de Policías de Victoria quedan arraigados," *HoyTamaulipas*, September 15, 2005; "Dictan 20 años De prisión contra el 'Z-48,'" *¡Ehui!*, February 23, 2008; PGR and Secretaría de Marina, Comunicado 283/09; various articles by veteran journalist Miguel Ángel Granados Chapa; and PGR bulletins. Mexican authorities first spoke of thirty-one original Zetas; however, the number in this cast of characters has varied from report to report. Outstanding William & Mary students Lindsey C. Nicolai and Gabriela Regina Arias assisted in preparing this table.

Appendix 2

Suspected Zeta Recruits

Name	Nickname	Captured/killed	Date
Abraham Santiago, José Jalil	El Négro	Captured by Mexican Army in Quintana Roo	September 9, 2009
Acevedo Juárez, Leticia		Captured by Tamaulipas State investigators in Tamaulipas	September 11, 2005
Aguilar Lara, Federico	El Pancho	Captured by Federal Police in Guanajuato	November 29, 2010
Alcorta Ríos, Mario	El Junior	Captured by Mexican Army in Vallecillo, Nuevo León	October 14, 2011
Alemán Narváez, Alfredo	El Comandante Alemán Alfredo N	Captured by Mexican Special Forces in Zacatecas	November 17, 2011
Alfaro González, José Arturo	El Arturo	Captured by Federal Police in Guanajuato	November 29, 2010
Alfaro Luna, Emilio		Captured by PGR in Tabasco	December 2, 2009
Alfaro Pérez, Carlos Ernesto		Captured by Federal Police in Tamaulipas	November 20, 2009
Almanza Huesca, Octavio	El Gori 4	Captured by PGR in Cancún	February 9, 2009
Almanza Morales, Ricardo	El Gori 1	Killed by Mexican Navy in Nuevo León	May 12, 2009
Alvarado Orta, Juan Héctor	El Muerto	Captured by Federal Police in San Luis Potosí	March 5, 2011

(Continued)

Suspected Zeta Recruits (*Continued*)

Name	Nickname	Captured/killed	Date
Aranda Rodríguez, René Reynol	El Dawn	Captured by Mexican Army in Monterrey	October 26, 2009
Arce Grajales, Rigel Denet	El Cangri	Captured by Mexican Army in Oaxaca	May 10, 2011
Arduño Corona, Jorge	El Gabo	Captured by federal and local police in Cancún	July 22, 2011
Avalos Piñeyro, Luis Fernando	El Noñín	Captured by Mexican Army in Monterrey	October 26, 2009
Barrón Solís, Amparo	La Güera	Captured by Federal Police in San Luis Potosí	March 5, 2011
Beltrán García, Miguel Ángel	El Pío	Captured by Federal Police in San Luis Potosí	March 5, 2011
Bernal Soriano, Óscar Manuel	La Araña	Captured by Federal Police in Monterrey	October 22, 2010
Berrones Ramírez, Julio Tadeo	Julio Rayas	Captured by Federal Police in Nuevo León	August 29, 2011
Blanco Flores, Luis Albert	El Pelochas	Captured by US ICE officials in Brownsville, Texas	July 23, 2010
Bravo Rivera, Antonio	El Tony Bravo	Captured by AEI in Nuevo León	August 26, 2009
Briones Espinosa, Francisco Rodrigo		Captured by Federal Police in Tamaulipas	November 20, 2009
Cabrera Escalante, Jaime (leader in San Nicolás)	El Comandante Kakino	Captured by Nuevo León State Antikidnapping Group in Nuevo León	December 9, 2011
Calderón Martínez, Gabriel (Casino Royale Bombing)	Bogar	Captured by Federal Police in Tabasco	December 11, 2011
Camacho Jaco, Antonio (Casino Royale Bombing)		Captured by Mexican Army	October 21, 2011

Suspected Zeta Recruits (*Continued*)

Name	Nickname	Captured/killed	Date
Campos Reyna, Patricia	La Güera	Captured by Nuevo León Antikidnapping Group in Nuevo León	December 9, 2011
Carmona Hernández, Marcos	El Cabrito	Captured by Federal Police in Oaxaca	March 7, 2011
Carranza, Eliseo de los Reyes		Captured by Federal Police in Tamaulipas	November 20, 2009
Carrazco Espinoza, Luis Carlos	El Chihuas	Captured by Federal Police in Nuevo León	August 29, 2011
Carranza Sandoval, Cristian Eduardo	El Toy Story	Captured by Mexican Army in Hidalgo	October 28, 2011
Castillo Flores, Oscar Alias: Arturo Castillo	El Apache	Captured by US ICE officials in Brownsville, Texas	July 23, 2010
Castrejón Peña, Victor Nazario		Dead	
Cequeda Gamboa, José	Juan Loco	Captured by Federal Police in Veracruz	May 2, 2011
Chairez Caldera, José Guadalupe	El Loco	Captured by Mexican Army in Torreón	November 28, 2011
Cruz Hernández, Rubén (Casino Royale Bombing)		Captured by Mexican Army	October 21, 2011
Cruz López, Arturo Abenamar	El Hugo/ Oscuro	Captured by Mexican Army in San Luis Potosí	November 21, 2010
Dávila Castillo, Ángel Cristian	El 28	Captured by Federal Police in San Luis Potosí	March 5, 2011
de la Cerda Hernández, Cristo Herbey	El Nano	Captured by Federal Police in Guanajuato	November 29, 2010
de la Garza Esquivel, Ina Lucia	(esposa de Villegas Vázquez)	Captured by Federal Police in Tamaulipas	November 20, 2009

(Continued)

Suspected Zeta Recruits (*Continued*)

Name	Nickname	Captured/killed	Date
de la Garza Esquivel, Jaime Anselmo		Captured by Federal Police in Tamaulipas	November 20, 2009
de la Peña Brizeula, Jorge Luis	El Pompín	Killed by Mexican Army in Tamaulipas	August 2, 2011
de los Santos Guerra, Rolando	El Roli	Captured by Federal Police and Mexican Army in Reynosa	March 24, 2009
De León Martínez, Gerardo (Casino Royale Bombing)	Papa	Captured by Mexican Army	October 21, 2011
Delgadillo Calderón, Benito	El Duende	Captured by Federal Police in San Luis Potosí	March 5, 2011
Desales Hernández, Enedina	La Paloma	Captured by Mexican Army in Oaxaca	May 10, 2011
Díaz Cuéllar, Rogelio	El Rojo	Captured by PGR in Tamaulipas	April 25, 2008
Díaz, Hipólito Muñiz		Captured by Mexican Army in Coatzacoalcos	September 22, 2009
Díaz Ramón, Javier	El Java Diaz	Captured by Mexican Army in Veracruz	December 22, 2008
Doria Santos, Hugo Santos	El Monky Manitas	Captured by Mexican Army in García, NL	November 10, 2011
Durán, Óscar Alejandro	El Gordo Panuchudo	Captured by Federal Police in San Luis Potosi	March 5, 2011
El Ostión (in charge of operations in Coahuila)		Captured by Mexican Army in Saltillo	October 12, 2011
Escandón Martínez, Alberto Iván	El Iván	Captured by Federal Police in Guanajuato	November 29, 2010

Suspected Zeta Recruits (*Continued*)

Name	Nickname	Captured/killed	Date
Espinoza Sabino, Óscar		Captured by Mexican Army in Veracruz	July 21, 2011
Estrada Luna, Martín Omar	El Kilo El Comandante Kilo	Captured by Mexican Marines in Tamaulipas	April 17, 2011
Estrada Sánchez, José Antonio	El Cuervo	Captured by local and federal forces in Palenque	March 15, 2009
Flores Jiménez, Vicente		Captured by Mexican Marines in Monterrey	May 5, 2010
Galarza Coronado, Antonio	El Amarillo	Captured by Federal Police in Reynosa	February 11, 2008
Galicia González, José Ezequiel		Captured by US ICE officials in Brownsville, Texas	July 23, 2010
Galván Torres, Adolfo	El Gufito	Captured by Federal Police in San Luis Potosí	March 5, 2011
Gálvez Ramos, Yoni de Jesús	La Cabeza	Captured by Mexican Army in Oaxaca	May 10, 2011
Gámez Vega, Jorge	El Extraño	Captured by Mexican Army in Vallecillo, Nuevo León	October 14, 2011
García Martínez, José Luis	El Gordo	Captured by Mexican Army in Monterrey	October 26, 2009
García Reyes, Margarita	La Mago	Captured by Federal Police in Guanajuato	November 29, 2010
García Rodríguez, Raúl	El Sureño	Captured by Mexican Marines in Monterrey	August 13, 2011
García Sorcia, Evencio		Captured by Mexican Army in Veracruz	July 21, 2011
Gómez Flores, Onofre	El Azucarado	Captured by Federal Police in Guanajuato	November 29, 2010
Gómez López, Daniel		Captured by Mexican Army in Veracruz	July 21, 2011
Gómez Uscanga, Mariano		Captured by Mexican Army in Veracruz	July 21, 2011

(*Continued*)

Suspected Zeta Recruits (*Continued*)

Name	Nickname	Captured/killed	Date
González Dúran, Jaime	El Hummer	Captured by Federal Police in Reynosa, Tamaulipas	November 7, 2008
González Nájera, Sindipersio Alias: Zindy Percy González Nájera		Captured by Mexican Army in Veracruz	July 21, 2011
González Juárez, Roberto	El Genio El Caprice	Captured by Tamaulipas Police, Tamaulipas	September 11, 2005
Gutiérrez Moraza, Rubén Elías	El Billy	Captured by Nuevo León Anti-Kidnapping Group in Nuevo León	December 9, 2011
Guerrero Pérez, Gabriela Abigail	La Gaby	Captured by Nuevo León Antikidnapping Group in Nuevo León	December 9, 2011
Hernández Barrón, Victor Manuel	El Flander II	Captured by army special forces in Matamoros	March 14, 2003
Hernández del Ángel, Ángelo Raúl (Casino Royale Bombing)	El George	Captured by Mexican Army in Vallecillo, Nuevo León	October 14, 2011
Hernández García, Jorge Armando	El Pavón El Negro	Captured by Mexican Army in Hidalgo	October 28, 2011
Hernández Martínez, Eduardo	El Lobito/ El Piedrero	Captured in Tamaulipas by Tamaulipas State investigators	September 11, 2005
Hernández Velázquez, Gilberto	El Conejo	Captured by Mexican Army in Monterrey	October 26, 2009
Hernández Villegas, Víctor	El Comandante Pérez	Captured by Mexican Army in Hidalgo	October 28, 2011
Herrera Martínez, Hilario Jesús		Captured by Federal Police in Tamaulipas	November 20, 2009

Suspected Zeta Recruits (*Continued*)

Name	Nickname	Captured/killed	Date
Huerta Montiel, Edgar	El Wache	Captured by Federal Police in Fresnillo	June 17, 2011
Hugo Espiricueta, Héctor	Commander Leo	Captured by Mexican security forces in Hidalgo	April 19, 2011
Jiménez Jaso, José Antonio	Don Toño	Captured by Federal Police in Guanajuato	November 29, 2010
Jiménez Martínez, Norberto	El Peje/ El Puma	Captured by PGR in Tamaulipas	September 21, 2009
Jiménez Pérez, Mario	El Mayito	Captured by Federal Police in San Luis Potosi	March 5, 2011
Juárez Llanas, José Luis		Captured by Mexican Marines in Monterrey	May 5, 2010
Juárez Mendoza, Román	El Chino El Gordo	Captured by Mexican Army in San Luis Potosí	November 21, 2010
Lara Flores, Lidia Verónica	La Wicha	Captured by Mexican Army in Torreón	November 10, 2011
Lara Hernández, Julio César	El Piñata	Captured by local and federal forces in Palenque	March 15, 2009
Lara Ochoa, Carlos Alejandro		Captured by Mexican Army in Coahuila	March 17, 2010
Lázaro Rodriguez, Antelmo	El Chamoy	Captured by elements of the AFI and the Mexican Army	March 5, 2009
Leal Puente, Luis Carlos	El Charli	Captured by Mexican Army in San Luis Potosí	November 21, 2010
Leal Torres, Juan Ángel	Casillas El Cash	Captured by Federal Police in Nuevo León	August 29, 2011
Loera Rodríguez, José Alberto (professional wrestler)	Voltaje Negro	Captured by Federal Police in Monterrey	October 4, 2011

(*Continued*)

Suspected Zeta Recruits (*Continued*)

Name	Nickname	Captured/killed	Date
López Martínez, Roberto Ezequiel	El Macetas	Captured by Mexican Army in San Luis Potosí	November 21, 2010
López Priego, Jorge Luis		Captured by SEDENA in Villahermosa, Tabasco	March 2008
López Ortiz, Ricardo Alias: Fernando Sandoval Martínez	El Pitufo	Captured by Mexican Army in Tabasco	October 30, 2007
Ludivina, Cinthya (age 13)		Captured by Nuevo León Antikidnapping Group	December 9, 2011
Luna Luna, Héctor	El Tori	Captured by Mexican Army in Monterrey	June 9, 2010
Maldonado García, Gregorio	El Panadero	Captured by Mexican Navy in Veracruz	September 30, 2011
Mandujano Lazcano, Jean Paul		Captured by Mexican Army in Coahuila	March 17, 2010
Marquez de la Rosa, Francisco Javier		Captured by Mexican Army in Torreón	November 25, 2011
Martínez Calzada, Óscar Alan		Captured by Mexican Army in Coahuila	March 17, 2010
Martínez de León, Francisco Daniel	El Gato	Captured by Nuevo León Antikidnapping Group in Nuevo León	December 9, 2011
Martínez Escobedo, Salvador Alfonso	La Ardilla	At large ($1.25 million reward)	
Martínez Hernández, Juan Carlos	El Camaleón	Captured by Mexican Army in Monterrey	October 26, 2010
Martínez, Juan Carlos Diego	El Chaparro	Captured by Federal Police in Guanajuato	November 29, 2010
Martínez Lugo, Raúl	La Chiva	Captured by Mexican Army in Monterrey	June 14, 2011

Suspected Zeta Recruits (*Continued*)

Name	Nickname	Captured/killed	Date
Martínez Martínez, Roberto		Captured by Federal Police in Tabasco	December 11, 2011
Martínez Martínez, Patricio Guillermo	El Memo	Captured by Mexican Army in Coatzacoalcos	September 23, 2009
Martínez Morales, Javier Alonso	El Javo	Captured by Federal Police in Nuevo León	August 29, 2011
Martínez Morales, Víctor Hugo	El Maza	Captured by Mexican Army in Nuevo León	April 13, 2011
Martínez Rueda, Carolina	Panther	Captured by Mexican security forces in Hidalgo	April 19, 2011
Martínez Sánchez, Juan	El Olivo	Captured by Mexican Army in San Luis Potosí	November 21, 2010
Martínez Serafín, Raúl	El Pika	Dead	
Martínez Torres, Juan Alberto		Captured by Mexican Marines in Monterrey	May 5, 2010
Medellín Ortiz, Ángel	El Güero	Captured by Federal Police in San Luis Potosí	March 5, 2011
Medina Rojas, Eleazar	El Chelelo	Captured by Mexican Army in Monterrey	June 9, 2010
Méndez Castañeda, Francisco Javier	El Paco/El Jotito	Captured by Federal Police in Guanajuato	November 29, 2010
Méndez Santiago, Flavio (in charge of Oaxaca, Chiapas, and Veracruz)	El Amarillo	Captured by Federal Police in Oaxaca	January 18, 2011
Mendieta Zentella, Carlos Alberto Alias: Carlos Alberto Herrera Zentella	El Paletón/El Güero	Captured by Mexican Army in Tabasco	May 10, 2009
Mendoza Aguirre, Napoleón de Jesús	El Napo	Captured by PGR	March 14, 2009

(*Continued*)

Suspected Zeta Recruits (*Continued*)

Name	Nickname	Captured/killed	Date
Mendoza Covarrubias, Juan José or Rodolfo Rolando Bernal Enríquez	El Pájaro	Captured by Mexican Army in Oaxaca	May 10, 2011
Mérida Rubalcaba, Pedro	El Piquetito	Captured by Mexican Army in Coatzacoalcos	September 23, 2009
Miraveles Reyes, Ezequiel	El Chabelo	Captured by Mexican Army in Hidalgo	October 28, 2011
Mireles Quiroz, José Andrés		Captured by Mexican Army in Vallecillo, Nuevo León	October 14, 2011
Montemayor Martínez, Joel Guadalupe		Captured by Mexican Marines in Monterrey	May 5, 2010
Montesinos, Elías	La China	Captured by Mexican Army in Oaxaca	May 10, 2011
Montoya Chávez, Héctor Javier		Captured by Federal Police in Monterrey	October 4, 2011
Montoya Ramírez, Horacio	El Gordo	Captured by Federal Police in San Luis Potosí	March 5, 2011
Mora Caberta, Ángel Manuel	Comandante Diablo	Captured by Mexican Navy in Veracruz	September 30, 2011
Mora Cortés, Sergio Antonio	El Toto	Captured by Mexican Navy in San Luis Potosí	February 28, 2011
Morales Blanco, Fermín		Captured by Federal Police in Tamaulipas	November 20, 2009
Morales Moya, María Guadalupe	La Lupe	Captured by Federal Police in Guanajuato	November 29, 2010
Morales Uscanga, Armando Cesar		Captured by Mexican Army in San Fernando, Tamaulipas	April 3, 2011
Moreno Carreón, Verónica Mireya	La Flaca/La Vero	Captured by Mexican Marines in Monterrey	September 10, 2011

Suspected Zeta Recruits (*Continued*)

Name	Nickname	Captured/killed	Date
Moreno González, Angel Jesús	El Chuy	Captured by Mexican Army in Monterrey	October 26, 2009
Morón Díaz, Abril Samanta		Captured by Mexican Marines in Monterrey	August 13, 2011
Mota Badillo, Gabriel	El Mota	Captured by Federal Police in San Luis Potosí	March 5, 2011
Muñiz Ruiz, Hipólito		Captured by Mexican Army in Coatzacoalcos	September 23, 2009
Muñoz Cuéllar, Juan Damián	El Damián	Captured by Federal Police in San Luis Potosí	March 5, 2011
Nájera Talamantes, Sigifredo	El Canicón	Captured by PGR in Cancún	March 20, 2009
Ocampo Ortiz, Hugo	El Gafe	Captured by Federal Police in Guanajuato	November 29, 2010
Ocaña de la Fuente, Pablo		Captured by PGR in Tabasco	December 2, 2009
Ochoa Celis, Tomás	El Tommy	Captured by Federal Police in Matamoros, Tamaulipas	December 11, 2009
Oliva Castillo, Carlos (chief in Nuevo León, Coahuila, and Tamaulipas)	La Rana	Captured by Mexican Army in Saltillo	October 12, 2011
Orea Morán, Audias	El Cachis	Captured by Mexican Army in Coatzacoalcos	September 23, 2009
Ortega Herrera, Pedro		Captured by Federal Police in Mexico City	July 4, 2011
Parra Rangel, Luis Roberto		Captured by Tamaulipas State investigators in Tamaulipas	September 11, 2005

(*Continued*)

Suspected Zeta Recruits (*Continued*)

Name	Nickname	Captured/killed	Date
Patiño Martínez, Renato	El Comandante Borrado	Captured by Mexican Army at a checkpoint in San Pedro de las Colonias, Coahuila	November 21, 2011
Peña Mendoza, Sergio Alias: Arturo Sanchez Fuentes	El Concord	Captured by Federal Police in Reynosa, Tamaulipas	March 14, 2009
Picaso Jiménez, Arnoldo	El Pikso	Captured by Nuevo León Antikidnapping Group in Nuevo León	December 9, 2011
Pineda Sánchez, Edith Alejandra	La Flaca	Captured by Federal Police in San Luis Potosí	March 5, 2011
Pérez del Real, Raúl	Run Run	Captured by Mexican Army and Federal Police in Zacatecas	November 15, 2009
Pérez Izquierdo, Víctor Manuel	El Siete Latas	Captured by Federal Police in Cancún	June 4, 2011
Pérez Zavala, Jesús Abad	Chuy Chilango	Captured by Mexican Army and Federal Police in Zacatecas	November 15, 2009
Pitula Carrillo, Carlos Arturo	El Bam Bam	Captured by navy in Veracruz	October 25, 2011
Ponce Jiménez, Víctor	El Víctor	Captured by Federal Police in San Luis Potosí	March 5, 2011
Quezada Espinoza, Liliana	La Lily	Captured by Federal Police in Guanajuato	November 29, 2010
Ramírez Franco, Jorge	El George	Captured by Federal Police in San Luis Potosí	March 5, 2011
Ramírez Lopez, René	Narizón	Captured by Mexican Army and Federal Police in Zacatecas	November 15, 2009
Ramos Cabrera, Miguel Alejandro (Casino Royale Bombing)		Captured by Mexican Military	October 21, 2011

Suspected Zeta Recruits (*Continued*)

Name	Nickname	Captured/killed	Date
Rangel Buendía, Alfredo	El Chicles/El Licenciado	Captured by Mexican Army in the Distrito Federal	August 16, 2008
Reyes Briones, Éric	El Tampico	Captured by Mexican Army in Coatzacoalcos	September 23, 2009
Reyes Pavón, Carlos Alberto	El Manotas	Captured by Mexican Army in Coatzacoalcos	September 23, 2009
Reyes, Luis Alberto	El Guerrero	Killed by four hitmen	May 10, 2003
Reyna Gutiérrez, Jonathan Jair		Captured by Federal Police in Nuevo León	August 29, 2011
Ríos Luna, Juan José	El Juanito	Captured by Mexican Army in Coatzacoalcos	September 23, 2009
Rivero Arana, Roberto (nephew of The Executioner)	El Bebo El Felino El Beto	Captured by Federal Police in Tabasco	March 29, 2011
Rodriguez Castillo, Héctor	El Conejo/El comandante Conejo	Captured by Mexican Army and FECDO in Chiapas	December 9, 2009
Rodriguez García, Jorge Omar		Captured by Mexican Marines in Monterrey	May 5, 2010
Rodriguez González, Roberto	La Conga	Captured by Mexican Army in Coatzacoalcos	September 23/24, 2009
Rojo Ocejo, Luis Miguel	El Oso Rojo	Captured by Mexican Navy in San Luis Potosí	February 28, 2011
Romero Sánchez, Omar Israel	El Flaco	Captured by Federal Police in Guanajuato	November 29, 2010
Romo Torres, Daniel	El Dany	Captured by Mexican Army in Coatzacoalcos	September 23, 2009
Ruiz Águila, José Arturo		Captured by Mexican Army in Veracruz	July 21, 2011

(*Continued*)

Suspected Zeta Recruits (*Continued*)

Name	Nickname	Captured/killed	Date
Ruiz, Noé San Martín		Captured by Federal Police in Tamaulipas	November 20, 2009
Saldaña Oliver, Araceli		Captured by Mexican Army in Hidalgo	October 28, 2011
Salinas Martínez, Martín	El Jícama	Captured by Mexican Army in Monterrey	October 26, 2009
Salmerón Rodríguez, Rafael	El Iguano	Captured by Mexican Army in Tamaulipas	August 2, 2011
Sánchez García, Ricardo	El Chaparro	Captured by Mexican Army in San Luis Potosí	November 21, 2010
Sánchez Hinojosa, Alberto	Tony/ Comandante Castillo	Captured by PGR and AFI in Tabasco	July 16, 2008
Sandoval Estrada, Leonardo	El Sharpey	Captured by federal and state police in Tabasco	September 2, 2009
Segura Téllez, Alejandro	El Cepillo	Captured by Federal Police in Hidalgo	March 5, 2009
Solis Luarte, Arturo	El Sani	Captured by Mexican Army in Coatzacoalcos	September 23, 2009
Soriano, Valdemar Quintanilla	El Adal	Captured by Mexican Army in Coahuila	August 2, 2011
Soto Mata, América Cristal	La Vaquita	Captured by Mexican Army in San Luis Potosí	November 21, 2010
Tenango Uscanga, Juan Daniel	El Oso	Captured by Mexican Army in Coatzacoalcos	September 23, 2009
Tejeda Vázquez, Héctor	El Pitufo	Captured by Mexican Navy in San Julián, Veracruz	September 12, 2011
Treviño Estrada, María Ricarda	La Rica	Captured by Mexican Army in Hidalgo	October 28, 2011
Tolentino Vergil, Alejandra Nohemí		Captured by Nuevo León Antikidnapping Group	December 9, 2011

Suspected Zeta Recruits (*Continued*)

Name	Nickname	Captured/killed	Date
Valdez Chávez, Ulises	El Chino	Captured by Federal Police in Guanajuato	November 29, 2010
Vargas Rubio, Rodrigo	El Diablo	Captured by Mexican Army in Oaxaca	May 10, 2011
Vázquez, Leonardo	El Pachis	Killed by Mexican security forces in Poza Riza	January 19, 2011
Velázquez González, Jesús	Campanita	Captured by Nuevo León Antikidnapping Group in Nuevo León	December 9, 2011
Vélez Morales, Rafael del Ángel Alias: José Manuel Figueroa Martínez	El Fayo	Captured by Mexican Army in Quintana Roo	May 8, 2009
Veloz Mezquitic, Jesús Adolfo	El Chuy	Captured by Federal Police in San Luis Potosí	March 5, 2011
Veytia Bravo, Rolando	El Manitas	Mexican Army killed him in Boca del Río, Veracruz	May 21, 2011
Villegas Vázquez, Antonio Daniel	El 20/El Travieso	Captured by Federal Police in Tamaulipas	November 20, 2009
Yáñez Martínez, José Guadalupe	El Dos	Captured by Mexican Army in Coahuila	August 2, 2011
Zapata Espinoza, Julian	El Piolín	Captured by Mexican Army in San Luis Potosí	February 23, 2011
Zapata Pantoja, José Ángel	El Cheché	Captured by Mexican Army in Tamaulipas	August 2, 2011
Zapata Picasso, Jonathan Uriel	El Doker	Captured by Federal Police in Guanajuato	November 29, 2010
Zatarín Beliz, Ernesto	El Traca	Dead	
Zavala Martinez, Diego		Killed by Mexican Army in Coatzacoalcos	September 24, 2009

(*Continued*)

Suspected Zeta Recruits (*Continued*)

Name	Nickname	Captured/killed	Date
Zeleta Hernández, Clarissa Yarmireth		Captured by Federal Police	March 19, 2011
Zetina Zetina, Hugo	Comandante Zetina	Dead	
Zúñiga Torres, Guadalupe		Captured by Tamaulipas State investigators in Tamaulipas	September 11, 2005

Source: Prepared by Lindsey C. Nicolai.

Abbreviation: ICE, Immigration and Customs Enforcement Agency.

Glossary of Key Terms

ABO/ABLs—(The Beltrán Leyva organization, led by Héctor Beltrán Leyva); debilitated by capture of key members; situational alliances with Los Zetas.

AFO—Arellano Félix Organization, also known as the Tijuana Cartel; weakened by killing/arrest of members of the Arellano Félix family; Sinaloa Cartel now dominates Tijuana.

ASE—(Agencia de Seguridad Estatal) Mexico State's Security Agency.

Costa Chica—A two-hundred-mile-long coastal region known for criminal activities; it begins just southeast of Acapulco, Guerrero, and extends to Huatulco in Oaxaca state.

DEA—US Drug Enforcement Administration.

DFS—(Dirección Federal de Seguridad—Federal Security Directorate); a notoriously corrupt Mexican intelligence agency formed in 1947 and dissolved in the mid-1980s.

Capo—Drug kingpin.

Cedes—(Centros de Ejecución de Sanciones or Centers for Carrying Out Sentences); correctional facilities run and operated by the Mexican government.

Ceresos—(Centros de Readaptación Social—or Centers for Social Readaptation); correctional facilities run and operated by the Mexican government.

CIDA—(Cártel Independiente de Acapulco—Independent Cartel of Acapulco); formed by Édgar "La Barbie" Vazquez Villarreal, captured on August 30, 2010, and specialized in murders and kidnappings in Acapulco and all of Guerrero State.

Colmillos—Small doses of cocaine.

Dual Sovereignty—When cartel leaders form a parallel government, particularly at the municipal level. (A Mexican "municipio" is analogous to a county in the United States.)

El Pollo—Literally, "a chicken"; refers to an illegal alien who has paid a "pollero" or "coyote" to smuggle him across the US border and/or into the United States.

Estaca—Specialized cell in Los Zetas organization, typically composed of five to seven members.

Frontera Chica—The "little border" composed of Miguel Alemán, Ciudad Mier, Camargo, Díaz Ordaz, and other municipalities in violence-torn northwest Tamaulipas State.

GAFES—(Grupo Aeromóvil de Fuerzas Especiales—Airborne Special Forces Group); Mexican Army Special Forces from which many original Zetas were recruited.

GOPES—(Fuerzas de Apoyo de la Policía Federal—Federal Police Support Forces); anticrime unit, also known as the Special Operations Group, under the Secretary of Public Security, coordinated by General Rodolfo Cruz López.

Gulf Cartel (CDG)—Drug syndicate based in Matamoros, Tamaulipas, and now headed by Eduardo "El Coss" Costilla Sánchez; an earlier kingpin, Osiel Cárdenas Guillén, who is now in prison in the United States, recruited Los Zetas as his Praetorian Guard.

Jesús Malverde—A Robin Hood-type figure with a shrine in Culiacán, Sinaloa, to whom some narco-criminals pay homage.

Juárez Cartel—A debilitated cartel led by Vicente Carrillo Fuentes and based in Juárez, Chihuahua; loosely allies with Los Zetas.

Kaibiles—Special operations forces of the Guatemalan Military whose deserters helped Los Zetas hone their ruthless techniques.

Knights Templars—Latest incarnation of La Familia Michoacana whose name derives from a medieval order known for acts of charity and savage fighting in the Crusades.

La Empresa—Michoacán criminal organization that morphed into La Familia Michoacana.

La Familia Michoacana/La Familia (LFM)—Michoacán-centered drug cartel, some of whose leaders claim that they are doing the Lord's work; underwent a serious split in 2011, with the strongest faction constituting the Knights Templars.

La Línea—A bloodthirsty gang with members in Ciudad Juárez and El Paso, which cooperates with the Juárez Cartel.

La Maña—A term sometimes applied to Los Zetas and other shadowy figures in Matamoros.

La Mano con Ojos—A gang founded by Oscar García Montoya that specializes in kidnappings in Mexico State; linked to the Beltrán Leyva Organization and Los Zetas.

La Polla—The $3,000 that Osiel Cárdenas Guillén gave each new Zeta recruit with which he could buy cocaine, cross into the United States, and find distributors.

La Resistencia—A criminal organization in Jalisco that emerged from the Milenio Cartel and that cooperates with Los Zetas, possibly providing resources to the paramilitaries.

La Última Letra—The last letter, a euphemism for "Z" or Zetas.

Los Mazatlecos—A gang in Mazatlán, Sinaloa, that works with the Beltrán Leyva Organization and whose leader Santiago "El Chaquín" Lizárraga Ibarra reportedly murdered the son of Sinaloa Cartel big shot Ignacio "Nacho" Coronel five days before Federal Police killed "El Chaquín" in Tepic, Nayarit, on April 12, 2010.

McZetas—Crooks who pose as members of Los Zetas, usually to extort money.

Mara Salvatrucha—Street gang that composed largely of Salvadorans, who first organized in Los Angeles before returning to Mexico and Central America.

Milenio Cartel—An organization, now extremely weak, that once specialized in methamphetamines; competed with La Empresa and La Familia Michoacana.

Montruo—A menacing tank-like vehicle used by Los Zetas in battling enemies.

NAFTA—North American Free Trade Agreement (January 1, 1994); trilateral trade bloc among the United States, Mexico, and Canada that took effect on January 1, 1994.

Narcobanderas—Banners unfurled in public places by cartels for the purpose of propaganda and recruitment.

Narcocorridos—Ballads that often praise cartels and their leaders.

Narcomenudeo—Small-time sales of drugs.

"Ni Nis"—a pejorative term applied to Mexican teenagers who neither work nor study but may be seduced by gangs and cartels.

Operación Lince Norte (Operation Northern Lynx)—Concerted effort by four thousand soldiers (mid-July to August 2, 2011) to crack-down on Los Zetas in the North—with the result of driving them into Veracruz.

*PAN—(*Partido Acción Nacional—National Action Party); center-right party to which ex-President Vicente Fox and incumbent Chief Executive Felipe Calderón belong.

PEMEX—(Petróleos Mexicanos—Mexican Petroleum); Mexico's extremely corrupt state oil monopoly.

PGR—(Procuraduría General de la República) Mexico's Attorney General's Office.

Piso—Money extorted by criminal organizations.

PJF—(Policía Judicial Federal—Federal Judicial Police); corrupt law-enforcement agency that President Vicente Fox disbanded in 2001.

Plaza—An area coveted by cartels for the storage, processing, and transit of drugs.

PRD—Democratic Revolutionary Party (Partido de la Revolución Democrática); a political organization composed of leftist and centrist currents that frequently war with each other.

PRI—(Partido Revolucionario Institucional—Institutional Revolutionary Party); party that controlled the presidency from 1929 to 2000 and is expected to regain this position in 2012.

Project Coronado (2009) and Project Delirium (2011)—Successful Department of Justice-led multiagency strikes against La Familia Michoacana in the United States.

Puente Grande/La Palma—Maximum-security federal prison located in Jalisco.

Santísima Muerte—"Saint of Death" venerated by some Mexican criminals.

Sicario—Hit man for a drug cartel.

SIEDO—Mexico's Assistant Attorney General's Office for Special Investigations on Organized Crime.

Sinaloa Cartel—Mexico's most powerful cartel led by Joaquín "El Chapo"/"El Tio" Guzmán Loera and Ismael "El Mayo" Zambada García; joined with the Knights Templars and the Gulf Cartel to combat Los Zetas in Northeast Mexico. The organization was once called "The Federation" or the "Sinaloa Federation"; however, since the split with the Beltrán Leyvas and the July 29, 2010 death of Ignacio "El Nacho" Coronel Villarreal (Guadalajara/Jalisco Cartel), this term is less frequently used.

Sopa marucha—An army staple made from tasteless packaged artificial noodles.

Suicide loads—Smaller amounts of marijuana or cash that traffickers know will get caught by local law enforcement but that tie up officers with hours of paperwork, giving traffickers time to move bigger loads undetected.

Matazetas—Foes determined to kill Zetas who come from the ranks of the Cartel of the New Generation of Jalisco (Cártel de Jalisco Nueva Generación—CJNG).

Tierra Caliente—A fertile area composed of parts of Michoacán, Guerrero, Mexico State, and Colima where La Familia Michoacana and other cartels grow marijuana and poppy; the LFM also imports cocaine precursor drugs through the state's major port, Lázaro Cárdenas.

The Fusion of Anti-Zeta Cartels—Fusión de Cárteles Anti-Zeta; the troika of organizations—the Gulf Cartel, the Sinaloa Cartel, and the Knight Templars—battling Los Zetas in Northeast Mexico for access to Nuevo Laredo and other portals on the US border; also known as "La Fusión de Cárteles" or simply, "La Fusión."

Zetabanderas—Banner unfurled by Los Zetas for the purpose of propaganda and recruitment of cadres.

Zetacorridos—Ballads praising actions of the paramilitaries.

Zetacuaches—Undisciplined punk criminals whom Los Zetas punish, sometimes by hanging them from bridges.

Zetapolicía—Police in thrall to the cartel.

Zetanización—The growing penetration of this criminal organization.

Zetitas—Teenage lookouts, couriers, and (sometimes) gunmen for the cartel.

Selected Bibliography

Books

Bailey, John J. and Roy Godson. *Organized Crime and Democratic Governability: Mexico and the U.S.-Mexican Borderlands*. Pittsburgh, PA: University of Pittsburgh Press, 2001.

Bowden, Charles. *Down by the River: Drugs, Money, Murder, and Family*. New York, NY: Simon & Schuster, 2003.

Brinton, Crane. *The Anatomy of Revolution* (rev. ed.). New York, NY: Random House, 1965.

Fernández Menéndez, Jorge and Víctor Ronquillo. *De los maras a los zetas*. Mexico City: Grijalbo, 2006.

Grayson, George W. *Mexico: Narco-Violence and a Failed State?* New Brunswick, NJ: Transaction Publishers, 2010.

_____. *Mexican Messiah: Andrés Manuel López Obrador*. University Park, PA: The Pennsylvania State University Press, 2007.

Grillo, Ioan. *El Narco: Inside Mexico's Criminal Insurgency*. New York, NY: Bloomsbury Press, 2011.

Logan, Samuel. *This Is for the Mara Salvatrucha: Inside the MS-13, America's Most Violent Gang*. New York, NY: Hyperion Books, 2009.

Poppa, Terrance E. *Drug Lord: The Life & Death of Mexican Kingpin: A True Story* (2nd ed., rev. and updated). Seattle, WA: Demand Publications, 1998.

Ravelo, Ricardo. *Osiel: vida y tragedia de un capo*. Mexico City: Grijalbo, 2009.

_____. *Los capos*. Mexico City: Debolsillo, 2007.

Wald, Elijah. *Narcocorrido: A Journey into the Music of Drugs, Guns, and Guerrillas*. New York, NY: Rayo, 2001.

Book Chapters and Monographs

Campbell, Lisa J. "Los Zetas: Operational Assessment," in Robert J. Bunker (Ed.), *Narcos Over the Border: Gangs, Cartels and Mercenaries*. New York, NY: Routledge, 2011.

Grayson, George W. *La Familia Drug Cartel: Implications for U.S.-Mexican Security*. Carlisle, PA: Institute of Strategic Studies, U.S. War College, 2010.

Oster, Patrick. "The Periodista" in *The Mexicans: A Personal Portrait of a People*. New York, NY: HarperCollins, 2002.

Journal and Magazine Articles

Campbell, Lisa J. "Los Zetas: Operational Assessment," *Small Wars & Insurgencies*, 21, no. 1 (2010): 55–80.

Lupsha, Peter. "Transnational Narco-Corruption and Narco-Investment: A Focus on Mexico," *Transnational Organized Crime* (Spring 1995).

McDonald, James H. "The Narcoeconomy and Small-Town Rural Mexico," *Human Organization*, 64, no. 2 (Summer 2005).

Government, Think Tank, Corporate, and Cartel Documents

Agencia Reforma, "Amplia Lazcano alcance de 'Zetas,'" *McAllear.com*, March 1, 2010.

De Amicis, Albert. "Los Zetas and La Familia Michoacana Drug Trafficking Organizations (DTOs)," capstone paper, Masters of Public and International Affairs, Graduate School for Public and International Affairs, University of Pittsburgh, March 12, 2011 (updated).

"Declaración del Embajador Antonio O. Garza," Comunicado de Prensa, U.S. Embassy, October 5, 2007.

Grayson, George W. "E-Notes: La Familia: Another Deadly Mexican Syndicate," *FPRI*, February 2009, http://www.fpri.org/enotes/200901. grayson.lafamilia.html.

———. "E-Notes: La Familia Michoacána: A Deadly Mexican Cartel Revisited," *FPRI*, August 2009.

———. "E-Notes: Los Zetas: the Ruthless Army Spawned by a Mexican Drug Cartel," *FPRI*, May 2008.

———. "E-Notes: Los Zetas and other Mexican Cartels Target Military Personnel," *FPRI*, March 2009.

———. "Mexico State Gubernatorial Election," *CSIS Americas Program Hemisphere Focus*, June 28, 2011, http://csis.org/files/ publication/110628_Grayson_MexStateGubElec_Hemisphere Focus.pdf.

Library of Congress, *Organized Crime and Terrorist Activity in Mexico*, 1999–2002, February 2003.

"Percepción Ciudadano sobre la seguridad en México," Consulta Mitofsky, August 18, 2009.

Policía Federal, "Cruces de los Integrantes de la Organización 'La Familia Michoacana,' Presuntamente Abatidos en el Enfrentamiento, del Día 09 de Diciembre de 2010," Secretaría de Seguridad Pública, Mexico City, n.d.

Presidencia de la República, "Suma Cártel del Golfo 5 golpes en su contra," October 30, 2004.

Secretaría de la Marina, "Personal de la Armada de México asegura en Coahuila arsenal pertenciente presuntamente al grupo delictiveo de los zetas, asi como más de una tonelada de marihuana en Nuevo León," *Comunicado de Prensa* 187/2011, June 6, 2011.

United States of America v. Juan Garcia Abrego. United States Court of Appeals, Fifth Circuit. May 6, 1998, http://altlaw.org/v1/cases/1090088.

Interviews and Electronic Mail

Co-author's interviews with abductee's family and business partner, who asked to remain anonymous.

Riley, Jack, DEA special agent, interviewed on "All Things Considered," *National Public Radio*, July 15, 2008.

Taylor, Jared. "Lawyers' Names," electronic mail to co-author, June 13, 2011.

Newspapers, Magazines, Electronic Media, and Blog Articles

Aguilar, Andro. "Militarización sin resultados," *Reforma* ("Enfoque"), April 10, 2011.

Alberto Cedillo, Juan. "Indagan 'atentado' en muerte de 14 internos," *El Universal.com.mx*, May 21, 2011.

———. "Pandillas al servicios del narco," *El Universal*, March 3, 2009.

Allard, Jean-Guy. "Cancún: las cubanas secuestradas, en red de prostitución de los Zetas," *Cuba Debate*, September 17, 2009.

Althaus, Dudley. "Mexican Officials Seize Arsenal, Arrest Gang Leader," *Houston Chronicle*, November 7, 2008.

———. "Mexican Victims Overwhelm Border Morgues," *Chron.com*, April 15, 2011.

Alvarado Alvarez, Ignacio. "Narcotráfico Heriberto Lazcano: Un poder tras la Sombra" *El Día Siete*, December 2005.

"Amenaza narco a periodistas y soldados," *Reforma.com*, May 28, 2009.

Andrade, Mario. "Vehicles to Battle Other Cartels, Military," *theintelhub*, May 25, 2011.

Ángel Castro, José. "99 ejecutados pese al pago de rescate," *Tabasco Hoy*, June 7, 2011.

"Aparecen 'Zetas' en panteón," *Reforma*, November 2, 2008.

Aponte, David. "Lideres narcos pactan el la Palma transiego de droga," *El Universal*, January 5, 2005.

"Aprueba Obispo legalizar drogas," *PrimeraHora.com.mx*, April 14, 2009.

Archibold, Randal C. "Mexican Prosecutors Train in U.S. for Changes in Their Legal System," *New York Times*, April 24, 2009.

"Arrestan a 'El Apache,'" *El Nuevo Heraldo*, August 4, 2010.

"Aseguran Marina más de 215 armas y uniformes de Los Zetas," *Notimex*, June 9, 2011.

"Authorities: Gulf Cartel, Zetas gang up on each other as arrangement dies," *The Monitor*, March 10, 2010.

"Authorities: Murders Related to Mexican Cartels," *The Monitor*, October 2, 2010.

Avilés Allende, Carlos. "Capturan a uno de los fundadores de Los Zetas," *El Universal.com.mx*, June 25, 2007.

Barajas, Abel. "Muestran 'Los Zetas' poderío," *Reforma*, September 12, 2004.

Baranda, Antonio. "Detallan 'Zetas' cobro a chinos," *Reforma*, January 10, 2010.

———. "Niega Poiré militarización," *Reforma*, June 7, 2011.

Beyliss, Marcelo. "Amenanzan con narcoflores a la policía de Sonora," *El Universal*, November 24, 2008.

Blanco, Yeilin. "Las bandas de narcos son empresas en México," *Minuto59*, January 22, 2010.

"Blowback Still Blows—Zetas, Kaibiles and MS-13," *NarcoGuerra Times*, November 26, 2009.

Bolaños, Claudia. "Cárceles, infierno de pobres," *El Universal*, May 16, 2009.

Brands, Hal. "Los Zetas: Inside Mexico's Most Dangerous Cartel," *Air & Space Power Journal*, October 1, 2009.

Brito, Luis. "Amotina el narco penales," *Reforma*, May 24, 2009.

———. "Detectan egreso de 'Los Zetas,'" *Reforma*, December 16, 2009.

Buch, Jason. "Breakout Was Latest Chapter in Mexican Prison's Sordid Story," *Corrections One News*, December 23, 2010.

Caballero, Sergio. "Nombran a militares en penales de QR," *Reforma.com*, April 26, 2011.

Cabrera, Javier. "Malova pide a los niños no imitar a los narcos," *El Universal*, May 1, 2011.

"Cae en Monterrey 'rey de gasolinas,'" *Reforma*, June 14, 2010.

"Cae presunto jefe de La Familia Michoacana," *Noroeste.com*, April 22, 2009.

"Caen dos 'narcoperiodistas' en Villahermosa, Tabasco," *Terra*, September 9, 2009.

"'Calientan' plaza 'Zeta' y 'Familia,'" *Reforma*, April 3, 2009.

"Capturan a contador de los Zetas en NL," *Milenio.com*, June 4, 2010.

"Capturan a presunto asesino de Valentín Elizalde," *Terra*, March 26, 2008.

Carrasco Araizaga, Jorge. "Veracruz, bajo control de 'La Compañía,'" *Demócrata Norte de México*, February 8, 2010, http://democratanortedemexico.blogspot.com/2010/02/veracruz-bajo-control-de-la-compania.html.

Castillo, E. Eduardo. "Decomisan arsenal en México a cartel de Los Zetas," *Associated Press*, June 6, 2011.

_____. "Mexico Cartel Issues Booklets for Proper Conduct," *Associated Press*, July 20, 2011.

_____. "Mexico Memorializes Soldiers Killed in Drug War," *Timesleader.com*, December 23, 2008.

_____. "Mexico Migrants Massacre: Drug Cartel Suspected," *Huffington Post*, August 26, 2010.

_____. "Official: Mexican Cartels Hiring Common Criminals," *Associated Press*, April 6, 2011.

César Carrillo, Pablo. "Elección con tufo a narco," *EXonline*, November 17, 2007.

"Ciudad Mier Evacuates After Zetas Threaten to Kill Residents," *The Monitor*, November 9, 2010.

Coley Pérez, José Gabriel. "El imperio del Lazca durante el foxismo," *Voltaire*, September 7, 2009, http://www.voltairenet.org/article1619.html.

"!Como México No May Dos!" *Mexfiles*, August 27, 2010.

"Controla crimen región fronteriza," *Reforma*, May 10, 2011.

Convoy, Bill. "U.S. Private Sector Providing Drug-War Mercenaries to Mexico," *The Narcosphere*, April 3, 2011.

Corchado, Alfredo. "Cartel's Enforcers Outpower Their Boss," *Dallas Morning News*, June 11, 2007.

_____. "Drug Cartels Operate Training Camps near Texas Border Just Inside Mexico," *Dallas Morning News*, April 4, 2008.

_____. "Mexico's Zetas Gang Buys Businesses along Border in Move to Increase Legitimacy," *Dallas Morning News*, December 7, 2009.

De la luz González, María. "La Sedena denuncia campaña en su contra," *El Universal.com*, April 4, 2011.

_____. "'Los Zetas' llegaron a Zacatecas desde 2007," *El Universal*, May 20, 2009.

Debussman, Bernd Jr. "Latin America: Mexico Drug War Update," *StoptheDrugWar.org*, November 6, 2009.

"Desertaron 100 mil militares con Fox," *Milenio*, July 20, 2007.

"Desertaron en 10 años 1,680 soldados de 'elite,'" *Milenio.com*, March 7, 2011.

"Detienen a presunto contador de 'Los Zetas' en NL," *El Siglo* (Durango), April 13, 2011.

"Dictan prisión contra Zetas," *Terra*, December 10, 2007.

Dillon, Sam. "Kidnappings in Mexico Send Shivers across Border," *New York Times*, January 5, 2009.

_____. "Matamoros Journal: Canaries Sing in Mexico, but Uncle Juan Will Not," *New York Times*, February 9, 1996.

Duarte, Enrique. "Los 10 estados con menos remesas," *CNNExpansión.com*, July 30, 2009.

"Ejecuciones 2010," *Reforma*, March 24, 2010.

"El Chapo Guzman Claims Credit for Butchering of 5 in Acapulco," *El Blog del Narco*, March 26, 2011.

"El dinero del narco, sin fronteras," *Diario de Yucatán*, December 26, 2009.

"El tráfico de migrantes da en México más ganancias que narco: ONU," *Excélsior*, March 28, 2011.

"Entrenan mercenaries a soldados en País," *Reforma.com*, April 6, 2011.

Eskridge, Chris. "Mexican Cartels and Their Integration into Mexican Socio-Political Culture," http://www.customscorruption.com/mexican_cartels_integr.htm.

Espinosa, V. and E. Flores. "Tapiza 'La Familia' Guanajuato, Guerrero y Michoacán con mantas contra 'Los Zetas,'" *Proceso*, February 1, 2010.

"Ex militar, de 36 años: el cruel líder de 'Los Zetas,'" *Diario Despertar de Oaxaca*, January 3, 2011.

"Ex militares sirven de sicarios a cárteles mexicanos," *SeguRed.com*, July 25, 2006, http://www.segured.com/index.php?od=9&link=7765.

"Executan a 'zetas' en cárcel in Mazatlán," *Reforma*, December 14, 2008.

Fairanu, Steve and William Booth. "Mexico's Drug Cartels Siphon Liquid Gold," *Washington Post*, December 13, 2009.

Fineman, Mark. "General Goes High-Profile in Mexico," *Los Angeles Times*, December 5, 1996.

———. "Mexican Drug Cartel Chief Convicted in U.S.," *Los Angeles Times*, October 17, 1996.

"Former Mayor of Rio Bravo, 2 AFI Agents Assassinated," *Mexico Trucker Online*, December 1, 2007.

"Fracturan cubanas nexo Zetas-Beltrán," *Reforma*, November 22, 2009.

"Fuerzas especiales del Ejército captura a 'El Mati,' lugarteniente de Osiel Cárdenas: Junto con el narco fueron capturados seis cómplices," *EsMas*, August 10, 2004.

Garduño, Silvia. "Controlan Zetas tráfico de migrantes," *Reforma*, June 19, 2010.

Gil Olmos, José. "Se escribe con Zeta," *Proceso* (special ed. no. 28, La Guerra del Narco), 2010.

González, María de la Luz. "La Sedena denucia campaña en su contra," *El Universal.com*, April 4, 2011.

Grillo, Ioan. "Mexico's Female Narcos," *Globalpost*, December 19, 2010.

Guzmán, Julio Manuel. "Pese a violencia, regresan habitantes a Ciudad Mier," *El Universal*, July 20, 2011.

Guzmán, Julio L. "Tamaulipas, tercer estados en consume de heroína," *El Universal*, August 27, 2008.

"Hallan a 6 decapitados," *Reforma*, February 7, 2010.

"Hallan cuatro decapitados en Zihuatanejo," *Reforma.com*, April 27, 2011.

Idalia Gómez, María and Darío Fritz, "Cuando la prisión era una fiesta," *El Universal.com.mx*, May 16, 2005.

"Identifican a los tres ejectados en Cancún; investan nexus con tráfico de cubanos," *Noticaribe*, June 19, 2009.

"Impact of the Financial Crisis: Remittance Growth 2008–2009 per State," *Remittance Gateway*, July 14, 2009.

"Inhiben señal de celular en 4 cárceles," *Reforma*, December 31, 2008.

"Invasion of the Body-Snatchers," *Reuters*, March 9, 2007.

"'Invierten' sicarios en cartel," *El Nuevo Heraldo*. March 1, 2010.

Jaramillo Alanís and María Guadalupe. "Regreso de migrantes generará conflictos sociales, Alcalde de Tula," *Asi es Tamaulipas*, October 15, 2008.

Jiménez, Benito. "Acusan a mandos de proteger a 'Zetas,'" *Reforma.com*, June 29, 2009.

———. "Cae coordinador de masacre de migrantes," *Reforma.com*, June 17, 2011.

———. "Identifica el Ejército tres rutas de cárteles," *Reforma.com*, April 29, 2007.

———. "Ubica reporte de PF expansión de 'Zetas,'" *Reforma.com*, February 27, 2011.

Lacey, Marc. "For Some Taxi Drivers, a Different Kind of Traffic," *New York Times*, March 1, 2009.

Lagunas, Icela. "Detectan 119 kilos de mariguana en aduana del Reclusorio Sur," *El Universal*, December 15, 2008.

"Las operaciones secretas del cartel del Golfo," *Revista Contralinea*, August 30, 2009.

Lawson, Guy. "The Making of a Narco State," *Rolling Stone Magazine*, March 4, 2009.

"Leyzaola Takes Post in Ciudad Juárez," *SanDiegoRed*, June 6, 2011.

"Libran a presuntos 'zetas,'" *Noticaribe*, October 24, 2009.

"Llevan cárteles a penales guerra por territorios," *El Universal*, October 18, 2008.

Logan, Samuel. "Mexico's Uppermost Threat is Organized Crime," *Mexidata.Info*, May 1, 2006.

———. "Soldiers Raid Los Zetas Training Camp near Higueras, Nuevo León—11 May 2010," *Southern Pulse*, May 16, 2010.

Logan, Samuel and John P. Sullivan. "The Gulf-Zeta Split and the Praetorian Revolt," *ISN/ETH* Zurich, April 7, 2010.

———. "Violence in Mexico: A Bloody Reshuffling of Drug Cartels," *Mexidata.Info*, April 12, 2010.

Lopez, Naxiely. "Report Details Drugs, Weapons and Explosives Seized by Mexican Military," *The Monitor*, April 5, 2011.

"Los Cárdenas Guillén: narcomenudistas que llegaron a capos," "*M Semanal*," November 14, 2010.

"Los Kaibiles: Las 'maquinas de matar,'" *Terra*, October 2, 2005.

"Los Zetas ordeñan ductos de Pemex," *Yahoo! Noticias*, August 7, 2009.

"Los Zetas pagan aguinaldo a 'sicarios' en Tabasco," *Proceso*, December 24, 2009.

Lupsha, Peter. "Transnational Narco-Corruption and Narco-Investment: A Focus on Mexico," *PBS Frontline*, http://www.pbs.org/wgbh/pages/frontline/shows/mexico/readings/lupsha.html.

Madrid, Lemic. "Detienen a Presunto Contador de Los Zetas," *Excélsior*, July 28, 2009.

Malkin, Elisabeth. "Mexico: Arrests in Reporter's Death," *New York Times*, June 13, 2009.

"Marineros detienen a presunto contador del líder de 'Los Zetas,'" *esmas*, May 30, 2010.

Marsh, Wendel. "Justice's 'Project Delirium' Targets Major Mexican Drug Cartel," *Reuters*, July 21, 2011.

Martínez, Sanjuana. "Si agarro a un *zeta* lo mato; para qué interrogarlo?: jefe policiaco," *La Jornada*, March 13, 2010.

McKinley, James C. Jr. "Keeping his Spies Close, and Maybe a Cartel Closer," *New York Times*, April 20, 2010.

————. "Mexican Drug Kingpin Sentenced to 25 Years in Secret Hearing," *New York Times*, February 25, 2010.

"Mexican Army Urged to Take Over Prisons," *USA Today*, August 1, 2005.

"Mexican Police under Suspicion in Mass Grave Case," *Australian News.Net*, April 14, 2011, http://www.australiannews.net/story/769368/ht/Mexican-police-under-suspicion-in-mass-graves-case.

"Mexican Troops Raid Camp Belonging to Los Zetas Gang," *Latin American Herald Tribune*, June 6, 2011.

"México: arrestan a 124 policías por vínculos con Los Zetas," *Adnmundo.com*, September 15, 2009.

"Mexico: Editor Abducted and Shot Dead," *International Pen*, October 15, 2008, http://www.internationalpen.org.uk.

"México: Incautan arsenal a cártel de los Zetas," *La Prensa.hn_internacionales*, October 22, 2010.

"México decomisa a Los Zetas cuentas para lavar dinero," *AOL Noticias*, February 16, 2011.

"Mexico: Smugglers Try Medieval Tech," *New York Times*, January 28, 2011.

"Mexico-Media Safety: Police Assault and Threaten Three Journalists," *IFEX*, March 19, 2009, http://www.newssafety.org.

"Mexico's Internal Drug War," *Power and Interest News Report*, August 14, 2006.

"Militares arrestan a presuntos 'Zetas' en posesión de armas y municiones en Fresnillo (Galería)," Universidad Tecnológica del Estado de Zacatecas, September 26, 2010.

"Militares detienen a cinco presuntos 'zetas' en Valle de Santiago," *El Universal*, February 3, 2010.

Miroff, Nick and William Booth. "At Mexican Grave Site, a New Level of Barbarity," *Washington Post*, April 25, 2011.

Moraga, Susana. "Sabían en Hidalgo de 'limosna': CEM," *El Diario. mx*, October 24, 2010.

Morales, Alberto. "Poiré: está Tamaulipas bajo control," *El Universal. com.mx*, April 27, 2011.

———. "Van a Tamaulipas 500 soldados más," *El Universal.com.mx*, May 13, 2011.

Moreno, Alejandro and María Antonia Mancillas. "Encuesta/Ven fines distintos en Guerra al narco," *Reforma*, April 1, 2011.

Muedano, Marcos. "Festejan 2 años de templo construido por 'El Lazca,'" *El Universal.com.mx*, February 3, 2011.

"Muere en Veracruz líder 'Zeta' en tiroteo," *Reforma*, November 4, 2009.

"Mujer opera secuestros de Los Zetas fuera del país: PGR," *Milenio. com*, March 8, 2010.

"Multiplica 'Familia' violencia en Edomex," *Reforma*, September 14, 2008.

Najar, Alberto. "Desertaron 100 mil militares con Fox," *Milenio*, July 20, 2007.

"'Narcoguerra' en Michoacán llega a 21 decapitados este año," *El Universal*, February 20, 2010.

"New Details Released about Gulf Cartel Leader's Death," *ValleyCentral.com*, November 7, 2010.

"Niega EU haber entrenado 'Zetas,'" *Excélsior*, May 20, 2008.

"Ocupa Tamaulipas cuarto lugar en agresiones hacia la mujer," *El Mañana*, August 5, 2009.

"Official: Mexican cartels hiring common criminals," *The Monitor*, April 7, 2011.

Osorno, Diego E. "In Two Years the Number of Gang Members Doubles in Monterrey," *The Narcosphere*, March 23, 2009.

"Pagan Zetas en dólares a kaibiles," *Terra*, October 4, 2006.

"Pelean Cancún mafia cubana," *Reforma.com*, November 22, 2009.

"Ponen 'Los Zetas' su sello a piratería," *Noticias de Tapachula*, April 11, 2010.

"Por la Inseguridad, may 500 mil con trastornos mentales en Tamaulipas," *Excélsior*, June 5, 2011.

"Por ordenes militares, Villa Castillo dejará Torreón," *La Jornada*, March 15, 2011.

"Por qué se fue Alejandro Junco," *Reporte Indigo*, September 12, 2008, http://www.reporteindigo.com.

Prado, Henia. "Toleran autoridades drogas en penales," *Reforma*, November 16, 2008.

———. "Rehúysen jóvenes empleo de policía," *Reforma.com*, May 23, 2011.

"Presentan a Zetas detenidos con arsenal en Cárdenas," *El Heroico. com*, October 23, 2010.

"Presunto narco fue capturado," *Univisión.com*, September 8, 2008.

"Quien es Heriberto Lazcano Lazcano, alias 'El Lazca,' 'El Verdugo' o 'Z-3,'" *El Blog de Terror*, July 25, 2010, http://www.diariodelnarco. com/2011/04/insignias-y-uniformes-del-narco.html.

Quiñones, Sam. "Jesús Malverde," *Front Line: Drug Wars*, PBS. http:// www.pbs.org/wgbh.

"Quitan puerto a 'Los Zetas,'" *Reforma*, October 4, 2009.

Ravelo, Ricardo. "El capo del panismo," *Proceso*, March 16, 2009.

————. "El Reparto del Mercado," *Proceso*, special issue no. 28, "La Guerra del Narco," 2010.

————. "Las entranos del ejército," *Proceso*, May 16, 2010.

"Reclutan 'Zetas' mujeres para integrar célula: 'Las Panteras,'" *Terra*, March 27, 2009.

"Reconoce PGR que tiene 2 averiguación en contra del gobernador Tomás Yarrington, pero aclara, "éstas se irán al 'archivo' por no encontrar delitos," *Es Mas*, October 20, 2004.

"Revelan creación del grupo de sicarias 'Las Panteras,'" *El Norte*, March 27, 2009.

Reyes Cruz, Juan Manuel. "Se disculpa Texas; quita letreros de Laredo para evitar a 'extraños,'" *Excélsior*, May 20, 2011.

Rodríguez, Olga R. "Mexican Senate Approves Judicial Reform," *Associated Press*, March 7, 2008.

Rodríguez García, Arturo. "Los Zetas, génesis de los conflictos en Topo Chico," *Proceso*, October 8, 2009.

————. "Tamaulipas: la masacre del narcopenal," *Proceso*, October 29, 2008.

Rodríguez Martinez, Marco Antonio. "El Poder de los Zetas," *Monografías.com*.

Roig-Franzia, Manuel. "Drug Trade Tyranny on the Border," *Washington Post*, March 16, 2008.

————. "Mexican Drug Cartels Making Audacious Pitch for Recruits," *Washington Post*, September 20, 2007.

Savio, Irene. "Confirman nexo 'Zetas' e italianos," *Reforma*, September 19, 2008.

Schiller, Dane. "A *Houston Chronicle* Exclusive 'I Knew What They'd Do to Me," *Houston Chronicle*, March 14, 2010.

Schwartz, Jeremy. "Musician Killings Highlight Unrelenting Violence in Mexico," *Banderas News*, December 2007.

"Se refuerza el cártel de Sinaloa," *EFE*, August 10, 2005.

"Security and Law Enforcement," *Frontera Norte Sur*, July 2003, http:// www.nmsu.edu/~frontera/jul03/secr.html.

"Sedena Identifies the Heads of Los Zetas," *Borderland Beat*, April 21, 2010.

"Shocking Culture of Impunity and Violence," http://www.freemedia.at/ cms/ipi/statements_detail.html?ctxid=CH0055&...&year=2008.

Simon, Jose and Carlos Lauría. "Mexican President Must Protect Freedom of Expression," *San Francisco Chronicle*, July 23, 2007.

"Sources: Zetas Head Lazcana Killed in Matamoros," *The Monitor*, June 17, 2011.

Stevenson, Mark. "Mexico Arrests Alleged Drug Lord Osiel Cardenas After Shootout near U.S. Border," *Associated Press*, March 15, 2003.

Sturgeon, William. "The Evolution of Security Threat Groups into the Twenty-First Century," *Corrections.com*, October 15, 2009.

Sullivan, Kevin. "Tijuana Gang Figure Held After Slaying of Journalist," *Washington Post*, June 26, 2004.

"Suman 187 cuerpos en fosas en Durango," *Reforma.com*, May 9, 2011.

"Suman 218 cadáveres en fosas de Durango," *Reforma.com*, May 15, 2011.

"Superan a Ciudad Juárez en violencia contra mujeres," *El Siglo de Torreón*, November 24, 2009.

Suverza, Alejandro. "El evangelio según La Familia," *Nexosenlinea*, January 1, 2009.

"Tamaulipas tundra en 2012 policía certificada, asegura García Luna," *Excélsior*, June 1, 2011.

Taylor, Jared. "Cartel Split Boosts Pot Traffic through Valley," *The Monitor*, June 12, 2011.

"Tenía ex militar negocio con 'Zetas,'" *Reforma*, April 5, 2009.

"The Dilemma Mexican Journalists Face: Self-Censorship, Exile or Certain Death," *Mexidata.info*, January 26, 2009.

"The World's Billionaires," *Forbes*, March 3, 2010.

Tobar, Héctor. "Mexico Gives Final OK to Judicial System Reform," *Tampa Bay Online*, March 7, 2008, http://www2.tbo.com/content/2008/mar/07/.

"Un narco violento que está en la mira," *Reforma.com*, December 6, 2010.

Venegas, Daniel. "Diputados exigen alto a la extorsión desde cárceles," *Milenio*, October 19, 2008.

Vulliamy, Ed. "Mexico's Zetas: Lords of a Brutal Narco-State," *The Observer* (London), November 17, 2009.

_____. "The Zetas: Kings of Their Own Brutal Narco State," *Mail&Guardian.online*, November 15, 2009.

Zapata Santiso, Claudia. "Refuta SET resultados sobre adicciones," *MetroNoticias*, October 26, 2009.

"Zeta Recalls His Life, Warns against It," *Brownsville Herald*, February 17, 2011.

"Zetas detenidos eran estacas," *Blog del Narco*, May 26, 2011.

Index

Lightning Source UK Ltd.
Milton Keynes UK
UKOW06f1325121015

260351UK00010B/345/P